Something Within

Something Within

Religion in African-American Political Activism

Fredrick C. Harris

New York   Oxford
Oxford University Press
1999

Oxford University Press

Oxford   New York
Athens   Auckland   Bangkok   Bogotá   Buenos Aires   Calcutta
Cape Town   Chennai   Dar es Salaam   Delhi   Florence   Hong Kong   Istanbul
Karachi   Kuala Lumpur   Madrid   Melbourne   Mexico City   Mumbai
Nairobi   Paris   São Paulo   Singapore   Taipei   Tokyo   Toronto   Warsaw

and associated companies in

Berlin   Ibadan

Copyright © 1999 by Oxford University Press, Inc.

Published by Oxford University Press, Inc.
198 Madison Avenue, New York, New York 10016

Oxford is a registered trademark of Oxford University Press

Library of Congress Cataloging-in-Publication Data
Harris, Fredrick C.
Something within : religion in African-American
political activism / Fredrick C. Harris.
p.   cm.
Includes bibliographical references and index.
ISBN 0-19-512033-7
1. Afro-Americans—Religion.   2. Afro-Americans—Political
activity.   3. Christianity and politics—United States.   I. Title.
BR563.N4H368   1999
306.6'089'96073—dc21   99-28043

1 2 3 5 7 9 8 6 4 2

Printed in the United States of America
on acid-free paper

In memory of my paternal great-aunt, Nellie Mae Harris-Mosley (1904–1992), who, unfortunately, never "lived to see it." An usher, deaconess, and devoted member of the Mt. Nebo Missionary Baptist Church in Atlanta, Aunt Nell's display of everyday forms of resistance throughout her years confirmed in my eyes and ears that there is truly "something within."

Acknowledgments

THIS PROJECT BENEFITED FROM THE SUPPORT of several individuals and institutions. At Northwestern University, where I completed the bulk of my research for this book as a part of my doctoral dissertation, I received research assistance from Maisha Goss, Henry Wong, and Charisse Gardner. They assisted me with collecting and transcribing material from observations at black churches in Chicago and with recoding data from several opinion surveys. Kathleen Bethel of the Northwestern University Library directed me to valuable sources on African-American religion and politics, which enhanced the scope of this book.

As chair of my dissertation committee, Jane J. Mansbridge has expressed a keen interest in this project and has been a model dissertation advisor and colleague. Her availability, insights, probing questions, and sustained enthusiasm kept me focused on the potential of this book, even in its early stage as a dissertation proposal. By encouraging me to incorporate qualitative material, Jenny's intuition greatly added to my findings and allowed me to develop a greater appreciation for observation as a research method. Not only did she read the dissertation more than once, she read several drafts in book manuscript form, even finding time to read one draft while in the process of moving from Evanston to Cambridge! Aldon Morris pushed me to consider the broader theoretical implications of my research. His wisdom regarding the importance of theory in the study of African-American life has nurtured within me an intellectual commitment to theory-building in African-American politics.

Funding for the early stages of research for this book was provided by the Indiana University Center on Philanthropy, the Aspen Institute for NonProfit Sector Research (93-NSRF-6), the Graduate School of Northwestern University, and Northwestern University's Department of Communications Studies, which funded survey questions on the 1991 Chicago Area Survey that were specifically designed for this research.

The Chancellor's Postdoctoral Program for Academic Diversity at the University of California at Berkeley provided me time off to work on the book at the university's Survey Research Center (SRC). I would like to thank Andrea Simpson, who also served as a Chancellor fellow with me, and Sam Lucus and Paul Sniderman, both SRC members, for providing me with an intellectual space to test my ideas. I would especially like to thank Andrea, who allowed me to interrupt her own work for what turned out to be a daily ritual of intellectual debate.

At the University of Rochester I benefited from the encouragement and assistance of several colleagues and students. Dick Fenno, the godfather of "soaking and poking," reinforced in me the importance of participant observation as a research method and gave valuable advice on the ethnographic and theoretical chapters of the book. The late Sam Nolutshungu offered insights and encouragement and lifted my spirits through his good sense of humor. His presence at Rochester is sorely missed. Richard Niemi, Harold Stanley, Gerald Gamm, and Dave Weimer commented on particular chapters. Sean Theriault, Marquitta Speller, and Lela Sims-Gissendanner assisted me with gathering opinion surveys, transcribing recorded material, and tracking down newspaper articles in Rush Rhees Library.

I have also benefited from presenting my work at various stages and in different venues. I would like to thank the African-American Studies Program at Loyola University of Chicago, the Workshop on Race, Ethnicity, Representation, and Governance at Harvard University, the Department of Political Science at the University of Washington, the Center for Political Studies' Senior Staff Seminar at the University of Michigan, the Annenberg School of Communications at the University of Pennsylvania, the Department of Political Science at Tufts University, the Department of Sociology at the University of California at Berkeley, and the Department of Political Science at Brown University for allowing me to present my work. I would also like to thank Lisa Featherstone for her editorial assistance and Kathleen Hall Jamison for bringing my manuscript to the attention of Tom LeBien at Oxford University Press. Tasheem Lomax and Karin Garver of the Russell Sage Foundation assisted me with final preparation of the manuscript.

© 1988 Studio 224, WARNER BROTHERS PUBLICATIONS U.S. INC., Miami, F.L. 33014, All Rights Reserved, Used by Permission.

The Johnson Publishing Co. granted permission to reproduce an illustration by Walt Carr in the *Negro Digest*—"I'm sorry, Reverend—but I guess I just ran out of cheeks to turn." I would also like to thank the University of Texas Press for allowing me to reprint material from my article "Something Within: Religion as a Mobilizer of African-American Political Activism" in the *Journal of Politics*, 56:1 (1994), pp. 42–68. Princeton University Press gave permission to reprint material which appeared as "Religious Institutions and African-American Political Activism" in *Classifying By Race*, edited by Paul E. Peterson.

This book has also been greatly enhanced by family, friends, and colleagues. I had the good sense to follow the advice of Charles S. Bullock who talked me out of going to law school while I was an undergraduate at the University of Georgia. Linda F. Williams, who I worked for as a research assistant at the Joint Center for Political and Economic Studies, "prepped" me for graduate school and has offered keen professional advice ever since. The Friday Evening Roundtable (1989–1993), a small reading group of African-American graduate students in the social sciences and humanities at Northwestern, provided a welcoming reprise from university seminars while I was in graduate school. My involvement with the Roundtable contributed enormously to my intellectual development and granted me exposure to perspectives on politics outside the often rigid confines of political science. I would especially like to thank Darrell Moore, now a professor of philosophy at DePaul University, who was the moving force behind that group and who over the years has helped me to flesh out my ideas.

Growing up I was always reminded that whatever the accomplishment, no one ever succeeds on their own. I am indebted to an assortment of friends both in and outside of the academy who, in their own way, enormously contributed to this book. Father Martini Shaw, rector of St. Thomas Episcopal Church, invited me to several religious and political events in Chicago during the research phase of my dissertation. Without Father Shaw's invitations I might not have gathered much of the ethnographic material that anchors the central ideas of this book. Don Weston, a friend from my days in Athens, Georgia, served as research assistant at large. Don was kind enough to send cassette tapes of church services and newspaper clippings of political events during his stays in New Orleans and Detroit. Reverend D. Darrell Griffith, pastor of the Antioch Baptist Church of Brooklyn, provided campaign materials from the 1994 National Baptist Convention and helped me to unravel the Byzantine-like practices of the Convention. Curtis Foy, Eric Snodgrass, Waldo Johnson, Jr., Carl Walton, and Herman "Skip" Mason urged me on and offered insights into their own experiences in black churches.

Finally, I would like to thank my family in Atlanta and my extended family in Washington, D.C., and Chicago. My mother, Charlene Harris, who had concerns about me moving "way up North," gave me both emotional and practical support. Her encyclopedic knowledge of the Bible assisted me with locating scriptures even when reference materials fell short. My requests led to invigorating discussions with her about religion, politics, and religion and politics. Each request gave her yet another opportunity to "bear witness." LeWanza Baskin, my best friend and critic, provided both emotional and intellectual support. While in medical school she found time to read and critique several chapters and, when I felt that there was no end in sight, she strengthened my resolve to finish the book. To her I will always be grateful. Although many contributed to this book, all mistakes herein lie with me.

New York, New York
February 1999   F. C. H.

Contents

Something Within

Introduction

Something within me, that holdeth the rein
Something within me that banishes pain;
Something within me, I cannot explain
All that I know, there is something within.

Lucie E. Campbell, 1919

ON A WARM SATURDAY MORNING in August 1992, on Chicago's South Side, several hundred people gathered in the basement of the Carter Temple CME Church.[1] Carter Temple, which borders Wabash and Michigan avenues along the Seventy-ninth Street corridor, is a part of the Christian Methodist Episcopal (CME) Church, a majority black denomination historically connected to the United Methodist Church South. This formerly all-white denomination broke with northern United Methodists over the issue of slavery on the eve of the Civil War. On this particular morning, before the regular Sunday service, the church's parking lot was packed with cars, many with stickers proclaiming their faith with such phrases as "God, my co-pilot," "Jesus on Board," and "Christ: Try Him, You'll Like Him." Surrounding streets provided parking spaces for latecomers.

In the entranceway to the basement, a set of tables were stocked with campaign brochures and buttons of various candidates for public office, along with voter registration information from the Chicago Board of Elections. Beyond these tables, a huge room overflowed with people, mostly men in suits, who were either chatting about church-related matters or the upcoming election. Some of the men wore white clerical collars; others wore ties. Some had a strip of African kente cloth, or a cross on a chain, around their necks; nearly all had campaign buttons adorning their suit lapels. Most of the women in the room were preparing food, setting up banquet-style tables, or directing attendees to their seats.

While the pianist played a soft but celebratory sacred tune, Bishop Arthur Brazier, minister of the ten-thousand-plus Apostolic Church of God, called participants to attention. Speaking in a deep, rhythmic voice, he reminded them that the event was "an opportunity for all of us to come together once more." Bishop Brazier had been "coming together" with these leaders for several decades. A tall man in his early seventies whose salt-and-pepper hair and intellectual vigor con-

3

cealed his age, Bishop Brazier had been involved in community organizing and electoral politics in Chicago since the 1950s. In the mid-sixties, he had organized for open housing with Martin Luther King; he had also worked with community organizer Saul Alinsky in what once was one of Chicago's most powerful community groups, The Woodlawn Organization (TWO).[2]

Since the 1960s, however, Bishop Brazier appears to have modified his political views. In that era Reverend Brazier advocated "black solidarity" against the "white power structure," which, he claimed, supported freedom and self-determination in principle "except for black people." He also referred to some black politicians in Chicago at that time as "Uncle Tom overseers [who keep] the ward quiet for the white boss" (1969, 138–144). By 1991, however, Bishop Brazier was one of the largest individual contributors to Richard Daley, the white incumbent mayor of Chicago who defeated two black mayoral candidates with less than 25 percent of the black vote during both the primary and general elections.

That August morning Bishop Brazier continued his involvement in electoral politics by supporting yet another candidate for public office. Behind the bishop was suspended a white poster board that spelled out boldly in red and blue letters: "Illinois Ministers for Carol Moseley Braun—Welcome Aboard." With the resonance of a biblical prophet, Bishop Brazier predicted the outcome of their collective engagement: "All together we will be able to see the great power that we have." He trumpeted the purpose of the event: "America is a political animal, a political society, a political country, and those who have seen political power must understand that in order to have great power we must be part of the political process. Do you understand that? Because that is why you are here."

These ministers and lay churchgoers understood Brazier's message well, and it is the message of this book: In a variety of ways religion assists African Americans with becoming a part of the political process. This book uncovers how religion assists African Americans in the political process by describing, analyzing, and explaining the various ways in which Afro-Christianity stimulates African-American political activism. The story I am about to tell is highly controversial. For many the links between religion and African-American political life seem obvious. Media accounts regard the political activities of black ministers and churches as routine features of black political life. However, scholars over the years have differed sharply on the role that religion plays in black political activism.

Two competing perspectives prevail. The first perspective, which I will refer to as the opiate theory, insists that Afro-Christianity promotes otherworldliness, functioning as an instrument of political pacification and fatalism. The second perspective, which I will refer to as the inspiration theory, makes exactly the opposite claim, arguing that Afro-Christianity has played a central role in black politics, catalyzing, for example, the collective involvement of African Americans in the modern civil rights movement.

RELIGION AS OPIATE

As Manning Marable has observed, "black religion is often viewed as the culprit, an agent of the oppressor, rather than a potentially liberating ideological force" (1989, 333). And as one minister critical of the opiate theory characterizes it: "Instead of cursing the white man, [blacks] shout at the Lord. Instead of kicking whitey, [blacks] kick over the pew."[3] Opiate theorists argue that religion works as means of social control, offering African Americans a way to cope with personal and societal difficulties and thus undermining their willingness to actively challenge racial inequalities.[4] This perspective has prevailed among several generations of leading social scientists in a range of disciplines, including anthropology (Powdermaker [1939] 1968; Fauset 1944), psychology (Billings 1934; Dollard [1937] 1949), sociology (Johnson [1934] 1966; Johnson [1941] 1967; Myrdal 1944; Frazier 1974), and political science (Bunche [1940] 1973; Lane 1959). The theory has its origins in the writings of Karl Marx, who saw religion as an instrument of economic and political domination over nineteenth-century British workers. Marx famously dubbed religion as "the opium of the people" (1963, 44). By minimizing temporal concerns and encouraging believers to focus on otherworldly pursuits, religion, in his view, pacified oppressed groups so that they would accept their subordinated status in society.

Echoing Marx, Eugene Gordon, writing in the 1920s, charged in an essay titled "A New Religion for the Negro" that Christianity teaches blacks to be "meek" and "humble" and "to turn the other cheek when [they] should retaliate in kind." He further characterized Negro Christianity as a "workable tool for others," blacks themselves as "religiously enslaved," their minds neglecting "the very real and very present now for the delirious pleasure of wandering in a vague, remote, and uncertain hereafter" (1972, 577).

Social science research during the Jim Crow period reinforced the idea that Christianity subverted black resistance. Political scientist Robert Lane concluded that religion offered urban blacks and newly arrived immigrants an "otherworldly solace for temporal ills," which encouraged political apathy (1959, 250–255). Although Gunnar Myrdal noted the black church's potential as a "power institution," he observed that "the [Negro] church has been relatively inefficient and uninfluential" as an instrument of collective action (1944, 873). But the harshest of the black-religion-as-opiate analyses came from sociologist E. Franklin Frazier, who viewed the black church as "having cast an entire shadow over the entire intellectual life of Negroes" as well as being responsible for the "so-called backwardness" of blacks ([1963] 1974, 90).

The first significant attempt to resolve this question through survey research was sociologist Gary Marx's study of belief systems in the black community (1967a, 1967b). More than any other study, Marx's findings provoked a debate between the opiate and inspiration schools that would last for decades.[5] In his 1964 metropolitan sample of African Americans, Marx found that intense religious belief had a negative relationship to support for the aims of the civil rights movement. Specifically, Marx established that in his sample, the greater the subjective importance of religion to black respondents, and the more often they went to church, the less militant they were in support of civil rights issues. Although Marx acknowledged that "many religious people are nevertheless militant," he concluded that until religion "looses its hold over these people, or comes to embody to a greater extent the belief that man as well as God can bring about secular change, and focuses more on the here and now," Afro-Christianity "would seem to be an important factor working against the widespread radicalization of the Negro public" (105).

More recently Adolph Reed, in his critique of Jesse Jackson's 1984 presidential campaign, emphatically dismissed the idea that Afro-Christianity encourages political participation among blacks. Instead, he argued, Christianity encourages "political quietism" among African Americans, stifling the possibility of mass activism. Though he grudgingly acknowledged the black church's "tactical support of political mobilization," Reed maintained that Afro-American Christianity is essentially an instrument of oppression. "The domain of the black church," he wrote, "has been the spiritual and institutional adaptation of Afro-Americans to an apparently inexorable context of subordination and dispossession" (1986b, 59). Reed sees a fundamental tension between the African-American church and politics, particularly because he sees clerical leadership as authoritarian and the tradition of the black church as antidemocratic.

RELIGION AS INSPIRATION

Taking the other side in the controversy, several generations of theologians have contended that Afro-Christianity inspires political liberation and activism.[6] Historians of American slavery have discovered that religion played a pivotal role in the survival and rebellion of African slaves (Genovese 1974; Raboteau 1978). Social scientists who have studied black churches have highlighted the influence of black ministers as catalysts for mobilizing African Americans into electoral and community politics (Hamilton 1972; Childs 1980). Looking primarily at the civil rights–era South, sociologists have noted that the urban church, as an indigenous organization, provided the leadership base, social interaction, and communication networks required for collective action (McAdam 1982; Morris 1984).

Describing southern blacks as a "God-fearing, churchgoing people," political scientists Matthews and Prothro maintained that the racially segregated black church may have "planted the seeds for the destruction of segregation" by serving the political organizational needs of southern blacks (1966, 232). Their survey of black and white southerners during the early years of the civil rights movement asked how often political campaigns were discussed at respondents' churches. While an overwhelming majority of both blacks and whites reported that political campaigns were not discussed in their church, 35 percent of black respondents (compared to only 18 percent of whites) reported hearing some discussion about political campaigns. Of those attending church services, 18 percent of blacks— but only 5 percent of whites—reported that their minister encouraged members to vote for a specific candidate. Matthews and Prothro estimated that "[a]lmost a fifth of the Negroes who go to church thus receive direct clues as to how they should vote, and over a third hear some kind of discussion of elections" (233). These findings on direct church involvement in electoral politics during the civil rights movement (but before the passage of the 1965 Voting Rights Act) provide some evidence that southern blacks were more amenable than their white counterparts to a politically active church.

Matthews and Prothro's findings during the 1960s are similar to patterns in contemporary black politics. Katherine Tate's analysis of black electoral behavior indicates that religious institutions are today an important organizational resource for disseminating information about elections, encouraging church members to vote, providing individuals a base to work with political campaigns, and allowing individuals to financially contribute to political candidates. Responses to the 1984 National Black Election Study found that these modes of church-based electoral activism varied in intensity, ranging from 60 percent of African Americans reporting that they were encouraged to vote at their place of worship to 10 percent reporting that they worked for a political candidate through religious institutions.[7] Although some scholars caution that not all black churches are politically engaged (Calhoun-Brown 1996), Tate's findings confirm the enduring significance of religious institutions as a mobilizer of black electoral participation in the post–civil rights era.

THE MULTIDIMENSIONALITY OF RELIGION

An important void in previous studies on Afro-Christianity and African-American political life has been the underestimation of the multidimensionality of religious beliefs and practices—the diversity of religion as belief and expression and the potential variety of ways different religious forms might affect political participation. The multidimensionality of religion has been a focus of religion scholars for more than two decades,[8] yet critics of Afro-Christianity and political behaviorists alike have tended to overlook it, viewing religion as discrete and unitary.

Despite the vast literature on political participation in the United States, only recently have students of American politics empirically addressed the impact of religion on political activism, especially for African Americans. Yet African Americans have been more involved in church activities and more intensely religious than other Americans. George Gallup and Jim Castelli report from their longitudinal and cross-national surveys on religious beliefs and practices that African Americans are "the most religious people in the [Western] world" (1989, 122–124). Blacks rank the importance of God in their lives far above where any other ethnic or national group ranks it. Black commitment to religion is so rooted that in a 1988 Gallup survey 75 percent of black respondents, compared to only 57 percent of the general population, said they believed that religion is capable of answering "all or most of today's problems."

This book goes beyond the opiate-inspiration debate by considering religion's multidimensionality and by incorporating perspectives on social movements, civil society, and cultural theory into our understanding of religion's effects on African-American political activism. It asks how religion—as a set of institutions, a source of self-empowerment, and a sign of indigenous culture—mobilizes African Americans into the political process.

Political scientist Kenneth Wald begins to develop a multidimensional approach to the study of religion and political activism by viewing religion as a "political resource." Wald explains that religiously based resources are "qualities possessed by religiously motivated people that can prove valuable in political action" (1987, 29). These qualities are represented, according to Wald, in three types of religiously based resources for political mobilization, namely, motivation, organization, and social interaction. Religious motivation, for instance, might work in two ways. First, it might encourage political activism by fostering a sense of personal or group empowerment. Political actors might feel that with spiritual guidance they could be effective in this-worldly pursuits, including politics. Second, religion might stimulate political action by leading participants to perceive political issues in moral terms. Religious leaders and political elites can articulate political issues, like abortion, as questions of morality, mobilizing religiously motivated actors for or against issues and for or against candidates who promote their moral perspective.

"Religious ideals," as Wald notes, "are potentially powerful sources of commitment and motivation," and they should not be underestimated as resources for participation. Religious ideals inspire people to act politically because of a unique set of participatory incentives. Religious ideals are so potentially powerful that "human beings will make enormous sacrifices if they believe themselves to be driven by a divine force" (1987, 29–30). And since these ideas are sacred to believers, and thus in their minds beyond doubt, they provide powerful cues for activism. "People to whom religion truly matters, people who believe they have found answers to the ultimate questions, or are very close to finding them," explains Stephen Carter, "will often respond to incentives other than those that motivate more secularized citizens" (1993, 275–276).

Religious institutions also have consequences for political action. "In terms of access and communication," Wald notes, "churches are powerful organizations with formal membership, headquarters, regularly scheduled group meetings, publications, and full-time professional leadership" (1987, 38). As scholars of civic participation have recently discovered, religious institutions are a laboratory for learning participatory skills. By participating in activities such as singing in a choir, serving on a trustee board, teaching and organizing Sunday school, or putting together a church fundraiser, churchgoers learn and sharpen organizing skills that can spill over into secular forms of participation (Peterson 1992; Verba, Schlozman, and Brady, 1995).

THE SCOPE OF AFRICAN-AMERICAN ACTIVISM

In contrast to most studies on religion and black political activism, this study considers both religion and political action as multidimensional factors. Black political activism embraces what Aldon D. Morris, Shirley J. Hatchett, and Ronald E. Brown describe as the "orderly and disorderly" sides of the political process (1989). By "orderly and disorderly" they mean that blacks have been socialized into employing political tactics that lie both within and outside of mainstream political processes. In other words, boycotting, picketing, and joining protest marches are just as legitimate as a tool of political expression as voting, campaigning for candidates, or contacting an elected official about a problem.

This mix of institutionalized and protest behavior has deep roots in African-American politics and society. It evolved as a participatory norm after the collapse of Reconstruction and—depending on the opportunities for political mobilization—has ebbed and flowed for much of the twentieth century.[9] The exclusion of African Americans from the nation's civic and social life with the onset of Jim Crow cemented a racialized public sphere. These norms were nurtured in what political scientist Michael Dawson has referred to as a "black counterpublic" (1994b, 195–223). This counterpublic, which included black religious institutions, social movements, civil rights organizations, black magazines and newspapers, masonic groups, social clubs, and so on, encouraged a variety of political tactics and strategies that challenged white supremacist discourse and practice.[10]

Black political activism—like all forms of political activities—also differs in the level of commitment actors devote to political action. Voting, for instance, takes relatively less effort than boycotting a store or organizing a neighborhood association. Taking part in a protest during the civil rights movement, for instance, required a greater level of personal commitment and risk than campaigning for a candidate in a northern city. Thus, religion's effects on black activism should vary not only because of religion's multidimensionality, but also because of the nature and context of political action.

METHODOLOGICAL APPROACHES

Exploring the multidimensional effects of religion on African-American political mobilization requires an interdisciplinary approach and diverse methods of inquiry. As religion scholar Wade Roof observes, religion is "so complex and convoluted that not only multiple dimensions but also multiple approaches are required for analysis" (1979, 18). This study's research draws on scholarship from sociology, anthropology, psychology, history, and political science. It uses both qualitative and quantitative methods. Participant observation has helped to explore religiously based resources in the context of political rallies and church services. Other primary sources include recorded church services, archives, religious publications, campaign finance records, newspapers, campaign literature, and personal interviews. Oral histories, biographies, autobiographies, church histories, and religious directories have been significant secondary sources. Opinion surveys from the 1960s to the 1990s have provided a rich database for systematic exploration of the institutional and psychological ties between religion and black political activism.

STRUCTURE OF THE BOOK

This book is organized in three sections. The first section (chapters 2–4) covers the theoretical focus of the book (that is, in what ways does Afro-Christianity supply resources for black political activism?) and reconsiders Afro-Christianity's effects on black activism during the civil rights movement. Chapter 2 delves further into what happened at the Carter Temple CME church that August morning in 1992, exploring the variety of political resources—material and nonmaterial—that Christianity made available to those who attended the event. Chapter 3 provides an interpretation of the event and sets the stage for the rest of the book by connecting themes that emerged from the event to themes that are covered in the succeeding chapters. It shows how religion provides both "macro" and "micro" resources for black political activism, and how those resources are linked to African-American political culture. Traveling back to the 1960s, chapter 4 offers an alternative view on whether Afro-Christianity acted as an opiate or mobilizer during the civil rights movement by combining perspectives on civil society, civil religion, and the oppositional character of social movements—perspectives that previous scholars on religion and black political activism have not considered.

The second section (chapters 5–8) takes a separate look at the institutional, psychological, and cultural dimensions of religious resources and considers how two of those dimensions—religious institutions and feelings of self-empowerment—work together in stimulating individual and collective political action. Chapter 5 examines the historical interaction between black churches and black political life and shows how the institutional dynamics of churches remain a powerful resource in contemporary black mobilization. Chapter 6 explores the links between religious devotion, feelings of self-worth, and believers' perceptions of their own political empowerment. Chapter 7 looks at how activism in church work and a religiously inspired sense of political empowerment work together to encourage black political activism. Shifting from an individual level of analysis to an examination of the behavior of elites, chapter 8 examines how religious symbols and rituals are used by ministers, community activists, and political candidates to construct strategies for political action.

In the concluding section, chapter 9 considers the role that gender plays in religion and African-American political activism by analyzing black women's participation in the church. Chapter 10 speculates on how current trends in both Afro-Christianity and black politics may alter black political activism in the future and raises questions about how inegalitarian norms in Afro-Christianity may undermine democratic practices in African-American politics and society.

SOMETHING WITHIN

In 1912, the French sociologist Emile Durkheim articulated his theory of religion as a mechanism encompassing a "collective force" that divinely confers inner strength upon believers (1972, 229–230). Seven years later lyricist and schoolteacher Lucie E. Campbell overheard a blind man in Memphis being taunted for singing gospel music, telling his tormentors that he had "something within" that made him sing. She was then inspired to turn that phrase into a gospel song. Campbell wrote during one of this century's worst periods of racial violence, shortly after legally enforced white supremacy, or Jim Crow, had returned to the South; her lyrics have symbolized black resistance to white domination ever since. As one music scholar interpreted it in 1992, "Life is a struggle, but we have something within us that tells us we are more than what is seen on the outside" (George 1992). This book takes its title from Campbell's song; the phrase reflects the book's aim of venturing deep within the contours of Afro-Christianity and its links to African-American political life.

2

When a Little Becomes Much

Religious Resources in Action

And they say unto Him, we have here but five loaves, and
two fishes.

Matthew 14:17

Each of the church leaders gathered at the Carter Temple CME
Church that August morning had, two weeks earlier, received a letter written on
Braun's campaign stationery addressed to them as "Dear Leader of Faith," inviting them to "a good morning of fellowship with Illinois Democratic nominee for
Senate, Carol Moseley Braun." The invitation had a head shot of the smiling
candidate on one side and a list of forty ministers who made up the event's
steering and organizing committees on the other; it was clear that the Braun
campaign was strategically targeting religious leaders to mobilize blacks for the
upcoming election.

This letter was signed by Braun's own minister, the Reverend Addie Wyatt of
the Vernon Park Church of God. Reverend Wyatt was chair of a group of ministers who would campaign on Braun's behalf; this committee was part of Braun's
official campaign organization. Her interdenominational work, activism in electoral and protest activities, and longtime involvement in Chicago's labor union
movement had probably made her a familiar colleague to these clerics. In addition
to her years of organizing for the Meat Packers Union, Reverend Wyatt had, two
years before, supported striking catfish workers in the Mississippi Delta.[1] She also
organized black women for Harold Washington's mayoral campaign. Under her
leadership, she estimated, these women raised more than one hundred thousand
dollars for the candidate.[2] In fact, Reverend Wyatt claimed to have delivered a
prophecy from God to Harold Washington, telling him, two weeks before he
announced his candidacy, "God has sent me to tell you that you suppose to be
mayor of Chicago." She assured the future mayor: "[God] will deliver the city
into our hands."

In her letter, Reverend Wyatt pointed out the historic nature of Braun's potential election: "Never before has an African-American woman been elected to
the U.S. Senate." She also recognized the indigenous ties of the clergy to Chicago's
black communities and the potential significance of the ministers' candidate en-

dorsements: "If you have not endorsed any candidate, we ask that you attend this breakfast and hear what Carol Moseley Braun has to say." Wyatt urged those who already supported Braun to "include her in your prayers and meditations, and join us."

The renown of Braun's minister probably helped to convince politically active clerics that the candidate had legitimate church ties. In addition, the steering and organizing committees for the event included locally based national leaders of various Christian denominations, including the bishops of the predominately black African Methodist Episcopal (AME) church and the Church of God in Christ (COGIC), as well as Roman Catholic priests and ministers of the National Baptist Convention, the Pentecostal Assemblies of America (both predominately black denominations), the United Methodist Church, and several nondenominational congregations.

Copies of the printed program for the breakfast were handed to participants as they entered the room. The cover read, "Religious Leadership Breakfast for Carol Moseley Braun"; the names of committee members appeared inside. Some parts of the program duplicated the structure of a religious service, with a congregational hymn, a scripture reading, an opening prayer, sacred music selections, and a benediction. In other ways, it read like a political event. Stuffed inside the program was a "Blitz for Braun" flyer requesting volunteers to distribute campaign literature.

After the audience sang a couple of verses of the hymn "Leaning on the Everlasting Arm," Bishop Brazier, the master of ceremonies for the event, observed that it was a great honor to be "a part of the election campaign of a great woman." Bishop Brazier then quoted scripture—Psalm 127. "Except the Lord build a house," he uttered in one breath, as a chorus of voices from the audience chimed in to help him finish, "they labor in vain that built it." He went on: "We know that the Lord is with us today. We know that we are on our way." He urged the assembled to labor for Braun's candidacy by registering eligible voters in their churches.

Carter Temple's minister, the Reverend Henry Williamson, who had recently been elected president of Operation PUSH (People United to Serve Humanity)— a nationally known civil rights group based in Chicago and founded by Jesse Jackson during the early seventies—was unable to attend the breakfast, so a representative gave the welcoming remarks in his place. Voter registration material was handed out to the audience by members of Project Vote, an organization registering black voters in Chicago for the November general election. Williamson's representative urged the audience to "participate and support our very own, God's child, Carol Moseley Braun," and asked interested ministers to see Project Vote's clerical coordinator.

The registration handout noted that "the unregistered in our communities potentially represent the critical swing vote in both the presidential and senatorial election." It outlined how churches could participate, instructing religious leaders to appoint a voter registration coordinator, devote a Sunday to registration at their church, put registration material in church bulletins, set up booths at church events or programs, encourage ten lay members to become volunteer deputy registrars, and publicize registration activities through their religious radio and television broadcasts. The leaflet appeared to be specifically designed for clerics, noting that "[c]hurches have historically been the key base for successful voter registration activities in the African American community" and adding that "[w]ith their large memberships and commitment to social justice, they provide both volunteer deputy registrars and a forum to reach the unregistered."

The leadership breakfast continued with a reading from St. John 27:20–26. Father Martini Shaw of the St. Thomas Episcopal Church read these passages, which were Jesus's prayer for unity among His disciples—and all believers—before His imminent crucifixion. Unity was a concern here, too; this may have been the first time since the death of Chicago's first black mayor that diverse factions of clerics had supported the same candidate. During the primary, thirty-six ministers had endorsed one of Braun's opponents, Al Hofeld. When asked by reporters why the group was not supporting Braun, the only black candidate, Reverend O'Dell White of the Spirit of Love Missionary Baptist Church had responded that "it is a simple percentage ratio . . . she can not win."[3] Father Shaw's reading appeared to symbolize the importance of oneness among politically fractured elements in the audience: "I do not pray for these only, but also for those who believe in me through their word. That they may all be one, even as thou Father are in me and I am in thee, that they also may be in us. So that the world may believe that thou has sent me, the glory which thou has given me, I have given to them, that they may be one even as we are one."

Father Michael Pfleger, a white Roman Catholic priest whose voice resonated like that of a Baptist preacher, led a prayer, which called for divine recognition and guidance for the candidate and her campaign. Pfleger's preaching resembles that seen in black charismatic Protestant churches. Reverend Willie Barrow, a black woman and former president of Operation PUSH, described it this way: "The first time I heard him, I had to look twice to make sure what was happening. Most white preachers, you know, don't have a lot of spirit and emotionalism. But this [white] boy, he can whoop!"[4] Father Pfleger serves as priest at the nearly all-black St. Sabina's on Chicago's South Side and often dresses in Kente cloth; he combines Catholic liturgy with West African music and rituals during mass. His renown comes from his work with Father George Clements to mobilize protest against stores and companies that sold and manufactured drug paraphernalia in Chicago's minority communities. These protest activities led to the passage of a state law that made the sale of such merchandise illegal.

Father Pfleger began his prayer that morning by acknowledging God's presence: "Father God we thank you and we pray to you first for the gift of this day.

We thank you, Lord, for each and every person here that you will allow to gather in your name. And we thank you for the purpose for which we gather. We have to thank you, Lord, that you would continue to reveal yourself to us in your all-divine way and fashion."

Father Pfleger then thanked God for sending a candidate of faith. "We thank you for our sister Carol. We thank you first of all that she knows you, that she loves you, and is faithful to you and your word. We thank you Lord that through Carol, you have given us the privilege and the opportunity to continue to renew the face of the earth, to open up the rivers of righteousness and the streams of justice."

Quoting fragments of Amos 5:24, which commands God's people to challenge social oppression, the prayer constructed Braun's candidacy as a divinely decreed challenge to societal inequalities. Father Pfleger's prayer then turned its focus to the gathering's participants, asking for divinely inspired commitment to political action and prophetically envisioning Braun's imminent victory: "All we ask Lord is that you continue to use us, from morning until sunset. We ask you Lord that you will stir up your word within us, that we might work with an urgency and not grow faint and in remembering that even as we stand the victory is already ours."

Father Pfleger then asked God to provide sacred protection and feelings of empowerment for the candidate: "Oh Lord, we thank you and we pray to you and we ask that you would protect our sister. Dispatch now your angels from Heaven to watch over her in her comings and in her goings. Strengthen her on the journey, and make her ever and always dependent upon you." The prayer ended: "For we are no longer ourselves, but now it is Christ who lives in us."

Next came the newly appointed bishop of the United Methodist Church, Charles Jordan. A former regional administrator of the United Methodist Church, Bishop Jordan had been instrumental in organizing black clerics in his denomination in support of Harold Washington's 1983 mayoral race.[5] Indeed, Bishop Jordan's involvement in secular politics extended back over two decades. Demonstrating the communication and social networks of ministers, Bishop Brazier noted, when introducing Bishop Jordan, that he had known him for over twenty-five years "and worked with him . . . when we were in the throes of organizing The Woodlawn Organization."

As if receiving a prophetic vision, Bishop Jordan proclaimed that one of the purposes of this gathering was to "celebrate that God is about to do something new in our midst" and that the candidate was a religious sacrifice "offering herself as a part of a fulfillment of God's new day."

Another reason for the event, the bishop said, was to organize support for Braun by "commit[ing] ourselves to the task" of mobilizing "our prayers, our time, our money, our energy, our votes—and we have to get the votes." After

Bishop Jordan's talk, some audience participants lined up for a breakfast of eggs, sausage, bacon, biscuits, orange juice, sweet rolls, and coffee, while others mingled.

Then the breakfast's featured speaker entered the room from a side door and was introduced by the master of ceremonies as "The next senator of Illinois!" Welcomed with thunderous and sustained applause from participants, most of whom were standing, the candidate sat down next to the speaker's podium, and participants began to settle back into their seats. As the applause slowly dwindled, Bishop Brazier introduced elected officials and candidates who were, as he put it, making "contributions to [the] city." These included several members of the Board of Education, the local head of the NAACP, a few candidates running for public office, and the newly crowned Miss Black Illinois. One candidate, Alderman Bobby Rush, the Democratic nominee for Illinois's First Congressional District who had been shaking hands and conversing with ministers throughout the event, stood and waved to the audience. As more seats began to fill and the breakfast line shortened, the musical selections began.

Sung a capella with collective hand-clapping and foot-tapping keeping the tempo upbeat, the first song, a slave spiritual, subtly repudiated otherworldliness and encouraged the political involvement of the faithful:

> Well, I keep so busy working for the master
> I ain't got time to die
> Oh, I keep so busy singing for Jesus
> Ain't got time to die
> Well, I keep so busy working for the kingdom
> Ain't got time to die

Someone unfamiliar with this culture might have read the song's verses as evidence of blacks' submissiveness to white domination. Phrases like "singing for Jesus" and "working for the kingdom" could be taken to refer to pie-in-the-sky desires, diversions from worldly concerns like electoral politics, distractions that might even amount to "working for the master" or serving "white" interests. But it is unlikely that anyone present experienced it that way, since the context of the performance was a political gathering to elect a black to the U.S. Senate. The soloist sang the bridge to the tune:

> Get out of the way, let me praise my Jesus
> Get out of the way, let me praise the Lord
> If I don't praise him the rocks are gonna cry out
> Glory and honor, Glory and honor
> I ain't got time to die.

Many in the audience responded with a wave of a hand, a nod, or a shout of "Yes, that's right." Any outsider bothered by the hint of submissive imagery in

"Ain't Got Time to Die" would have been immediately reassured by the next number, "Ordinary People." In this performance the soloist, this time with piano accompaniment, sang several of the first verses in a melancholy yet earnest mood. They seemed to articulate the merits of collective action through divine guidance, especially for those who might lack material resources:

> Just ordinary people, God uses ordinary people
> He chooses people, just like me and you
> Who are willing to do everything that he commands.
> God chooses people that will give Him their all
> No matter how small it all seems to you
> Because little means much when you place it in the Master's hand.

"Yes, it does," "That's all right," "Amen," the audience fervently agreed. The next verses of the melody seemed to symbolize the link between collective action and divine guidance. Referring to biblical miracles that illustrate personal sacrifice and divine intervention, the soloist continued:

> Just like the little lad, who gave Jesus all he had
> Oh multitudes were fed with a fish and loaf of bread
> What you have may not seem much
> But when you yield it to the task
> The master's loving hand appears
> Then you understand how your life could never be the same.

Repeating the first stanza, the tune slowed and modulated to a higher octave. The soloist improvised verses by stretching syllables and emphasizing phrases, bringing most of the audience to its feet. Listeners swayed back and forth, shouting "Glory" and "That's right" in chorus. The boundary between performer and audience blurred, symbolizing more clearly the mission of the political gathering.

Rocking side-to-side, with a microphone in one hand and gesturing with the other hand to emphasize particular phrases of the song, the singer trumpeted:

> Just ordinary people, my God uses
> Plain old ordinary people
> He uses the rich and the poor,
> The black and the white, the strong and the wounded
> I just stopped by to tell you that
> My God uses people who will give them their all
> No matter, no matter how small it may seem to you
> Because little becomes much
> When you place it in the Master's hand.

As the performance ended, the master of ceremonies returned to the podium, and members of the audience began to settle back into in their seats. With approving murmurs still stirring the gathering, Bishop Brazier began to chant, as if he were about to deliver a sermon, "if this were Sunday morning . . . I would be ready." Repeating a line from the previous selection—"A little becomes a lot"—Bishop Brazier continued the program with an introduction that granted further sacred legitimacy to Braun's candidacy, and he continued on to liken Braun's victory against incumbent Allen Dixon to David's victory over Goliath in the Old Testament. As he spoke, some listeners joined him in call and response.

BRAZIER: As I sat there I began to think of how so often we fail to see the hands of God.

RESPONSE: Think about it.

BRAZIER: Because sometimes he moves in mysterious ways.

RESPONSE: Oh, yes, yes!

BRAZIER: When this candidate started out . . .

RESPONSE: Yes, think about it!

BRAZIER: I would expect that ninety percent of the people in this room thought it was a useless task.

RESPONSE: Well.

BRAZIER: She was coming up against a giant . . .

RESPONSE: Yes, oh yes, a giant.

BRAZIER: . . . one who had never lost an election . . .

RESPONSE: Come on Bishop.

BRAZIER: . . . who was already ensconced on the throne . . .

RESPONSE: Yes. Come on Bishop!

BRAZIER: . . . who was an incumbent, an incumbent rarely loses.

RESPONSE: That's right.

Attempting to renegotiate the gender distinction between Braun and the biblical warrior, the bishop proclaimed: "[H]ere comes a little, almost unknown person, who, I hate to call on Jesus, but is it possible to say Davidess? If it wasn't so un-biblical I would talk about a little David who comes along and strikes a mighty giant. I can see the hand of God . . . that was the hand of God, leading us out of the wilderness."

Then, referring to Braun as "our keynote speaker," Bishop Brazier introduced the candidate as "Our next United States senator from the state of Illinois!" The event immediately began to feel like a political rally as participants shouted and clapped in unison—"Carol! Carol! Carol!" Braun took the floor; the wide stripes of her blue and white dress coordinated strikingly with the red, white, and blue lettering on the poster above the podium.

She thanked the organizing committee for putting the event together. Recognizing—and perhaps exaggerating—the political resources of the ministers, Braun claimed that "this room right now easily represents . . . five million people." On a rush of applause from the audience, she added that reaching out to churches had helped her win the Democratic primary; she thanked Bishop Brazier and other ministers for letting her "come to their pulpit" to "talk to [their] congregations about my platform and my programs for Illinois and why I was running . . . for the United States Senate." Seeking similar support for the general election, Braun quickly reminded the ministers that her campaign still needed their support, telling "everyone else in the room that I was not able to contact [or] did not contact [or] did not have a chance to interface with in the primary" that "I am so grateful to you because really the race is not over 'til it's over. It's not over until November and I am going to need all your help."

Braun then started to give what appeared to be a modified campaign speech. "You know, Reverend Brazier," she exclaimed, "when [you] talked about David, really the fact of the matter is, [you] really struck a responsive cord in me." Weaving the biblical story of David and Goliath into a narrative that justified her race for the Senate, she declared: "[w]e really did just start out with an idea and concept of doing that which was right. Doing the right thing, that's all that we were trying to do." She contended that her campaign was for "stand[ing] up for the principles about the appropriate role of government, and how government should serve all people, and what should be done."

Commenting on the program's musical selections, Braun began to "testify" about how her religious beliefs had sustained her physically and emotionally during the campaign. Noting that "this campaign trail has been a rough one" and that with the long hours campaigning "every now and then I get weak in the knees," Braun began to describe how her religious beliefs had supported her through the hard work of the primary: "We walked into a church in Urbana-Champaign last week, and as I walked in the church, the scripture on the church program—now I don't have it with me, and I don't know my Bible well enough to know where this book comes from, but it had to do with—we shall win the race if we don't faint." The scripture that Braun tried to recall was from Galatians 6:9. It speaks about the perseverance of those who seek to "do good." The scripture reads: "And let us not be weary in well doing; for in due season we shall reap, if we don't faint." As the audience exploded with laughter and shouts of "Amen," Braun continued her testimony:

> Now I don't know where that comes from . . . but I'm sure that somebody
> will let us know, because I would like to find that again. But it had lifted

FIGURE 2.1. *Carol Moseley Braun at Ministerial Breakfast. Photo by author.*

me up. For that whole day of activities in Urbana-Champaign, and that quote, walking into that church that morning, lifted me up and held me up for the rest of the service. And I have to tell you, all during the dark days of that primary it was that faith that lifted me up and carried me through even when my own strength was failing me. When my own strength was failing me, I was able to keep going.

Attributing her physical health to this faith, Braun continued to recognize divine intervention in her election victory: "I didn't even get a cold once this year and

I've had chronic bronchitis ever since I was sixteen. I did not get a cold once. Because it was my faith that carried me through it. Yes, that carried me through it."

Braun went on to talk about the goals of her candidacy. Throughout her thirty-minute stump speech, she kept returning to the theme from one of the musical selections played earlier: "I can't get over the notion that an ordinary person went out there to do the right thing." Braun described the Senate as a closed institution "without the voices of working people, ordinary people," saying she entered the senatorial contest to get democracy to "serve ordinary people." She charged that the Bush administration didn't understand the economy because "they don't hear ordinary people" who "built this country to begin with," and that Bush advocated only for "the one percent at the top that got richer in the last ten years."

Toward the end of her talk, Braun began to focus on the organizational resources of churches. She first asked ministers in the audience to help "get the word out" about her campaign. Then, recognizing the participants' networking capacity and their ability to bring campaign and voter information to potential voters, Braun made this request:

> I need your help; there are a hundred and two counties in this state. I have to try to be in as many of them as I can. I will not always be able therefore to be here in Chicago physically or even in Cook County and so I thought . . . about how to do this. The church is the single most important institution we have, and so if you are willing to help me spread the word in your respective denominations, to spread the word through your own congregations, to help spread out and spread the word and make introductions for me even in southern and central Illinois [and] throughout the state, that will give me the ability to have the kind of statewide network so that Illinois will be able to send a signal . . . that will be unmistakable.

Braun then returned to her seat while the audience applauded enthusiastically. Bishop Brazier then introduced ministers who would talk about how everyone present could get involved in Braun's campaign.

Reverend Elmer Fowler of the Third Baptist Church, who had recently served as president of the Chicago chapter of the NAACP, spoke first. He talked about the electoral challenge that lay ahead. Referring to the rift that had arisen among both religious and secular black leadership over who would be Harold Washington's successor as mayor of the city, Fowler quipped, "We have a second chance in Chicago," adding, with an edge of ridicule, to the mostly male audience: "If the Lord don't use men, He will use women!" Many in the audience laughed and amened; others nodded in agreement. Reverend Fowler recalled famous black women of the past who were African-American leaders: Harriet Tubman, Sojourner Truth, "who never apologized for being a woman," Mary McLeod Bethune, Madame C. J. Walker, and "that school teacher from Memphis, Tennessee, who wrote 'There is something within me that holdeth the reins, there is something within me that I cannot explain.' These are the women who have come [before us]."

Urging members of the audience to "talk to every black person you see and get them registered to vote," Reverend Fowler also asked them to make a financial contribution to Braun's campaign, declaring that "you got to have money to get into the game," so "give some money for the cause." He then went on to caution them not to give out of self-interest, asserting "you ain't supposed to get nothing for yourself." Indeed, "you're supposed to get something for the folks and in turn they will give something to you." After he announced an upcoming political rally at his church, Reverend Fowler's voice turned angry as he contested the religious claims of political conservatives: "[T]hese Republicans . . . think that being a conservative is a blessing, a gift from God to this earth. But ain't nothing to no Republican conservative, to conserve, you got to have something to conserve. I'm so sick and tired of Bush. . . . Yes, I am a liberal and I hate Republican conservative voters as well, as much as they hate them liberal Democrats."

Reverend Fowler's spirited talk ended with these partisan remarks, which provoked an eruption of laughter and applause from his listeners. Bishop Brazier then introduced the next speaker, the Reverend Shelvin Hall, who had served as president of a West Side ministerial group and during the mid-sixties had been active in Martin Luther King's Chicago crusade. Before Reverend Hall reached the podium, Reverend Brazier informed the audience that he had to leave for a previous engagement but was contributing a thousand dollars to Braun's campaign.

Asking all the ministers from his own Baptist organization, the Illinois Baptist Association—some thirty—to stand before the audience, Reverend Hall noted in his talk that his denominational group had had Braun as a guest speaker at one of their statewide meetings in East St. Louis, Illinois. He informed the audience that his was the "largest [organization of] structured Baptist churches in the state," suggesting that he represented a vast communication network. He also noted that Braun's appearance at his group's statewide Baptist convention would help her win in November, because ministers from key cities throughout the state would be in attendance. He ended his remarks by announcing that he too would pledge a thousand dollars to Braun's campaign.

At that point Reverend Leon Finney, a political operative for the Braun campaign, took over as master of ceremonies and introduced the final speaker, Reverend Willie Barrow. A minister from the Church of God and the former president of Operation PUSH, Reverend Barrow, known as the "little warrior" for her short stature and tenacity on civil rights issues, had been involved in both electoral and protest politics in Chicago for decades. She approached the podium, which nearly hid her figure from the audience's view, and started raising funds for Braun's campaign.

Quoting a snippet from the Book of Revelation that seemed to justify Braun's underdog victory in the primary, "the last shall be first, and the first shall be last," Reverend Barrow explained how the candidate was last in political organization, campaign advertising, endorsements, and funds. But now, Barrow maintained, Braun was the first woman during the election year to break "the glass ceiling," allowing other women to win primary victories for nominations to the Senate.

Proclaiming that twenty-five thousand dollars would be raised from breakfast participants, she then asked the audience to bow their heads in prayer for the candidate. Acknowledging the racial and gender importance of Braun's candidacy, Reverend Barrow prayed for perseverance: "Eternal God our father, we pause because we know that the strength of God endures forever. This is a woman of God. You have placed her in this position not for herself, but for all of your people, black, white, brown, rich, poor. Here's a woman that's not taking it. She lives on our side, don't live in the suburbs. She lives right here on the South Side with a black child. . . . Preserve her strength."

Reverend Barrow then began to target those present for thousand-dollar contributions. Disclosing the names of the ministers who had already given that amount, Barrow thundered: "I know that we've got about ten people here who could give a thousand dollars," asking the hushed audience, "How many of you will join the thousand-dollar crowd?" Reverend Barrow then asked those willing to raise their hands. In Barrow's first ten minutes of soliciting, a dozen or so individuals gave or pledged a thousand dollars each.

Adopting a fundraising technique used at many black churches, Barrow began to lower dollar amounts in increments to encourage more people to give. Many of the several hundred participants of the breakfast came forward to put their contribution into a round wicker basket, as if it were collection time at a regular Sunday morning worship service. This ritual went on for about twenty minutes, as the candidate left for another campaign stop and the participants slowly drifted out of Carter Temple's basement.

Up to the last Sunday before Election Day, Braun made appearances at several more black churches. She reserved one of her last visits for her own church, the Vernon Park Church of God. While radio, television, and print media gathered in with congregants and elected officials, Braun arrived at the church after both the morning sermon and a stump speech given by then Virginia Governor L. Douglas Wilder on behalf of presidential candidate Bill Clinton and other Democratic candidates.[6]

Before Braun came forward, the minister, Reverend Addie Wyatt, reflected—while the choir softly sang "We Are All More Than Conquerors through Jesus

Christ"—on how Vernon Park church had served as a resource for advancing black political interests throughout the years:

> We've been here a long time involved in the struggle. During the dark days of Emmett Till and even before when workers were on the forefront, trying to make life better for themselves and their families, Vernon Park Church of God, you were there. When Ralph Metcalfe in his struggles came to us, thank God we were there. When Harold Washington during his struggle— poor Harold sometimes would come to our services and [his] security [guards] could not get him out of the services—there's something about the presence of God in every life that makes a difference. So we love you for being there, for God's people, for God's call.

These recollections provided the congregation with collective memories of events that have shaped black Chicago's political consciousness and informed some and reminded others of Vernon Park's connection to those events. Reverend Wyatt then reminded the congregation that it was about to make history again by having one of its own a member of the United States Senate.

"We have brought home today Carol Moseley Braun," Reverend Wyatt declared, "who before the world ever knew her would sit in our presence and ask for prayer, and ask for strength." As the choir's singing came to a close, Wyatt introduced Braun, reminding the congregation that Vernon Park had nurtured the candidate by being her "spiritual family." For Braun, this was an opportunity to express thanks to her church for years of both political and personal support. The candidate told the assembled that her experience at Vernon Park had given her strength that had sustained her during periods of crisis. She thanked the congregation, saying: "[Y]ou have provided the kind of support over the years in ways that I don't think you realize." Then Braun began to reflect: "I was remembering, coming up the stairs, Reverend Wyatt, how ten years ago, if not more—we were on Seventy-sixth Street—and I sat next to Ricky Wyatt. And I was really in trouble in that time of my life and [Reverend Wyatt] said to me, 'Lean not on your own understanding.' It opened my eyes and gave me the ability to overcome through times of stress and times of trouble."

Braun told the congregation how their support assisted her in times of political crisis, thus providing symbolic meaning to the troubles that plagued her campaign for the Senate. Quoting again the same scripture that encourages believers to rely on God for personal strength and guidance, "Trust in the Lord with all thine heart; and lean not unto thine own understanding" (Proverbs 3:5), Braun acknowledged that divine guidance had helped her to face adversities during her campaign. "As I reflect on all that I have been through . . . the scandalizing of my name and the exposure and all of that. All I can think of is lean not on your own understanding, there's a reason for everything. There's a reason for suffering, there's a reason for strife, for all of those things. . . . I feel blessed to be in a position to be an agent for change."

Braun thanked the congregation for "holding up the light over all these years," because, she asserted, her run against opponent Richard S. Williamson represented a battle between good and evil. She explained: "And that's what its really all about. . . . The more things get complicated the more you can reduce them to simplicity. And the bottom line is that it is the same struggle between good and evil and right and wrong. Between those who will do for the people, and those who will not. It is the same struggle, getting played out in another kind of way."

Braun ended her comments by telling the congregation that she felt "good about the election because the Lord is in the blessing business." Joining hands with church elders and politicians, including former mayor Eugene Sawyer and state representative Don Trotter, both members of Vernon Park, she heard a special prayer for her candidacy. Reverend Wyatt, declaring that "we want people [in office] who will respect and appreciate God and will work for God's people," instructed a female clerical assistant to lift a divine request for the candidate. Delivered by a woman, the prayer articulated the significance of Braun's campaign to many women by lending it biblical symbolism:

Our father and our God, we don't even know how to offer this thanksgiving of praise to you for what you have done for us. To see the scriptures unfold before our eyes. When we read in Jeremiah the thirty-first chapter that this new thing was going to be created in the earth. A woman—glory to God— would compass a man, not surpass, but go around and about in your kingdom-building work and be effective.

Citing an Old Testament prophecy that heralds the emergence of women as leaders (Jeremiah 31:22), the minister continued to pray on Braun's behalf by characterizing her as a biblical heroine:

We thank you for the wonderful opportunity that we have of presenting Carol to you, Jesus. We thank you, Lord God, we lift her up, she our modern-day Esther, standing in the gap for us. We bless her right now in the name of Jesus. We connect with every other prayer of faith that has already been prayed in her behalf, and we believe that you are going to deliver us on Tuesday. We claim the victory.

When a Persian king, struck by her beauty, chose her to be his queen, Esther used her influence on the royal court to save her people from extermination. Wyatt likened Braun to Esther; like the Old Testament queen, she was "standing in the gap for us," and, by implication, she would represent her people's interests in times of crisis.

Not surprisingly, not everyone was convinced that Braun had a political alliance with God. Her Republican opponent, Richard S. Williamson, characterized her religious remarks as "really strange. . . . Apparently she claims she was endorsed by God, and I think it's getting stranger," adding, "I think it's a little goofy."[7]

Yet the prophecies did not end. When Braun made perhaps her last campaign visit to a church that same Sunday, her forthcoming victory—two days away— was divinely revealed. The Reverend Milton Bronson of the Christ Tabernacle Church announced to Braun a message from the Divine: "The Lord has told me to tell you that you have won [the election]." To some this spiritual revelation of Braun's victory was more reliable than any scientific poll could ever be.

3

Prophetic Fragments

Macro and Micro Foundations of Religious Resources

Gather up the fragments that remain, that nothing be lost.

John 6:12

THE RELIGIOUS LEADERSHIP BREAKFAST FOR senatorial candidate Carol Moseley Braun was more than a routine campaign event. Later, after the breakfast, I listened again and again to the recording of Braun's visit to her own church the Sunday before the election, and I doubted that a survey of churchgoers or ministers could have fully captured the dynamics of either of those events. On the surface, the leadership breakfast could be interpreted as just another way for Braun to target ministers—as she might any other group of powerful people—as potential supporters of her congressional campaign. Yet my observations suggest that there was more going on here than a politician's self-interested pursuit of elites; indeed, they shed light on something far more complex—religion's effects on collective action and black political mobilization.

The tools of ethnography, as well as what political scientist Richard Fenno describes as "soaking and poking," the practice of immersing oneself in the milieu of political actors, help uncover the effects of religion on black political mobilization beyond the confines of ministerial leadership. They provide a starting point from which we can begin to systematically explore how political actors forge religiously based resources and how, during the mobilization process, these resources interact with one another institutionally, psychologically, and culturally. Resource mobilization theory is also helpful here; scholars use it to describe the resources that social movements draw on to organize individuals. It has concentrated on tangible, material sources of mobilization, or "macro" resources, such as indigenous leadership, communication, social networks, meeting places, and financial support. Though resource mobilization theory does not emphasize cognitive, emotional, or "discursive" resources (Billings 1990), my adaptation of this approach (outlined in figure 3.1,) assumes that these kinds of resources are as significant as organizational resources. Scholars of the evolving micromobilization perspective (Mueller 1992), who argue that political actors draw on resources other than organizations and institutions, have inspired this adaptation. "Micro"

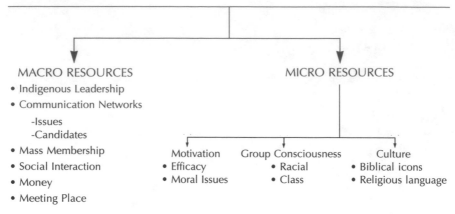

FIGURE 3.1. *Aspects of Religion as Resources for Political Mobilization.*

level resources, which are nonmaterial and thus less tangible—some examples are group solidarity, the symbolic articulation of political goals, and feelings of confidence in one's ability to affect political matters—play a crucial role in political mobilization.

Activities during the leadership breakfast and Braun's visits at worship services illustrate some of the ways that micro resources help actors to negotiate and formulate political goals. Members of a cultural group construct collective identities, formulate grievances, and articulate possibilities of political success through their own cultural milieu. When mobilized, these identities, grievances, and estimates of potential success interact with macro resources—funding, meeting space, and networks—that are lodged in the organizations and institutions of politicized groups (Mueller 1992, 10–11). Thus when one minister urged participants at the breakfast to commit their "prayers, time, and energy" to Braun's campaign, he identified both micro and macro foundations of political mobilization as mutually supportive sources for cooperative action.

MACRO RESOURCES

Macro resources for political mobilization are readily recognized by students of social movements and political participation. Locating them, because they are often tangible, is easier than uncovering micro resources, which are subtle and often unrecognized as sources of collective action even by the actors themselves. The ministerial breakfast easily revealed how a church could furnish political actors with organizational and institutional resources. The indigenous leadership, communication networks, easy availability of mass memberships, and social interaction of political actors at the breakfast were there for all to see. Anyone looking through the door could identify key campaign actors socializing with ministers of various denominations, broadening the capacity of networks, disseminating information about their campaigns to various churches and denominational groups, and facilitating the direct involvement of ministers and congregants in the political process. It is obvious that as a political entrepreneur in search of electoral support, Braun received "hard" resources—like a meeting place for the ministerial breakfast and financial support—from the participants.

The leadership breakfast also confirmed what past scholars of social movements have demonstrated: preexisting networks are a key part of the mobilization process. As Aldon Morris (1984) notes in his study of the modern civil rights movement, black ministers' formal and informal networks facilitated civil rights protest organizing in many southern communities. The ministerial breakfast for Braun demonstrates how, in the post–civil rights era, preexisting clerical networks continue to function as a source of black mobilization.

During the breakfast, these formal clerical networks assisted Braun's mobilization efforts on at least two levels. At the religious level, participants were linked through groups like the West Side Ministers Alliance and denominational organizations such as the statewide Illinois Baptist Association, the African-American Religious Connection, the United Methodist Church, and the governing districts of the AME church. On the political level, networks also brought together ministers who had been previously involved in Chicago politics. Many had been involved in labor and civil rights mobilization efforts for decades—ranging from Saul Alinsky's group TWO and Martin Luther King's crusade against slum housing during the sixties to electoral campaigns in the eighties (Harold Washington's bids for mayor, for instance) to demonstrations against stores and companies that sold and manufactured drug paraphernalia in minority communities in the nineties. Still other ministers at the breakfast were active in civil rights organizations like the NAACP and Operation PUSH.

Furthermore, the social networks of ministers at the breakfast reflected, to some extent, the socioeconomic diversity within Chicago's African-American communities. This is an important component of successful collective action in any black community. Clerics at the breakfast represented religious institutions that included large working- and middle-class congregations like Bishop Brazier's Apostolic Church of God as well as small storefront churches with less affluent congregants like Lucius Hall's First Church of Love and Faith, a spiritualist sect. As I will show later in my detailed discussion of black religious institutions and their impact on black political activism, mobilization through church networks— which bring together people of various socioeconomic backgrounds—helps poor African Americans, who compared to whites and middle-class blacks have fewer personal resources for participation like income and education.

(As scholars of the micromobilization perspective argue, social networks are important not only because they facilitate collective action through institutional alliances but also because they bring in participants who are "socially embedded" within their groups and communities. As I shall discuss shortly, these socially embedded actors, during the process of collective action, exploit micro resources for themselves as well as for others.)

Although the networking of ministerial leadership does promote political mobilization, it was not the only church-based macro resource in operation at Braun's campaign events. Communication networks were also very much in evidence. During the breakfast, several actors emphasized the special capacity of religious institutions to disseminate information. As a political entrepreneur attempting to mobilize black voters, Braun was quick to acknowledge the important role that church communication networks could play in transmitting information about her candidacy to black communities statewide. She told those assembled that they "easily" represented "five million people" who could be mobilized through their efforts. Asking the audience to "spread the word in your respective denominations . . . in your own congregations . . . and make introductions for me . . . throughout the state," Braun understood that the churches would give her "the ability to have the kind of state wide [communication] network [to win]" the election.

Perhaps recognizing the "logic of mobilization," a strategy in which political entrepreneurs pour resources into mobilizing individuals who are predisposed to supporting targeted goals (Rosenstone and Hansen 1993), the voter registration group Project Vote also attempted to use church-based resources. The group asked ministers at the breakfast to designate a Sunday for voter registration at their church, put voter registration material in Sunday bulletins, set up voter registration booths during morning worship services, and recruit church members as volunteer registers. (As I will show later in my discussion of African-American religious institutions, the flow of information through church networks promotes African-Americans' involvement in politics to a far greater degree than it does that of Anglo-whites or Latinos.)

Finally, the event also allowed the participants themselves to become part of the political process. The leadership breakfast linked ordinary people to electoral politics by giving some of them the opportunity to make political speeches, contribute money to a candidate, and work for a political campaign—behaviors scholars recognize as modes of political participation. Equally important, but less obvious, were the simple and (some might think) trivial acts of collecting money, preparing food, setting up chairs and tables, performing a song, or leading a prayer. These activities are normally not thought of as political actions but rather routine activities of church life; nevertheless they contributed both to the overall success of Braun's campaign and to the political education of the participants. As Sidney Verba, Kay Lehman Schlozman, and Henry Brady (1995) illustrate in their work on civic voluntarism, participation in church groups facilitates political activism through the learning of civic skills, indirectly promoting political participation through organizational activity. They find that in their churches blacks cultivate these organizational skills—by giving speeches, planning and chairing meetings, and writing letters—more than Anglo-whites and Latinos do.

(As several analysts of black religious institutions have pointed out, these "trivial" tasks, which help sustain religious institutions throughout black communities, are overwhelmingly performed by women, although men hold the bulk of powerful leadership positions within these institutions. This gender inequality, which is examined in chapter 9, exists despite the fact that women outnumber men considerably in regular church attendance and membership. Although religious institutions provide black women with the opportunity to develop civic and organizing skills, they also reinforce the ideals and practices of male authority, thus legitimizing male domination of women.)

African Americans who attend activist churches gain considerable "social capital" through their church involvement. Social capital refers to what Robert Putnam defines as "features of social organization such as networks, norms, and social trust that facilitate coordination and cooperation for mutual benefit" (1995, 67). Indeed, because of the social and communication networks in black churches, black religious institutions provide church members with social capital that can be used to coordinate social and political activities in African-American communities throughout the United States.

The internal structure of most black churches and the relative autonomy of black churches from white actors partly account for the involvement of African-American religious institutions in the political sphere. These dynamics were shaped by the policies and practices that historically excluded African Americans from mainstream, white-dominated political and religious institutions in the United States. Many of these religious institutions, which formally emerged during Reconstruction as Protestant denominations independent of white control, have long been critical resources for providing organizational experience and social capital needed for African-American political development.

The National Baptist Convention, USA, the largest religious organization of African Americans in the United States, which has 8.5 million members, has over thirty thousand churches and is geographically organized around more than 120 state conventions and district associations, many of which were founded during the late nineteenth century (Payne 1991, 32–47). The other two major Baptist organizations, the National Baptist Convention of America, (3.5 million) and the Progressive Baptist Convention (1.2 million), two organizations that broke from the National Baptist Convention, USA, are similarly organized. The churches in these African-American Baptist conventions have complete organizational autonomy from national and state associations over their governance and are congregationally centered. Many have their own constitution that dictates the duty of the pastor, deacons, deaconesses, trustees, and clerical and support staff. These rules and structures therefore give African-American Baptists the opportunity to develop and nurture skills that can be used in the political sphere (Mukenge 1983).

Other black religious groups are organized more hierarchically, although congregants have the opportunity to practice organizing skills through local congregations and district associations. Founded in the late eighteenth century in protest against the racially discriminatory practices of the Methodist Episcopal church, the AME church is the oldest organized black religious denomination. It has 3.5 million members with over eight thousand churches in nineteen episcopal districts (Payne 1991, 54–64). The General Conference, the supreme body of the AME Church, meets every four years (coinciding with the U.S. presidential elections). Delegates are elected to represent their districts at the General Conference, and denominational officers, including bishops, are elected by convention delegates. District and quarterly meetings are held between the General Conferences. The 1.2 million AME Zion church (1796) and the 1 million CME church (1870) are similarly structured.

The largest black Pentecostal denomination, the COGIC, was founded at the end of the nineteenth century (1897) and for most of its existence was considered by religion scholars to be a cult. Today, the COGIC is considered a part of the black religious mainstream. As one of the fastest growing denominations in the United States, it has over four million members who belong to over ten thousand congregations. The governing structure of the COGIC is organized hierarchically; it is led by an eleven-man board of bishops, and the church's General Assembly, the supreme legislative body of the denomination, is composed of bishops, pastors, elders, missionaries, and designated lay members. Although lay members have fewer opportunities to participate in the workings of denominational activities than do Baptists and Methodists, the autonomy of local congregations provides COGIC members the opportunity to nurture organizing skills. However, since local pastors have the authority to appoint and remove all church officers, the COGIC has a less democratic structure than the other mainstream black denominations.

All of these predominantly black denominations, as well as majority black congregations affiliated with majority white Protestant groups, give blacks the opportunity to learn organizing skills within their local churches, and in many cases, in their denominational bodies. These institutions also provide spaces for the development of other macro resources.

Secular political and civil rights organizations cannot match the organizational resources of African-American churches, which consistently provide black communities with the kinds of social capital needed for political mobilization. Nationally based civil rights and social service organizations like the NAACP, the Southern Christian Leadership Conference (SCLC), and the Urban League are non partisan in nature, which limits their ability to mobilize African Americans directly into action in electoral politics. National, regional, and local associations of black elected officials, such as the Congressional Black Caucus (CBC), the National Conference of Black Mayors, the National Association of Black County Officials, or the National Black Caucus of State Legislators, do not have the institutional infrastructure to organize beyond their own limited constituencies. These groups themselves rely on church networks to pursue their political goals.

Moreover, their elite-centered leadership structure, reliance on paid professional staffs, and dependence on government and corporate funding render these secular political groups incapable of consistently teaching the kinds of organizing and civic skills African Americans regularly learn from working with their religious institutions. These formal political groups also lack the institutional autonomy from mainstream actors that most African-American churches have, as well as the capacity to disseminate information about political goals throughout black communities. Since churches meet weekly and occupy a greater share of African-American associational life than any other black institution, they have distinct advantages over civil rights groups and elected leadership in their ability to engender the social capital that sustains participation.

MICROMOBILIZATION

To mobilize individuals and groups, political participants also draw on resources other than organizations and institutions. Since actors need to find ways to articulate their goals and to believe that they have the power within themselves to influence political outcomes, they also require the psychological and cultural resources that many scholars call micro resources.

Others have noted some of the ways micro resources can mobilize political action. Aldon Morris's study of the civil rights movement, for example, acknowledges the importance of nonorganizational resources, arguing that movement leaders were able to assemble organizational resources for mobilization through their charismatic leadership (1984). Braun's campaign events graphically illustrate how micro resources interact with macro resources to produce cooperative action. From the performance of a melody that symbolized the virtue of "ordinary people" participating in the political process, to the praise for a "Davidess" who miraculously triumphs over a politically entrenched Goliath, the political actors at the breakfast meeting constructed meanings for collective action from their group's cultural repertoire. The breakfast event also demonstrates how religion can engender feelings of personal efficacy in actors, providing them with psychological resources for political action.

Religiously Inspired Efficacy

In his book *The Elementary Forms of Religion*, Emile Durkheim recognized religion's capacity to empower believers. To Durkheim, belief in God is "not merely an authority upon whom we depend, but a force upon which our strength lies."

More precisely, "[t]he man who has obeyed his god and who for this reason believes the god is with him, approaches the world with confidence and with the feeling of increased energy" (1972, 229–230). Durkheim's perspective highlights the potential effects of religious beliefs on political life. The feeling that one has the power to influence political outcomes—what political scientists describe as political efficacy—is an obvious yet mostly overlooked resource that can be strengthened by religious beliefs.

During both the leadership breakfast and Braun's campaign visit to her own church, several people articulated the belief that one can be divinely endowed with the strength to overcome emotional obstacles to participation and to make a difference in the political world. From prayers that asked for personal fortitude in behalf of the candidate ("strengthen her on the journey"; "we know that the strength of God endures forever") to the candidate herself "bearing witness" to how her religious beliefs sustained her commitment to the campaign during moments of uncertainty ("during the dark days of that primary it was that faith that lifted me up and carried me through even when my own strength was failing me"), different actors in the event used religious language to express the possibilities of political success.

In contrast to the negative perspective on religion prevalent among social scientists before and during the civil rights movement, I argue that in the post–civil rights era, a strong psychological attachment to religion encourages African Americans to believe that they can influence the political process through action.

The effects of attachment to religion on political participation have probably changed over time. During the sixties, religious belief seems to have undermined modes of political action—such as protesting and political campaigning—that require time, effort, and, at that historical juncture—risk. The data presented in chapter 4 indicate that in the 1960s, the psychological effects of religion undermined these forms of participation among the general public even as the organizational and socialization effects of religion simultaneously promoted them. On the other hand, as narratives of movement activists reveal in chapter 5, among the politically committed, the psychological dimensions of religion fostered feelings of psychological strength, reassuring them of divine approbation in risky undertakings. This resource nurtured the activists' determination to keep resisting the ongoing systems of domination in the South.

If we compare religion's negative impact on political activity among the general public in the 1960s to the positive effects that southern activists report, and if we compare surveys of the effects of religious belief among the general public from the 1960s, 1980s and 1990s, we see that there are two, perhaps complementary explanations. First, the psychological dimensions of religion during the sixties may have had different effects on activists and nonactivists. A strong attachment to religion may have undermined such modes of participation as protesting and campaigning among the general population, but it empowered many activists in the movement to risk their own lives and material well-being for social change.

Second, religion's psychological impact on political action may have changed since the sixties. Instead of undermining some forms of political activism, as they did during the civil rights movement, today the psychological dimensions of religion, at least in the aggregate, indirectly promote black political activism by supporting feelings of political efficacy. Chapter 7 examines data from 1987 on the causal connections between internalized religious feelings and psychological resources for participation. It also suggests how these feelings and resources interact with church-based organizational resources to inspire individual and collective political action.

RELIGIOUS CULTURE AS A MICRO RESOURCE

The influence of religious culture on political mobilization is perhaps the least explored aspect of the interrelation of religion and political behavior. Nonetheless, it has become apparent that religion has played an important role in the formation of a group's oppositional consciousness in various movements for social change (Corbin 1981; Billings 1990; Levine 1992). West Virginia coal miners, for instance, employed Christian beliefs and practices in their revolt against mining companies at the turn of the century. The prayer, biblical interpretations, and sacred songs of evangelistic Protestantism assisted miners with strengthening bonds of solidarity, articulating their grievances and goals, and legitimizing their struggle for better working conditions. Christianity for these insurgents "promoted collective thought and action, gave cohesion and strength to a social class, and permitted the miners to resist the servility and the feelings of inferiority that class oppression often breeds in the oppressed" (Corbin 1981, 169).[1]

During the early 1980s, Poland's solidarity movement incorporated religious symbols and rituals in its opposition against totalitarianism. Catholic masses were held before protest rallies, wooden crosses were consecrated in memory of deceased activists, and painted icons of Christ and the Black Madonna served as symbols of defiance. The cross, in fact, provided multiple meanings for the movement—as a symbol both of support of and opposition to the state. Jan Kubik notes that the cross served as a "permanent element of Solidarity's decor," functioning as a "sign of defiance toward the Communist regime and the authorities," a "metaphor of national martyrdom," and a "symbol of Poland as messiah of nations" (1994, 189).

In the faith-based communities throughout Latin America, religious symbols are also employed as a means to interpret and legitimize political action. Daniel Levine, in his analysis of base communities in Colombia and Venezuela, reports how community organizers use bibical scriptures as a means to "link faith to action" and to express "solidarity, sharing, and sacrifice in the community" (1992, 139). Levine reports participants legitimizing their involvement in political action through their readings of the Exodus and their reinterpretation of the life and death of Christ. Reading the Bible during community meetings "and making reference to it thoughout the session gives activism and participation a sense of rightness they might not otherwise enjoy" (142).

Culture cannot easily be investigated through quantitative tools of analysis like survey research, but its effects were apparent in my own participant observation study of candidate visits at black churches in Chicago. When Alderwoman Dorothy Tilman of Chicago's fourth ward introduced Danny Davis, the black mayoral candidate for the 1991 Democratic primary, for example, she drew on African-American religious language, culture, and symbols: "There is a quiet storm going on in our community. There's a storm that folks who don't understand God don't understand. . . . We don't have no money, but neither did Jesus, he was born in a manger. [Audience responses: "All right!" "Yes Lord!"] "We don't have money for colorful television commercials or colorful radio commercials, but we have God and we have Jesus."[2]

Theologian James Cone, writing about the meanings of spirituals to African slaves, reminds us: "Religion is not a set of beliefs that people memorize and neither is it an ethical code of do's and don'ts that they learn from others. Rather religion is wrought out of the experience of people who encounter the divine in the midst of historical realities" (1972, 29). Cone's interpretation of African-American Christianity provides a framework in which to explore how and why sacred symbols and rituals are or can become politicized, action-oriented vehicles of meaning that help actors interpret their political goals and construct strategies for action.

African-American religious worldviews—perspectives carved from blacks' acceptance of Christianity and their historical experience with racial and economic domination—have provided, and continue to provide, actors in black communities with an oppositional culture through which to articulate grievances, opportunities, and collective identities during episodes of protest and electoral activism. Scholars of social movements call these articulations "collective action frames"—"emergent action-oriented sets of beliefs and meanings that inspire and legitimize social movement activities and campaigns" (Snow and Benford 1992).

The use of religious symbols and rituals during Braun's campaign events showed how a group can construct collective action frames out of its traditional cultural material. Prayers, for example, expressed solidarity among the politically fractured group of ministers ("that they may be one even as we are one") and articulated grievances regarding racial inequality ("to open up the rivers of righteousness and the streams of justice"). Musical lyrics symbolized collective identities ("God uses plain old ordinary people"), the importance of coalitions to electoral success ("God uses the rich, poor, black, white, the strong and the wounded"), and the virtue of cooperative efforts given limited material resources ("a little become much when you place it in the Master's hand"). Biblical scriptures, sacred icons, and prophetic insights framed political opposition (like the opposition of David and Goliath) and expressed possibilities for electoral success ("God is giving us another chance"; "our modern-day Esther, standing in the gap for us").

Unlike the cultural studies movement that is sweeping the humanities, political science has not concerned itself greatly with how mass culture influences overt political action. Nor has black cultural studies concerned itself much with how religious symbols and rituals influence black political mobilization (see Dent 1992). While the civic culture perspective, which I shall explore in detail later, tells something of how social institutions and system-supporting attitudes strengthen and maintain civil society (Almond and Verba 1963), scholars of political participation have often overlooked how popular culture—expressed in symbols and performed through rituals—shapes individual and collective political action.

Political scientist Sidney Tarrow suggests that collective action frames can be best observed "through the study of how people struggle, against whom they struggle, and in the name of which symbols and points of concern they struggle" (1992, 197). On this model, chapter 7 examines how religious symbols and rituals have historically fostered black political activism and how they continue today to frame political ideals and commitments in African-American communities. By combining the preferences of groups with the cultural materials that actors employ for mobilization, I assemble a framework in which to explore the ways that individuals in groups mobilize their own indigenous culture for cooperative action.

A macro and micro perspective of religion's impact on political mobilization provides a broader perspective on religion and black political activism and shows that research focusing only on the activism of clergy—an approach that has dominated the study of religion and black political life—gives, as we see, an incomplete view. By primarily studying ministers who hold leadership positions in political organizations outside of their church (e.g., the NAACP, the Urban League, the SCLC, Operation PUSH), who preside over large congregations, or who frequently take public positions on political issues (Hamilton 1972, 110–145; Childs 1980), scholars of black political life see only one side of the links between Afro-Christianity and mass political activism.

OPPOSITIONAL CIVIC CULTURE

Two perspectives—that of civil religion and civic culture—have influenced our thinking on the stability and maintenance of democratic societies. Although both perspectives generally imply that social institutions in liberal democracies instill citizens with behaviors and attitudes that sustain the civic order, scholars of both concepts have studied them as if they functioned independently of one another. As scholars of civil religion argue, religion performs various functions in a democratic polity, including providing citizens with national symbols and beliefs (Bellah 1967), a moral basis for citizenship, and a foundation for legal principles. Civil religion then gives citizens a sense of social cohesion and commitment to democratic norms (Richey and Jones 1974; Gehrid 1979; Wald 1987; Bryant 1995). In reviewing the literature on civil religion, Gail Gehrid captures the link between religion's civic capacity and its ties to civic order. Gehrid notes that since "societies attempt to legitimize their institutional arrangements in terms of an ultimate set of values, legitimization falls within the realm of religion" (1979, 35). Religious sources of legitimacy strengthen and maintain the civic order by "molding, socializing, and educating . . . citizens into those ethical and spiritual beliefs that are internalized as republican virtue" (Bellah 1980, 16). Simply put, religion "cement[s] loyalty to the nation" (Wald 1987, 61).

One might have expected scholars of civic culture to link religious sources of civic loyalty to their conception of civic culture. Gabriel Almond and Sidney Verba, who coined the term (1963), considered social institutions and positive orientations toward the existing political regime to be major factors that contribute to a society's civic culture. The civic dimensions of religion, however, do not fit into their theory of civic culture. This omission is hard to understand. If obligations to the political system are formed through social institutions and system-supporting attitudes, then one would expect some religious factors to foster citizens' commitment to the polity. Likewise, one would expect the religious dynamics of civic associations to stimulate citizen activism by giving church members the opportunity to learn and practice civic skills through their religious institutions.[3] Thus, as thriving components of civil society, religious institutions—and the legitimizing values they promulgate—should complement civic culture in the United States.

Given that the state and exclusionary practices in civil society legitimize and often structure systems of human domination, one might also expect the norms of civic culture and civil religion to influence the culture and institutions of subordinated groups in ways that make it harder for them to fight their oppression. The dominant culture's civic orientations might also diminish the ability of marginal groups to adopt political ideas and strategies that call for action outside normal political channels. As civil religion theorists argue, religion can legitimize a society's civic order, thus by implication rationalizing systems of domination that thrive within that order. By legitimizing the polity's investments in the structure and maintenance of racial domination, the civic dimensions of Afro-Christianity might have fostered quiescence not by acting as an otherworldly "opiate" but rather by cultivating within religious blacks feelings of loyalty to the political order.

Peter Paris raises the possibility that Christianity promoted among African Americans a loyalty to the nation's civic order so strong that it made protest unviable. In his book *The Social Teachings of Black Churches* (1985), Paris asserts that black churches have not only demanded of blacks "a high measure of adoption to the nation's major political and moral values" but also directed the political ideas and strategies that religious adherents are likely to adopt in behalf of social change: "[T]he loyalty of the black churches to the nation's laws and customs has often limited them in the kinds of action that they could advocate, especially when those laws and customs have been in conflict with the demands of racial justice. Strategies such as civil disobedience, armed struggle, and various forms of underground activity have rarely been considered viable options by the black churches" (30–31).

On the other hand, research on social movements demonstrates how the indigenous culture and institutions of marginal groups are critical to the formation and the legitimization of social movements. Just as organizations and institutions of civil society help integrate citizens into the civic order, so do the churches and other autonomous organizations and institutions of dominated groups help these groups in their revolt against civil society and the state. Each provides insurgents with leadership, communication networks, meeting spaces, and funding (McAdam 1982; Morris 1984; Evans and Boyte 1986).

These material resources for collective action are not the only sources of mobilization that members of marginal groups assemble in their opposition to systems of domination. They must also cultivate and sustain perspectives that defy the dominant society's justification of their subordination (Morris 1992; Tarrow 1992). As Aldon Morris explains in his theorization of "oppositional consciousness," these perspectives emerge from a "set of insurgent ideals and beliefs constructed and developed by an oppressed group for the purpose of guiding its struggle to undermine, reform, or overthrow a system of domination" (1992, 363). Like the material resources that preexist in the institutions of marginals and are then mobilized for collective action when political conditions are ripe (McAdam 1982), oppositional consciousness also matures and materializes as a source of collective action. Oppositional consciousness "often lies dormant within the institutions, life-styles, and culture of oppressed groups" in which "the groundwork for social protest has been laid by the insurgent ideas rooted within [marginals'] churches, labor unions, voluntary associations, music, informal conversations, humor, and collective memories of those elders who participated in earlier struggles" (Morris 1992, 370).

Many scholars have noted how Afro-Christianity gave the civil rights movement similar resources for insurgency (McAdam 1982; Morris 1984). As "free spaces," that is, as environments where subordinates could act with "a new self-respect, a deeper and more assertive group identity, public skills, and values of cooperation and civic virtue" (Evans and Boyte 1986, 18), the spaces of Afro-

Christianity generated material resources and an oppositional consciousness and culture for the civil rights movement. Although clerical leaders were often reluctant in their support of the movement (Payne 1995), churches as institutions furnished insurgents with leadership, communication networks, funding, and a mobilizable mass constituency (Morris 1984).

Afro-Christianity also supplied the movement with alternative worldviews that challenged the logic of white supremacy. These worldviews—which were and still are the bedrock of the Afro-Christian tradition—affirmed and established for black Christians "the equality of all persons under God" (Paris 1985, 16). This "counter norm" of equality, which endured in the face of the dominant society's white supremacist practices and discourse, was a part of Afro-Christian culture long before the emergence of the modern civil rights movement (Levine 1977).[4]

This book argues that the relatively mainstream religious institutions in African-American life affected and still affect black political activism in two seemingly contradictory ways. They serve as a source of civic culture by giving African Americans the opportunities to practice organizing and civic skills and to develop positive orientations toward the civic order. The same institutions, however, also provide African Americans with material resources and oppositional dispositions to challenge their marginality through modes of action and thought that call for inclusion in the political system instead of exclusion from the polity. I call this dualistic orientation of the culture and institutions of dominated groups an oppositional civic culture.

The idea of an oppositional civic culture reflects what Jean Cohen and Andrew Arato (1995) call the "two-sided character" of civil society. In discussing the links between civil society and social movements, Cohen and Arato, following Jürgen Habermas, contend that a dualistic approach to civil society "goes beyond the one-sided stress on alienation . . . or domination . . . and an equally one-sided focus on [social] integration" (526). To Cohen and Arato the dualism of civil society reflects "self-limiting radicalism" in which movements for social change "acknowledge the integrity of [existing] political and economic systems" (493). By acknowledging religion's oppositional capabilities as well as its civic functions and by examining diverse modes of black political action and thought, my analysis demonstrates that Afro-Christianity was a far more complex factor in black activism than both critics and defenders have previously assumed.

Braun's minister articulated the concept of an oppositional civic culture when she reminisced about how her church had served as a source of political resistance in the past. While the choir softly sang "We're All Conquerors through Jesus Christ," she reminded the congregation that their church had been engaged "a long time in the struggle." This struggle involved participation in the labor union movement during the forties, as well as reaction to Emmett Till's lynching in Mississippi during the mid-fifties, former Congressman Ralph Metcalf's controversial break from Chicago's Democratic machine during the seventies, Harold

Washington's mayoral campaigns, and white reaction to his leadership during the eighties. Now this institution and its culture would also provide resources to elect a U.S. senator who, "before the world ever knew her," Braun's minister informed her congregation, "would sit in our presence and ask for prayer, and ask for strength."

4

Religion Reconsidered

Black Protest and Electoral Activism in an Age
of Transformation

*And unto him that smiteth thee on the one cheek offer also
the other.*

Luke 6:29

To keep you from fighting back, he gets these old religious
Uncle Toms to teach you and me ... to suffer peacefully.

Malcolm X, "Message to the Grassroots," 1963

The government is happy with most Baptist churches,
Cuz they don't do a damn thing to try to nurture
Brothers and sisters in a revolution.
Baptist teaching dying is the only solution.
Passiveness causes others to pass us by.

Arrested Development, "Fishin' 4 Religion," 1992

IT SEEMS UNLIKELY THAT ANYONE at Carol Moseley Braun's breakfast
considered religion an opiate, likely to soothe its partakers into an apathetic
slumber, incapacitating them for politics. In the 1960s, however, many activists
and scholars were arguing just that. In 1963, a peak year of protest activism in
the South and the same year that Malcolm X blasted "those religious Uncle
Toms," sociologist Nathan Hare criticized black ministers for having "naively or
selfishly played up poetic dictums rationalizing the Negro's lot and soothing his
psychological injuries, such as: it is better to give than receive and the meek shall
one day inherit the earth—apparently by simply remaining meek and doing nothing to warrant the prize" (1963, 12).[1]

Indeed, many southern clerics were reluctant to participate in the civil rights
movement. Martin Luther King, himself a minister, was critical of the black
church leadership's resistance to protest. In recounting the difficulties in mobilizing support for the Birmingham bus boycott, King inveighed against the "ap-

FIGURE 4.1. *Cartoon by Walt Carr: "I'm sorry, Reverend—but I guess I just ran out of cheeks to turn." Negro Digest,* July 1963.

parent apathy of the Negro ministers" whose indifference "stemmed from a sincere feeling that ministers were not to get mixed up in such earthy, temporal matters as social and economic improvement" (1958, 35). King argued that strictly otherworldly religion worked against protest, insisting that "any religion that professes to be concerned with the souls of men and is not concerned with the slums that damn them, the economic conditions that strangle them, and the social conditions that cripple them is a dry-as-dust religion. Such a religion is the kind the Marxists like to see—an opiate of the people" (36).

Advocating separation from American society, the black nationalist ideology of the Nation of Islam provided the most biting and public criticism of Christianity's effect on mainstream black thought and action. Both Elijah Muhammad, leader and founder of the Nation of Islam, and Malcolm X, Muhammad's national spokesman, preached that Christianity perpetuated white domination by encouraging black passivity. In his study of the Black Muslim movement in the 1950s, C. Eric Lincoln (1961) summed up the Nation's position: "The black Christian preacher is the white man's most effective tool for keeping the so-called Negroes pacified and controlled, for he tells convincing lies against nature as well as against God. Throughout nature, God has made provision for every creature to protect itself against its enemies; but the black preacher has taught his people to stand still and turn the other cheek" (79).

Challenging the civil rights movement's nonviolent direct action strategies, Malcolm X maintained that, unlike Islam, Christianity taught blacks to be docile when they needed to learn to take "an eye for an eye, a tooth for a tooth, and a head for a head, and a life for a life." He preached: "Any time a shepherd, a pastor, teaches you and me not to run from the white man and, at the same time, teaches us not to fight the white man, he's a traitor to you and me. Don't lay down a life all by itself. No, preserve your life, its the best thing you've got. And if you've got to give it up, let it be even-steven" (1963, 12–13).

This chapter provides a corrective to the debate on whether Afro-Christianity inspired or subverted black political activism during the civil rights movement. Going beyond the opiate or inspiration positions that have marked the debate, I argue that Christianity's effects on African-American political action and thought were affected by both the nature of religious commitments and the direction of political ideas and action. By distinguishing between political ideals and actions that support the civic order and those that undermine such support, I suggest, more broadly, that a marginal group's culture and institutions can potentially serve dual purposes in democratic societies. Religious practices and beliefs, for example, can both help counter the prevailing system of domination *and* help socialize believers into the society's prevailing norms and values. This dual function, what I termed in chapter 3 an oppositional civic culture, then influences the tactics and strategies marginal groups embrace in their quest for social change.

AFRO-CHRISTIANITY AND MOVEMENT ACTIVISM

It was during the height of the civil rights movement that Gary Marx (1967a, 1967b) conducted his study of belief systems in the black community, the first significant piece of survey research on the impact of religion on black protest. Data from his nonrandom metropolitan sample,[2] taken in 1964, supported the idea that religiosity, for African Americans, worked as an opiate in relation to civil rights militancy. Specifically, Marx found that the greater subjective importance of religion to black respondents, and the greater the frequency of their church attendance, the lower they scored on militancy. Marx also concluded that respondents who belonged to black-controlled religious denominations, particularly the Baptists and Methodists—the overwhelming majority of blacks who claimed denominational affiliation—were less "militant" than those who belonged to white-controlled denominations like the Catholic, Episcopalian, Presbyterian, and Congregationalist churches. Marx noted that "it is somewhat ironic that those individuals in largely white denominations . . . appear somewhat higher in militancy than those in Negro denominations, in spite of the greater civil rights activism of the latter" (1967b, 98). Marx found that the respondents who belonged to "sects and cults" scored even lower on militancy than those who belonged to the mainstream black denominations.

Marx's analysis of religion's impact on "black militancy" is problematic for several reasons, not the least of which is his monolithic view of religion. Much of the criticism of Marx's analysis points to his insufficient grasp of the diversity that exists in religious belief and behavior, the different effects that different components of religion have on black militancy, and the need to simultaneously control for demographic and socioeconomic factors that influence both religious factors and black opinion on civil rights (Madron, Nelsen, and Yokley 1974; Nelsen, Waldron, and Yokley 1975; Nelsen and Nelsen 1975; Hunt and Hunt 1977). Marx's choice of indicators for religious beliefs and his collapsing of several different indicators of religion into one all-inclusive index obscured the influence that religious resources, psychological and organizational, had on black activism in the sixties. Marx's "religiosity" index lumped church attendance in with questions on orthodoxy of beliefs, measured by agreement with statements about the belief in the existence of God, the devil, and life after death (Marx 1967a). Although Marx later separated out the religious measures in a second analysis (but still did not simultaneously control for socioeconomic and demographic factors), he continued to find and conclude that religion operated against support for "militant" ideals among blacks (Marx 1967b).

Marx's findings have been only partially replicated in other studies. Nelsen and Nelsen (1975) and Nelsen, Waldron, and Yokley (1975), reanalyzing Marx's data, found that when they simultaneously controlled for education, gender, age, and region, none of his indicators were significantly related to black militancy. Analyzing their own data from a small urban southern community, these authors looked at both "sectarian" and "temporal" facets of religion. Sectarian religious views promote withdrawal from the secular world, surrendering temporal concerns to divine authority, while temporally oriented religious beliefs should, in theory, promote engagement in this-worldly matters, including politics. The Nelsen studies examined the psychological and organizational contexts of religiosity as well as its temporal and otherworldly components. Their analysis employed several indexes. An "index of associational involvement" combined church attendance with involvement in church groups. An "orthodoxy" index gauged "churchlike belief" by affirmative responses to questions about belief in heaven and hell, the importance of going to church rather than being active in politics, the inerrancy of the Bible, and the belief that biblical guidelines about behavior should be followed.

A "sectarian" index gauged the otherworldly component of religious beliefs by adding up respondents' affirmative answers to the following questions: 1) "Should testifying about one's religious experience be part of regular religious services?" 2) "Does God send misfortune and illness as punishment for sins?" 3) "Should ministers be "called" rather than trained in the ministry?" 4) "Will the world soon come to an end?"

Taking into account demographic and socioeconomic factors, the authors discovered that "associational involvement," "orthodoxy" (adherence to Christian doctrines), and "sectarianism" (otherworldly tendencies) had different effects on black militancy. The associational involvement index, measuring the organizational context of religion, was not, according to their data, significantly related to militancy. Orthodoxy positively predicted militancy. Sectarianism was negatively related to militancy. From these findings the authors concluded that "religious belief is not especially potent in either fostering militancy or muting it," insisting that the "direction of the effect depends on the character of the beliefs held" (1975, 146).

Hunt and Hunt's (1977) reanalysis of Marx's data examined both the psychological and organizational components of religious involvement and considered religious indicators that Marx did not use. By separating the sample into four categories—which they called the organizational, psychological, churchlike, and sectlike facets of religion—they demonstrated how religion simultaneously promoted and undermined civil rights militancy. Their this-worldly measure of religious involvement, which they call "churchlike activity," combined various degrees of church attendance, involvement in church groups, and participation in secular groups into an overall index measuring churchlike involvement. Respondents exhibiting high levels of involvement on the churchlike activity dimension were most inclined to civil rights militancy. Their measure of "sectlike" activity—that is, activity removed from secular affairs—combined degrees of church attendance and participation in church and secular organizations into an index that showed the extent to which respondents were active in their church in ways that precluded involvement in the outside world. The authors found that respondents scoring high on sectlike activity were the least likely to engage in temporally oriented activities and thus were the least militant about civil rights.

Regarding the psychological dimension, Hunt and Hunt's reanalysis also considered two separate effects of Christian doctrines on militancy, using Marx's measure. Their measure of "churchlike beliefs" (as contrasted with churchlike activity) summed affirmative responses to whether respondents acknowledged the Ten Commandments as a part of Judaism, believed that there is life after death, recognized that the Old Testament identifies Jews as God's chosen people, and acknowledged the existence of God. Their index of "sectlike beliefs" summed affirmative responses to questions about whether respondents believed in "the Devil," thought that one had to believe in Jesus to be "saved," believed that atheists should be prohibited from teaching, and agreed that a wrathful God punishes Jews for not accepting Christ.

Their analysis confirmed that churchlike and sectlike beliefs have different effects on black militancy. Paralleling the patterns with churchlike and sectlike activity, churchlike beliefs boosted militancy, while sectlike beliefs undermined such action. Moreover, the churchlike and sectlike belief measures were not significantly related to each other.

Among respondents who belonged to sectarian or "retreatist" denominations, churchlike activity was positively related to militancy. Yet for those who belonged to the three mainstream denominational categories, sectlike activity had no significant negative effect on militancy. For members of the three mainstream black denominations, churchlike beliefs were positively related to militancy. For those who belonged to white and sectarian black denominations, sectlike beliefs were negatively related to militancy. Hunt and Hunt's results reflect better the complex relation of religion to militancy than do the analyses offered by either Marx or the Nelsen studies. Arguing that "where religious orientation is more churchlike . . . religiosity is associated with high levels of militancy," Hunt and Hunt concluded, using Marx's own data, that "the opiate interpretation of black religion is a limited one-sided image of black religion, which in many of its forms has probably made a significant contribution to the mobilization of the black community for protest" (1977, 13).

While subsequent reanalysis and replication of Marx's findings did recognize the multidimensionality of religion and clarify the different effects of different religious beliefs and orientations on black people's "militant" ideals, these studies left Marx's approach to militancy unchallenged in crucial ways. They continued to use attitudes toward issues of civil rights in their analyses rather than direct measures of participatory behavior. And while black nationalist sentiments and urban rebellions were distinct and vibrant forms of black activism during the sixties, these revisionist works ignored how Afro-Christianity might have affected these more radical modes of African-American thought and action.

MILITANCY IN AN ERA OF TRANSFORMATION

Marx's concept of "black militancy" fits uneasily within contemporary discourse on African-American political thought and action. Marx's survey, taken in 1963, attempted to gauge what he called "conventional militancy" by measuring black attitudes toward racial segregation and discrimination. His index summed agreement with the following attitudinal statements: blacks could get "ahead as easily as any one else," people should spend more time praying than demonstrating, restaurant owners should not have to serve blacks if they don't want to, blacks have to demonstrate that they "deserve" equal rights before getting them, property owners have the right not to sell to blacks, the government's pace in pushing integration was sufficient, and that there should be fewer rather than more mass demonstrations. Marx also surveyed people's attitudes toward the effectiveness of civil rights demonstration, and asked if they were afraid to take part in such protests.

Although most of these questions reasonably gauged support for the aims of the early period of the civil rights movement, at least two of the questions do not properly separate support from opposition to civil rights. Asking respondents to agree or disagree with whether "Negroes should spend more time praying and less time demonstrating" forced respondents to choose one form of activity over another, thus assuming that the two were mutually exclusive. In discussing the typical "militant Negro," Marx argued that militants encouraged "civil rights demonstrations and [their] concern for the here and now leads [them] to think that Negroes should spend more time in secular activity of demonstrating than in the otherworldly one of praying" (1963, 42). Some religious respondents might have felt that praying was a better use of time than demonstrating, but a preference for the former would not necessarily preclude the latter, especially given that, in its early phase, the movement's demonstrations themselves stressed Christian principles.

Marx's question on whether respondents were "afraid to take part in civil rights demonstrations" also potentially underestimated support for civil rights activism. Fear of participation in demonstrations would not necessarily impede support for civil rights or, for that matter, involvement in protest activities, since fearful respondents could, in theory, overcome their fear and participate anyway. Moral incentives to participate might potentially overcome the fear of material sanctions (Chong 1991).

Marx also did not separate behavior from attitudes. He asked questions regarding membership in civil rights organizations, voter participation, and frequency of reading black newspapers and reported that these behaviors were correlated with the attitude scale, but he never reported on how these behaviors were affected by religiosity. By limiting militancy to the attitudes of support for antidiscrimination and segregation policies and strategies and by not looking at the effects of religion on reported participation, Marx's study did not consider a more detailed investigation into the impact of religious involvement on black political activism.

Two years after Marx did his nonrandom surveys in a few cities, the 1966 Harris-Newsweek Race Relations Survey sampled a more representative group. This survey, taken during a critical phase of black political mobilization, provides a base from which to explore the effect of religious behaviors and beliefs on both conventional political participation—electoral activism—and unconventional participation in the form of nonviolent direct action. The survey was taken the year that the nonviolent direct action phase of the civil rights movement began to taper off. That phase reached its peak with the Selma to Montgomery mass demonstration for voting rights in March 1965; a new era began with the August 1965 Watts rebellion, which lasted five days and resulted in thirty-four deaths, over one thousand injuries, and over four thousand arrests (Bergman 1969). Urban rebellions escalated after the Watts rebellion, with more than 290 occurring between 1966 and 1968 (McAdam 1982, 182). Sociologist Doug McAdam (1982) empirically documented the decline of the movement's nonviolent direct action phase, giving as causes, among other factors, the decentralization of the movement's organizational structure, the movement's geographic diffusion, its lack of consensus on goals after the successful passage of the 1964 Civil Rights Act and the 1965 Voting Rights Act, and the rise of conservatism in American electoral politics.

An explosion of black electoral activism, which had been slowly on the rise since World War II (Gosnell and Martin 1963), coincided with the urban rebellions and the decline of the nonviolent direct action phase of the movement. In the year after the passage of the 1965 Voting Rights Act, blacks' voter registration rate doubled in nearly every southern state, going up to 50 percent. The turnout of registered black voters also increased significantly, and after the 1966 elections, the number of blacks elected to public offices in the South doubled (United States Commission on Civil Rights 1968).

Blacks' electoral progress during this period, though incremental, could also be observed in their growing influence within the Democratic party. Pressured by the Mississippi Democratic Freedom Party's challenge to the all-white Mississippi delegation at the 1964 Democratic National Convention, and by the increase in black support for Democrats after the Johnson-Goldwater presidential race, the national Democratic leadership initiated reforms that advanced black inclusion and influence within the party (Crotty 1978). As a result, 6 percent of the delegates at the 1968 Democratic convention were black—twice as many as in 1964—and by the 1972 convention, that percentage was up to nearly 15 (Joint Center for Political Studies 1988). These developments were the antecedents to the unprecedented levels of black electoral activism of the seventies.

The emergence (or re-emergence) of electoral politics during this era has been overshadowed by discussions of the decline of the direct action phase of the movement, the rise of urban rebellions, and the black power phase of the movement. Yet the 1965 Voting Rights Act reduced structural barriers to black voter participation in the South and made electoral politics a sound strategy for advancing black interests.

It was at the beginning of this transitional period that the Harris-Newsweek survey examined the impact of religion on electoral participation. Their survey took place two years after "Freedom Summer," in which several thousand southern blacks were registered to vote, one year after the passage of the 1965 Voting Rights Act; and one year before Carl Stokes of Cleveland, Ohio, and Richard Hatcher of Gary, Indiana, became the first elected black mayors of major American cities. During this period blacks also began to win less visible elected offices in both the North and the South. In 1967, even Mississippi, perhaps the southern state most resistant to racial change, elected its first black to the state legislature since Reconstruction (Bergman 1969). Historian and activist August Meier noted of this era that "as the millenialistic expectations earlier associated with nonviolent direct-action waned, many [blacks] came to pin their hopes on political action—on using the Negro bloc vote as a lever for social change" (1970, 2).

Acknowledging the contested quality of black ideas and strategies during the mid-1960s raises a central question about the relationship of Afro-Christianity to the different types of political behaviors during the 1960s. Did religion undermine support for all these modes of political action—as opiate theorists would have us believe—or did religion support some behaviors and undermine others? Given religion's capacity to nurture civic loyalty, did Christianity prevent black Christians from engaging in and supporting modes of political action and thought that were protest-oriented or exclusive from participation in mainstream American society?

The 1966 Harris-Newsweek survey provides some answers. It interviewed over one thousand black adults over eighteen years of age from a national random sample. The interviews, consisting of over two hundred questions, were conducted face to face and mostly by black interviewers (Brink and Harris 1964, 1967). No survey during this time period contained both an extensive array of possible political actions, including five forms of protest activism, and several measures of religious commitment, including membership in church groups. This survey asked about such an extensive array of protest actions because this was a period in African-American civic life when such actions were very salient. My analysis of this survey will view religion, in its varied forms, as a source for black political activism. It will explore the impact of varied forms of religious orientations and behaviors on several strategic modes of black political action and thought during the 1960s—specifically voter participation, campaign activism, demand-protest activism, political violence, and separatist black nationalism.

CONTESTED MODES OF POLITICAL ACTION

The passage of the 1965 Voting Rights Act opened up many new ways to articulate black interests, allowing violent rebellion, protest or demand activism, electoral activism, and black nationalist thought to emerge as different, and contested, modes of black political involvement. As Adolph Reed, Jr., maintains, these contested modes, or what he describes as "oppositional tendencies in black activism," were "discrete options among a number of embedded possibilities in contention to steer the movement's articulation" (1986a, 5).

This analysis investigates the effects of religion on both inclusive and exclusive modes of political action and thought. The 1966 Harris-Newsweek survey asked respondents a battery of questions about their participation in, and support for, both of these modes. To measure modes of participation *inclusive* of the civic order, my analysis used two sets of questions. One set measures *conventional*, the other *unconventional*, modes of participation. Conventional participatory acts include electoral activism. They are those acts that are accepted as appropriate by the dominant political culture (Conway 1985). They seek to influence governmental decisions through established political processes. In the area of conventional participation, the survey asked respondents questions on voting, as well as whether they had ever belonged to a political group, worked for a political candidate, asked people to register or vote, gone to a political meeting, written or spoken to a congressman, or given money to a candidate or a political party. Unconventional participatory acts inclusive of the political system include protest or demand activism. They are those means of political expression historically viewed as unsuitable by the dominant culture—tactics that seek to reform both governmental and nongovernmental policies and decisions from outside the system (Conway 1985).

To measure unconventional participation, the survey asked, "[I]n the cause of Negro rights, have you personally or a member of your family ever" taken part in a sit-in, marched in a demonstration, picketed a store, stopped shopping at a store, or gone to jail? A follow-up question asked respondents whether they would participate in such activities if asked. The questions regarding involvement in protest-demand activities are an imperfect measure of individual involvement in protest or demand activism, because we cannot know, from the structure of the question, whether the respondent personally or someone else in the household was involved in such activities. Nevertheless, the questions provide some indication of the frequency of such activities in comparison to other strategic modes of participation.

To measure modes of participation and ideas *exclusive* of the civic order, I looked at questions that tapped explicitly separatist attitudes and support for separatist organizations as well as attitudes supportive of rioting. Questions on separatism asked whether blacks should depend on themselves rather than working with whites, whether they approved of black nationalists and Black Muslims, and whether they supported a separate black state. Questions about rioting asked whether black people should resort to violence, whether riots have helped or hurt the cause of Negro rights, and whether they themselves would join a riot.

Using the Harris survey, table 4.1 indicates the degree and nature of both inclusive/exclusive and conventional/unconventional political action and thought among African Americans during the sixties. The table demonstrates that, overall, respondents reported greater involvement in conventional than in unconventional acts, although more respondents engaged in certain forms of unconventional acts than in others—for example, refusing to patronize stores (31 percent) and marching in demonstrations (22 percent).

Those conventional participatory acts that attracted the most involvement, namely voting (in 1964, 66 percent), asking citizens to register and vote (42 percent), going to political meetings (37 percent), and asking citizens to vote for a specific candidate (30 percent), required less commitment than protest-demand acts, which required not only time, money, and skills but—in this historical context—risk as well. Unconventional participatory acts like taking part in sit-ins (14 percent), picketing a store (13 percent), and going to jail (7 percent) are potentially extremely risky. Exclusionary attitudes, such as support for a separate black state (7 percent) and willingness to join a riot (15 percent) had limited to moderate support. I analyzed these measures of action and thought for their internal consistency, confirming the multidimensionality of African-American political thought and action during this period of political transformation (see appendix A for question wording and for the intercorrelations of inclusive/exclusive and conventional/unconventional political measures).[3] The following two sections explain the measures I developed for inclusive and exclusive modes of black political action and thought.

INCLUSIVE FORMS OF POLITICAL PARTICIPATION

Voter Participation and Campaign Activism

My voter participation index sums responses to questions about whether respondents were registered voters and whether they voted in the 1960 and 1964 presidential elections. My campaign activism index sums responses to questions asking whether respondents worked for a political candidate, asked others to register and vote, asked others to vote for a particular candidate, went to political meetings, or belonged to a political club or group. Again, these modes of action are institutionalized within the existing political system and are considered "normal" ways for citizens to express their grievances and political preferences.

Protest-Demand Modes of Activism and Support

Protest-demand activism is direct action, organized around specific political goals, either protesting measures that produce harm or demanding measures that produce good. This type of activism is characteristic of social movements. Participants engage in such activities when normal political channels are not responsive to their demands. My index of protest-demand acts sums questions asking

Table 4.1. Frequency of Conventional and Unconventional Modes of African-American Political Action and Thought, 1966

	%
Conventional participation	
Voter participation	
Registered voter	76
Voted in 1960	62
Voted in 1964	66
Campaign activism: "Have you ever . . . ?"	
Asked people to register and vote	42
Gone to political meetings	37
Asked people to vote for a candidate	30
Written or spoken to a congressman	20
Worked for candidates	19
Given money to candidates	17
Unconventional participation and attitudes	
Protest activism (inclusive): "In the case of Negro rights, have you personally, or has any member of your family . . . ?"	
Stopped buying at store	31
Marched in a demonstration	22
Taken part in sit-ins	14
Picketed a store	13
Gone to jail	7
Separatist black nationalism (exclusive)	
Negroes should depend on own people	10
Approve of black nationalist	6
Approve of black Muslims	5
Favor separate black state	7
Political violence (exclusive)	
Riots helped the cause of black rights	34
Violence has to be used to win rights	21
Would join a riot	15

Source: 1966 Harris-Newsweek Race Relations Survey
N = 1,037

whether respondents or someone in their household had—"in the cause of Negro rights"—taken part in a sit-in, refused to buy from a store, marched in a demonstration, picketed a store, or gone to jail.

Because participation in these types of activities often depends on opportunities people have to join movements, I also included an index of respondents' willingness to engage in protest. My index of protest-demand support sums questions asking respondents whether they would, hypothetically if asked, participate in such activities. Reported involvement in protest activism and a willingness to protest are moderately related, suggesting that my protest activism index potentially underestimates respondents who were sympathetic to protest strategies and also that "willingness to protest" may function as a form of "cheap talk," perhaps not to be considered as seriously as reported involvement.

EXCLUSIONARY FORMS OF POLITICAL THOUGHT AND ACTION

Politically Motivated Violence

Given the spontaneity and unpredictability of violent rebellions, it is difficult to study the relationship between religion and politically motivated violent behavior. An analysis of attitudes supporting riots, however, indicates a possible connection. Politically motivated violence represents one of the most extreme forms of civic disorder. Like protest-demand activism, it is a mode of action that is not only unconventional but also, unlike protest-demand activism with its nonviolent ethos, is an act that does not recognize any legitimacy in the political system. My index of support, or sympathy, for politically motivated violence sums questions asking respondents if they thought "Negroes today can win their rights without resorting to violence," if "riots that have taken place in Los Angeles and other cities have helped or hurt the cause of Negro rights," and if they themselves would join a riot.

Separatist Black Nationalism

Gary Marx's concept of black militancy, applied in his 1964 survey and undoubtedly devised earlier, gauged support only for the integrationist ideology of the civil rights movement and not for black nationalism. Yet by 1965 the tenor of the movement had shifted from the integrationist philosophy of nonviolence to the beginnings of nationalism. The separatist ideology manifested in the 1965 Watts rebellion and Stokely Carmichael's 1966 call for "black power" had grown increasingly influential. As Marx said in a footnote, his definition of militancy differed from the black nationalist one, which by 1967, when he wrote up his results, was gaining currency; he warned readers that "[i]t should be clearly understood that by militancy . . . we are not referring to black nationalists or extremist attitudes, although our measure of militancy does not preclude the holding of such attitudes" (1967a, 41).

Although its political meaning was ambiguous and incorporated both pluralist and separatist viewpoints as well as economic, cultural, and social perspectives (Aberbach and Walker 1970; Holden 1973; McCartney 1992; Van DeBurg 1992), one tenet of black nationalist thinking espoused "an actual physical and political withdrawal from the existing society" (Essien-Udom 1962, 7). Matthew Holden viewed separatism as one of several varieties of "withdrawal politics," or blacks' conscious separation from the basic values and institutions of dominant American culture. Separatism calls for "full separation from the United States' political institutions, on the assumption that they are inescapably corrupt and/or doomed" (1973, 68). The index of "separatist black nationalism" that I have constructed from the 1966 Harris-Newsweek survey sums questions on whether respondents agreed that blacks should "give up working together with whites and just depend on their own people," approved of black nationalists, approved of Black Muslims, or favored a separate black state. These ideas and groups were major tenets of black separatist ideology in the 1960s.

RELIGION RECONSIDERED AS A RESOURCE FOR ACTIVISM

Since Marx's original 1964 survey, more recent scholarship on both religion and politics[4] and black political behavior[5] has suggested that religion, in its various manifestations, promotes political activism by fostering civic attitudes, political socialization, and organizational involvement, all of which directly influence political participation. Using the 1966 Harris-Newsweek survey, my analysis tests such predictions, along with the prediction that religion acts to demobilize some modes of political action—those acts that compete with the time and commitment of the most devout believers—and inhibits support for separatist black nationalism and political violence—acts and beliefs that challenge the legitimacy of the civic order. Recognizing the multiple ways in which religion effects political life, I have estimated the impact of five religious characteristics on black activism during the 1960s: sectarianism, church attendance, denominational affiliation, and membership in church and church-related groups.

Sectarianism

One might expect people who are deeply involved in their religion, especially those whose orientations are marked by apocalyptic expectations, not to be politically active. Indeed, as Nelsen and Nelsen (1975), Nelsen, Waldron, and Yokley (1975), and Hunt and Hunt (1977) demonstrated, sectlike and churchlike elements of religion have different effects on black thought. A sectlike religious orientation—one removed from secular affairs—should discourage activism in both conventional and unconventional modes of participation while also negatively affecting, or having no effect on, political violence or perhaps separatist black nationalism. The Harris-Newsweek survey questions do not allow us to measure sectlike orientation precisely. They do, however, measure respondents answering to being "deeply religious" rather than believing that their religion is not that important. About 83 percent of the respondents reported that they felt deeply about their religion. In this era it seems reasonable to hypothesize that identifying oneself as deeply religious would—independent of socioeconomic factors and temporally oriented religious behaviors—directly discourage all forms of political participation.

Church Attendance and Civic Behavior

Nearly half (43 percent) of the respondents in the Harris-Newsweek survey reported attending church at least once a week. Several studies have found a positive and direct link between church attendance and voter turnout (Milbrath and Goel 1977; Macaluso and Wanat 1979; Houghland and Christenson 1983; Martinson and Wilkening 1987; Strate et al. 1989). Most of these studies concluded that regular church attendance promotes civic-oriented participation, giving citizens a sense of civic obligation that leads them to participate regularly in elections (Macaluso and Wanat 1979; Houghland and Christenson 1983; Martinson and Wilkening 1987). As John Strate and others theorized in their analysis of factors contributing to voter participation, "church attendance involves a sense of personal affiliation with an institution in which communal values and social obligations are regularly emphasized" (1989, 452), thus facilitating the orientations that influence civic duty. However, as several studies have demonstrated, church attendance is not related to more demanding forms of political participation like campaigning and contacting public officials (Houghland and Christenson 1983; Martinson and Wilkening 1987). Houghland and Christenson hypothesize that church attendance promotes only those modes of participation that involve "minimal investments of time and resources," concluding that "church attendance does not encourage political action which is likely to increase one's power within the political system" (416).

Given these findings on the relationship between church attendance and voter participation, we would expect church attendance in 1966 to promote voter participation but not to promote more demanding modes of activism among blacks. We might, however, expect church attendance to promote protest-demand activism, since this mode of action might depend—as does voter participation—on a sense of moral or civic obligation. This is plausible since civic engagement among African Americans has historically incorporated both electoral and protest-oriented modes of political activism. Finally, since church attendance fosters civic-oriented attitudes and behavior, it should dampen support for political violence and separatist black nationalism, a mode of behavior and an ideology antithetical to civil society.

Denominations and Black Political Socialization

Denominational orientation has a significant impact on the socialization of churchgoers (Wald, Owen, and Hill 1988, 1990). The theological and social homogeneity of churches allows them to function as "communities of belief" in which "messages from the pulpit and social interaction with congregants promote a common political outlook among church members" (1990, 545). Theoretically, this socializing function of denominational orientation should serve as a resource only for certain forms of black political activism, namely those that promote inclusion rather than exclusion from civil society.

The mainstream denominational orientations of African Americans, overwhelmingly represented by the black-controlled Baptist and Methodist churches, have served as socializing agents for reform-oriented politics both through protest-demand activism and through conventional participation (Morris, Hatchett, and Brown 1989). Committed to an ideology of protest and reform politics, these denominational orientations have "housed a substantial portion of the institutionalized consciousness of black people," which has resisted racial domination subtly through culture and at times overtly through direct involvement. As Morris, Hatchett, and Brown further explain, "[t]he concrete expression of that consciousness—music, sermons, prayers, and the like—reveal that a protest philosophy undergird[s] black religion." They contend that this philosophy is "an enduring dimension of the black protest tradition" (284–285). More recently Allen, Dawson, and Brown (1989) have demonstrated that religious beliefs promote the racial identity and consciousness of black churchgoers. Their work demonstrates—as scholars of black life have acknowledged in past studies—that the black church cultivates racial identity and consciousness.

We might expect the mainstream black denominations to support only those modes of thought and action that legitimize the prevailing social order. While examining the protest and accommodation tenets of black religious traditions, Baer and Singer (1992) note how mainstream black denominations have socialized African Americans into accepting the basic precepts of American society by functioning as "agencies of ideological hegemony." Although committed to a program of social reform, they have also "legitimized social arrangements in American society by participating in reformist politics, rather than in radical or revolutionary ones" (98).

In this 1966 survey, therefore, we would expect membership in a black mainstream denomination to encourage voter participation and protest-demand activism and to discourage participation in political violence and separatist black nationalism, both of which oppose the prevailing political order. Challenging Gary Marx's finding that blacks affiliated with white-controlled denominations (e.g. Catholics, Episcopalians, Presbyterians) were more militant than blacks from black-controlled denominations, we would expect respondents who reported being Baptist or Methodist, typically black-controlled denominations, to be more active in conventional and protest-demand activities than those who belonged to the Catholic church, a white-controlled denomination. Given the more other-worldly nature of "fundamentalist" religious orientations, we would expect respondents who belonged to such denominations not to be socialized into the political process. Thus, a fundamentalist orientation should discourage participation in both conventional and unconventional modes of activism, as well as support for black autonomy.

Respectively 60 percent and 16 percent of the survey respondents were identified as Baptist and Methodist, while 5 percent were classified as Catholic and 1 percent as "fundamentalists." Since the Harris-Newsweek survey separated respondents into Baptist, Methodist, Catholic, and "other denominations" (a category that was positively related to education), it is probable that the fundamentalist category (which is negatively related to education) reflects respondents who are affiliated with Pentecostal or holiness churches.

Church and Church-Related Groups

Scholars have documented the role of the church as an indigenous, mobilizing agent of protest during the civil rights movement. As scholarship on political participation shows, any organizational activity, whether religious or secular, is likely to promote political participation. In examining the organizational capacity of church life, Peterson argues that "participation in decision making within a church [can] spill over and enhance the odds of an individual becoming involved in political activities" (1992, 124). In his analysis of the 1987 General Social Survey (GSS), Peterson demonstrates how church organizational activism is associated with both voter participation and more demanding forms of political participation like campaigning for candidates and contacting public officials.

Given the dynamic effects of organizational activity and the involvement of local congregations and ministerial groups in the civil rights movement, we would expect membership in a church organization to promote both conventional modes of political participation and protest-demand activism. Conversely, we would expect church membership to impede involvement in political violence and deter support for separatist black nationalism.

In addition to church group membership, my analysis will consider the role of masonic groups, which are quasi-religious organizations, as religiously based organizational resources for black activism. Black masonic groups, which are loosely connected with black churches and are ritualistically associated with black religious traditions (Muraskin 1975; Wesley 1961), have generally been ignored by scholars of black political mobilization.

Some masonic groups, such as the Prince Hall Masons, predate the founding of independent black churches and were instrumental in mobilizing northern black freedmen and freedwomen in the antebellum period. With their roots extending as far back as the eighteenth century, black masonic groups have operated both as sites for civic engagement and as sources of organized and ideological resistance to racial inequality. Masonic groups were aligned with Marcus Garvey's black nationalist movement after World War I and served as a recruitment vehicle for A. Phillip Randolph's Brotherhood of Sleeping Car Porters during the 1930s. Masonic orders also include women's auxiliaries, like the Order of the Eastern Star, which have historically given black women a space for political organizing. In her history of black women's labor activism after the civil war, Tera Hunter notes how women's secret societies promoted civic engagement. "Through the complex body of procedures and rules that regulated the conduct of meetings, rituals, and standards of membership, these groups promoted self-governance and discipline of the highest order" (1997, 72–73).

Many Baptist and Methodist ministers who belong to historically black denominations are members of masonic lodges. The Prince Hall Masons, the largest of the black masonic groups, have over four thousand five hundred lodges that encompass over three hundred thousand members. Like church groups, masonic groups provide the opportunity to learn organizational skills, indirectly promoting political activism. As Muraskin explains,

Masonry as an institution has been concerned with . . . inspiring and training its membership in leadership roles. Through the fraternity, members have learned to perform many bourgeois social roles with which they have limited or no prior experience. By teaching these roles, and by promoting an arena for their enactment, Masonry has worked to bring leadership potential within its membership to practical fruition. (1975, 27)

Given their religious orientation and commitment to nurturing leadership, masonic groups should encourage both conventional and protest-demand activism independently of either political or nonpolitical organizations. As is the case with church group membership, masonic group membership—measured by respondents' reporting membership in either the Masons or the Eastern Stars, a women's auxiliary group to the Masons—should, because of the civic orientation of these groups, discourage support for both political violence and separatist black nationalism.

My analysis considers the effects in 1966 of these religious resources and orientations on modes of political activism, independently of membership in both explicitly political organizations and nonpolitical, secular groups. I have created an index of civil rights group membership by combining membership in the NAACP, the Congress of Racial Equality (CORE), and the Urban League, all traditional civil rights groups that have employed various tactics and strategies for advancing the civil rights of African Americans (Meier 1963). I have created a similar index of civic/partisan group membership by summing membership in a civic group and membership in either a Republican or Democratic club.

In addition to comparing the impact of church and masonic group membership with explicitly political group membership, I have included in my analysis an index of membership in secular, nonpolitical organizations so the independent effects of church and masonic membership could be measured against general activity in organizational life, which also functions as a resource for political participation. My analysis also demonstrates how in 1966 different religious behaviors and orientations—independent of demographic and socioeconomic status (SES) factors (e.g., gender, income, education, age, region, urban location) that influence both religious behavior (Gallup 1989) and political participation (Verba and Nie 1972; Milbrath 1977; Conway 1985)—were having different effects on individual and collective political action, conventional and unconventional activism, and support for black nationalism.

THE EFFECTS OF RELIGION ON INCLUSIVE MODES OF ACTION

Table 4.2 presents regression estimates of the four religious factors influencing voter participation, an individualistic mode of conventional activity, and campaign activism, a collective mode. Two religious factors encouraged black voter participation in 1966: church attendance and affiliation with either a Baptist or Methodist denomination.

Being "deeply religious," as a measure of "otherworldliness," had, contrary to what opiate theorists would expect, no independent effect on voter participation, countering the assumption that such religious feelings impede *all* political action. In contrast, church attendance, a religious behavior associated with civic action, rivaled education in fostering voter participation. As a conventional, easy-to-practice religious act, church attendance promoted participation with the most easy-to-practice political act—voting. Similarly, being a Baptist or Methodist (two mainstream black-controlled denominations) rather than a member of a strictly fundamentalist or white-controlled denomination (in this case Catholic) encouraged voter participation.

Church attendance and membership in a church group had positive effects on campaign activism. However, deeply religious feelings discouraged participation in campaign activities, confirming what opiate theorist would predict, that religion impedes political action. Moreover, affiliation with a denomination, whether black-controlled, white-controlled, or "fundamentalist," had no impact on campaign activism, suggesting that socialization within black denominations did not in 1966 promote political activity more personally demanding than voter participation.

Given the importance of organizations in facilitating collective action efforts, I should stress that church group membership and masonic group membership stimulated participation on the one mode of participation that is most like their

Table 4.2 The Effects of Religious Resources and Orientations on Voter Participation and Campaign Activism: Blacks, 1966

Independent variables	Voter participation	Campaign activism
Religious factors		
Dimensions		
Deeply religious	−.04 (.11)	−.41 (.18)**
Church attendance	.14 (.02)***	.07 (.09)*
Denominations		
Baptist	.24 (.09)**	−.15 (.14)
Methodist	.39 (.13)***	−.12 (.18)
Catholic	.13 (.16)	.23 (.24)
Fundamentalist	−.38 (.39)	.08 (.52)
Organizational resources		
Religious/quasi-religious		
Church group member	.14 (.08)	.47 (.14)***
Masonic	.04 (.01)	.48 (.19)**
Political		
Civil rights	.13 (.09)	.93 (.14)***
Partisan/civic	.17 (.11)	1.01 (.19)***
Nonpolitical secular	.10 (.06)	.52 (.11)***
SES and demographics		
Region (South)	−.51 (.08)***	.07 (.12)
Gender (male)	.18 (.06)***	.67 (.10)***
Education	.12 (02)***	.23 (.04)***
Age	.27 (.03)***	.29 (.05)***
Urban	−.16 (.09)*	−.14 (.14)
Number of cases	909	1020
Adjusted R^2	.19	.37

Entries are unstandardized regression coefficients with standard errors in parentheses. Total sample = 1,059.
*$p < .10$, one-tailed test.
**$p < .05$, one-tailed test.
***$p < .001$, one-tailed test.

own—campaign activism. These two church-based organizational resources encouraged campaign activity among blacks independently of—though less potently than—their involvement in more explicitly political organizations like the NAACP or a voters' league. The impact of masonic groups membership in promoting campaign activism confirms these groups' role as nurturers of civic action.

Table 4.3 presents the effects of religious resources and orientations on protest-demand activism and support, modes of political action that are both unconven-

Table 4.3 The Effects of Religious Resources and Orientations on Protest Activism and Support: Blacks, 1966

Independent variables	Protest activism	Support for protest
Religious factors		
Dimensions		
Deeply religious	−.59 (.18)***	−.13 (.39)
Church attendance	.08 (.05)*	.07 (.09)
Denominations		
Baptist	−.09 (.15)	.79 (.32)**
Methodist	−.12 (.18)	.83 (.39)**
Catholic	.23 (.25)	.46 (.54)
Fundamentalist	−1.16 (.54)**	−.80 (1.16)
Organizational resources		
Religious/quasi-religious		
Church group member	.21 (.14)	.16 (.30)
Masonic	.16 (.20)	−.12 (.43)
Political		
Civil rights	1.41 (.15)***	.89 (.32)***
Partisan/civic	.75 (.19)***	.30 (.41)
Nonpolitical secular	.19 (.11)*	.56 (.24)**
SES and demographics		
Region (South)	.08 (.12)	−.14 (.26)
Gender (male)	.37 (.19)***	.25 (.22)
Education	.24 (.04)***	.20 (.08)**
Age	−.08 (.05)	−.46 (.11)***
Urban	.19 (.14)	.97 (.31)***
Number of cases	1020	1020
Adjusted R^2	.31	.08

Entries are unstandardized regression coefficients with standard errors in parentheses. Total sample = 1,059.
*$p < .10$, one-tailed test.
**$p < .05$, one-tailed test.
***$p < .001$, one-tailed test.

tional and inclusive of the political system. In many ways the patterns for protest-demand activism look much like those for campaign activism. Sectarianism and church attendance had opposite effects on black protest in 1966. Being deeply religious discouraged participation in protest activities, while church attendance, a religious behavior associated with civic activity, encouraged such participation. However, although affiliation with a fundamentalist denomination had no association with campaign activism, it was negatively associated, as expected, with protest activism.

The nonsignificant effects of religiously based organizational resources on protest-demand activism present a puzzle, given the black church's documented role in this period in mobilizing protest through indigenous leadership and financial resources. As one would expect, membership in civil rights groups had a greater impact on protest-demand activism than any other factor in the model. Involvement in partisan and civic associations also encouraged participation in protest activism, confirming the importance of the associational dynamics of civil society in providing "free spaces" for collective action.

In regard to support for protest-demand activism, rather than reported involvement in it, a different pattern emerges. As the model shows, neither deeply religious feelings nor church attendance affected whether blacks supported protest activities in 1966. However, membership in mainstream black denominations was positively associated with such support. These findings contrast with Gary Marx's findings that affiliation with black denominations dampened support for civil rights in several cities in 1964. Affiliation with both the Baptists and the Methodists encouraged support for protest-demand activism, suggesting that these denominations served as socializing agents to legitimize such activism as a strategy for the articulation of black interests. In the case of members who belonged to the National Baptist Convention, the largest of the black Baptist organizations, the finding that the Baptist laity supported protest tactics is in contrast to the civil rights conservatism of Joseph H. Jackson, then president of the Convention and nemesis of Martin Luther King.

As was the case with reported participation, neither church group membership nor masonic group membership predicted support for protest-demand activism. Only involvement in civil rights groups, organizations directly involved in civil rights activities, and nonpolitical secular groups, which reflects the wide variations in black civil society, were associated with such support.

THE EFFECTS OF RELIGION ON EXCLUSIVE MODES OF THOUGHT

Table 4.4 indicates that religious resources and orientations had little or no positive impact on blacks' support for political violence in 1966. As we might expect, church attendance, the most conventional of the religious acts, discouraged support for one of the most extreme and unconventional political acts—political violence. Deep religious feelings, denominational affiliation, and church-based organizational resources had no significant impact on political violence. Given that church attendance is a civic-oriented resource for participation, its negative association with political violence is expected, since political violence is an act of participation that rejects the existing civil order.

Table 4.4 The Effects of Religious Resources and Orientations on Political Violence and Black Autonomy: Blacks, 1966

Independent variables	Political violence	Black nationalism
Religious factors		
Dimensions		
Deeply religious	−.22 (.18)	−.23 (.18)
Church attendance	−.12 (.04)***	−.17 (.04)***
Denominations		
Baptist	.22 (.15)	−.30 (.15)**
Methodist	.22 (.17)	−.33 (.18)**
Catholic	.45 (.25)*	.36 (.25)
Fundamentalist	.37 (.53)	−.37 (.54)
Organizational resources		
Religious/quasi-religious		
Church group member	−.14 (.14)	−.14 (.14)
Masonic	−.14 (.19)	.07 (.20)
Political		
Civil rights	−.15 (.15)	.02 (.15)
Partisan/civic	.20 (.19)	.07 (.19)
Nonpolitical secular	−.13 (.11)	.02 (.11)
SES and demographics		
Region (South)	.19 (.12)*	.15 (.12)
Gender (male)	.25 (.10)**	.08 (.10)
Education	−.10 (.04)***	−.16 (.04)***
Age	−.19 (.05)***	.08 (.05)*
Urban	.14 (.14)	−.30 (.14)**
Number of cases	1020	1020
Adjusted R^2	.04	.04

Entries are unstandardized regression coefficients with standard errors in parentheses. Total sample = 1,059.

*p < .10, one-tailed test.
**p < .05, one-tailed test.
***p < .001, one-tailed test.

The fact that membership in political, nonpolitical, and religious-based groups had no effect on support for potential violence confirms the unpredictability and spontaneity of mass political violence. Some patterns have been noted, however. As other studies have found (Kerner Commission 1968), as education increases, the likelihood that an individual joins a riot diminishes; in addition, men are more supportive of rioting than women.

Table 4.4 also presents the effects of religion on support for separatist black nationalism. As we might expect, church attendance, a behavior that fosters support for civic action, discouraged support for separatist black nationalism in 1966. This confirms the theory that church attendance usually works against racial separatism, or any ideology that advocates withdrawal from American society. Affiliation with a black-controlled denomination similarly inhibited support for separatism. Mainstream black-controlled denominations may have operated as socializing agents against an ideology of separatism, on the one hand serving as hegemonic institutions that fostered inclusionary rather than separatist politics and on the other hand serving as socializing agents for the legitimacy of protest. As with political violence, organizational membership, whether religious or secular, had no impact either way on support for separatism, while education negatively predicted support for separatism, and being male increased support for political violence.

Sectarianism and the Demand Modes of Activism

Reporting a deeply religious feeling (or sectarianism), which is probably linked to an otherworldly religious orientation, undermined participation in campaign and protest-demand activism but had no effect on blacks' participation in voter activities. This finding suggests two, not mutually exclusive, possibilities. First, as previously mentioned, deep commitments to one's religion might discourage involvement in any form of secular activity, including politics, that competes with religious obligation. Second, the fact that deeply religious feelings have a negative impact on high-initiative modes of action like campaigning and protesting might reflect a difference between the private and the public dimensions of religion. Slightly over 40 percent (42 percent) of respondents who reported feeling deeply about their religion attended church less than once a week. This suggests, as others have noted (Tate 1993), that public commitments to one's religion in the form of regular church attendance and participation in religious activities have a more *direct* influence on stimulating political action than privatized religious commitments.

Afro-Christianity and an
Oppositional Civic Culture

These findings on the effects of religious factors on activism during a pivotal period of black political mobilization are multifaceted and, in some instances, ambiguous. They show that these effects depend on the form that religion takes, contradicting critics who have argued that religion in general fosters passivity. Rather than acting as an opiate, religion stimulated many kinds of black activism in the sixties. My analysis found religion promoting mainstream and protest activity, though it did repress support for political violence and separatist black nationalism.

Part of the misunderstanding about religion's impact on black activism during the sixties is the lack of clarity regarding the nature of religion and political activism. Critics of black religion have charged that religion operated as an opiate on "militancy," "radicalism," and "revolution" among blacks without having adequately defined these concepts, leading to the impression that religion generally operates as a sedating force on all aspects of political activism. By not separating modes of behavior and attitudes that support civil society from those that undermine civil society, critics of religion's influence on black activism have overlooked the different modes of political activism and the different influence of religion on these diverse modes of action.

The positive effects of distinctive religious forms on both voter participation and campaign activism point to religion as a resource for conventional political action. Church attendance and affiliation with a mainstream black denomination promote voting; they serve as political resources by nurturing civic obligation and legitimizing the social order. Church attendance, church group membership, and masonic group membership encourage campaign activism; during this period of black political activism, they fostered civic duty and provided organizational resources for such activism.

The effects of religion on inclusive forms of unconventional political behavior are ambiguous. While church attendance is the only religious factor that positively predicted actual demand-protest activism, only affiliation with a Baptist or Methodist denomination predicted a willingness to participate in such activism. This suggests that affiliation with a black rather than white mainstream denomination socialized religious blacks into viewing protest politics as a legitimate means of advancing black interests. No religious component positively predicted support for political violence, and church attendance was negatively associated with support for political violence, illustrating how religion can stifle civil disorder.

But the positive impact of some religious factors on conventional participation and protest activism and the negative connection between church attendance and support for political violence suggest that religion can support a unique civic culture for African Americans. As Almond and Verba explain, the term "civic culture" refers to "political orientations—attitudes toward the political system and its various parts, and the attitudes toward the role of the self in the political system" (1963, 12).

For African Americans, certain religious elements seem to foster a civic culture that promotes not only civically directed participation, like voter participation and campaign activism, but also participation in and support for protest-demand activism, a mode of behavior that occurs outside of the institutionalized political system. The finding that black denominational affiliation affects support for protest more than actual protest echoes Almond and Verba's discovery of a gap between support for political action and actual political action. Almond and Verba concluded that citizens felt an obligation to participate in the polity, whether they did so or not. This obligation to participate is transmitted through "a complex process that includes training in many social institutions," specifically "family, peer group, school, work place, as well as the political system itself" (1963, 367).

Although Almond and Verba did not specifically identify religion as a vehicle for civic culture, my analysis reveals its potential influence. And although Almond and Verba were thinking of mainstream civic cultures, my findings suggest that an analysis similar to theirs applies to what Aldon Morris calls "oppositional consciousness" (1992). An oppositional civic culture may develop attitudes and behaviors that simultaneously support civil society and oppose a system of domination within that society. Dominated groups may oppose their domination through conventional and unconventional modes of activism that attempt to reform society rather than undermine or overthrow it. Given that in 1966 various religious factors promoted conventional political action among blacks, as well as their involvement in and support for protest-demand activism, and that church attendance, in particular, discouraged political violence, it appears that religion, in its various manifestations, fostered a particular form of oppositional civic culture among blacks during the sixties.

By rejecting violence as a political strategy and supporting protest-demand activism, this oppositional civic culture among black Americans promoted inclusion within the polity rather than separation from existing political structures. This oppositional civic culture is also reflected in the negative link between church attendance and separatist black nationalism. By rejecting withdrawal from civil society, some elements of black religion encouraged civic-directed participation, which, as the decade of the sixties proceeded on into the 1970s, contributed to the unprecedented level of black electoral engagement.

These findings suggest, more broadly, that the culture and institutions of dominated groups can nurture political beliefs and strategies that at the same time both support and oppose the existing civic order. One would expect norms of civic culture that bind ordinary citizens to the polity to be fragile among dominated groups whose subordination is legitimized and sanctioned by that polity. Yet African-American religion in the period of the civil rights movement fostered both loyalty to the regime *and* opposition to aspects of that regime. Although scholars have debated for several generations the effects of Christianity on the political activism of African Americans, they have focused on whether Christianity dampened or stimulated black activism. Most have neglected to investigate the capacity of religion to do both at the same time.

Afro-Christianity, in this crucial period of contest for the loyalties of African Americans, encouraged inclusive political activities but discouraged exclusionary ones. This makes it necessary to understand in more complex ways the nature of insurgent institutions and how they may operate in liberal democratic societies. Just as oppositional outlooks and resources are lodged in the culture and institutions of dominated groups, so too are more system-supporting civic norms, skills, and outlooks lodged in the culture and institutions of the larger society that insurgents acquire even as marginal members of that society. This dual capacity suggests that it is important to uncover the difference between those social norms and institutions that lead both to loyalty to the polity and reformist opposition and the contrasting norms and institutions that undermine civic loyalty.

The idea of an oppositional civic culture also raises questions about how social movements are incorporated into the existing political system. Students of social movements have emphasized the ways macrostructural factors such as government repression of movements, the cooptation of movement leaders, and the contraction of movement resources contribute to movement institutionalization. They have somewhat overlooked the capacity of civic norms to influence the direction of insurgents' behavior. In the case of black nationalist and revolutionary movements of the 1960s and early 1970s, the federal government's counterinsurgency plan to disrupt radical activism increased the risk for insurgents involved in such activities (McAdam 1982). This disruption no doubt contributed to groups like the Black Panthers receiving only soft support in black communities during this era of political contestation. My analysis, however, suggests that the civic norms embedded in the relatively mainstream institutions and culture of most African Americans also helped institutionalize the movement by guiding blacks away from modes of action and thought that would undermine the civic order and toward modes of action that called for inclusion in the American political process.[6]

5

Blessed Assurance

Religion, Personal Empowerment, and African-American Political Activism

If ye have the faith as a grain of a mustard seed, ye shall say unto this mountain, remove hence to yonder place; and it shall remove; and nothing shall be impossible unto you.

Matthew 17:20

If you take one step, He'll make two.

African-American religious saying

We stood up. Me and God stood up.

Ethel Gray, civil rights organizer, Greenwood,

Mississippi.

ONE MINISTER IN BROOKLYN, NEW YORK, asked by a newspaper reporter whether he felt "scared" organizing to rid a half-abandoned apartment building of drugs and prostitution, mentioned a source of political empowerment that scholars rarely acknowledge. Reverend Hardy Smallwood answered that it was "but the grace of God" that kept him from danger.[1] He noted that he could not have succeeded alone; it was the "police and community working together" that made his organizing effective. Police and sympathetic neighbors may well have provided the minister with earthly reassurances in the face of the dangers of vengeful drug dealers and pimps, but Reverend Smallwood made it quite clear that, more than anything else, his belief in divine protection was what enabled him to overcome fears of retribution for his political activism. Game theorists, following self-interest models of political action, argue that the promise of co operation with others can move some people to participate in collective action. Likewise, for activists like Reverend Smallwood, the perceived cooperation of a divine force—what could be described as *sacred assurance*—may provide incentives for participation.

This chapter examines how religion can inspire African Americans to feel politically effective, and how such a feeling may contribute to the process of mobilizing micro resources (see chapter 3). It explores a concept that I call religiously inspired political efficacy, a confidence that one can affect the political order through the guidance and/or protection of an acknowledged sacred force.[2] It considers religion's psychological effects on black activism: how faith and religious practice foster feelings of strength and confidence in people who organize for social and political change in black communities. What I describe as religiously inspired political efficacy is different from the way political scientists have generally understood political efficacy. Political scientists define political efficacy in two dimensions—either as an internal or as an external force that makes citizens feel politically competent. Internal political efficacy, which is closely related to my idea of religiously inspired political efficacy, is a feeling that one has within oneself the power to influence the political process. External political efficacy depends on the perception one has of political institutions and elites where feelings of empowerment rest on external factors—on how one perceives government institutions and officials responding to the needs of people like oneself.

My perspective on religion's empowering effects on black political activism is drawn from two methods of analysis. Narratives of activists during the modern civil rights movement suggest that religion promotes feelings of political efficacy during risky episodes of political engagement. Although fervent religious orientations probably discouraged protest in the larger black population during the 1960s (chapter 4), religion gave many committed activists the courage to risk their material and physical well-being in protest. Data from a survey taken in 1979 suggests that the negative effects of intense religious beliefs on the political participation of the black population in the 1960s may have changed in the post–civil rights era. The models suggest causal linkages between privatized religious feelings and practices (religiosity), feelings of personal empowerment (personal efficacy), feelings of competence in political matters (internal political efficacy), and political activism.

THE PSYCHOLOGY OF RELIGION

In their exhaustive review of research in the psychology of religion, Bernard Spilka, Ralph Hood, and Richard Gorsuch give limited attention to the empowering effects of religion on human behavior. Summarizing research on faith, the authors distinguish between intrinsic and extrinsic forms of private faith. "Extrinsic faith" has a utilitarian motive—the desire for the material and psychic benefits of divine intervention. "Intrinsic faith," by contrast, transcends the self-centered desires of individuals by its emphasis on faith as "ultimate significance, a final good, supreme value, the ultimate answer" (1985, 18–19). Intrinsic faith could, in theory, benefit collective action efforts by de-emphasizing self-centered incentives for participation in favor of more transcendent religious values. The potential effect of this aspect of religious faith on collective action must remain speculative given the paucity of research on religion's capacity to motivate individuals to act collectively.

As Spilka, Hood, and Gorsuch indirectly recognize, religion may promote feelings of efficacy. The authors theorize from their review of the research that "[r]eligion is . . . a source of meaning, an agency of control for people through worship and prayer, and, through the provision of meaning and capability, self-esteem is maintained and enhanced in the face of threat and insecurity" (1985, 21). These speculations provide a psychological basis for analyzing the causal linkages between religiosity, efficacy, and black political activism. The idea that religion may promote political activism, thereby empowering African-Americans with a sense of political efficacy, is a fresh perspective, for much of the earlier research on the psychological dynamics of religion among African Americans has viewed religion primarily as a distraction from worldly social change.

PSYCHOLOGICAL EXPLANATIONS OF AFRO-CHRISTIANITY

The observations of scholars who have subscribed to the opiate theory tell a complicated story about the psychological dynamics of Afro-Christianity. Historian Carter G. Woodson concluded from his research during the 1930s that Christianity had different psychological effects on rural and urban blacks. Describing the urban black church as an "uplift agency," Woodson concluded that the rural church was merely a "mystic shrine" ([1930] 1985). Writing during a period of rapid economic change and disorder in the South, Woodson commented that for rural blacks, who were mostly sharecroppers, Christianity operated as a means of escape from the drudgery of their labor. Woodson observed that rural believers "have no time for the problems of this life except to extricate themselves from the difficulties which will ever beset them here until that final day" (333). Likening spirit possessions to "paroxysms which could hardly be expected outside of an insane asylum," Woodson offered this description: "With the spirit of the people thus fired up they can retire to their homes sufficiently uplifted to face the toils of another week or month. On assembling for similar services again they will have their spiritual strength renewed" (333).

Woodson's account of the rural black religious experience during this period of black subordination reveals a psychological dynamic that would serve some activists well during the modern civil rights movement, a generation later. Despite his pessimistic outlook on the lives of rural believers, Woodson's observations suggested that religion could nurture feelings of self-worth and personal efficacy, both connected to feelings of internal political efficacy.

R. A. Billings, a professor of medicine at Howard University, provided Freudian and class interpretations of black religion. In his essay "The Negro and His Church: A Psychogenetic Study," Billings argued that religion, for blacks, compensated for feelings of sexual aggression, hatred of whites, and resentment of their lot as members of a despised group. Billings observed black churches during the 1930s through the lens of the basic premise that religion is "the plastic apparatus that always freely promised those things which people desire or needed most but were lacking" (1934, 425).

Billings concluded that fervent emotionalism shielded the poorest African Americans (who, he pointed out, were usually darker-skinned than middle- and upper-class blacks) from the psychic effects of both class and color prejudice. This escape mechanism was so essential, he reasoned, that without it poor blacks "would have been able to go on [in life] but would in desperation bash their heads against a stone" (1934, 430). Noting that their religious fervor "bolstered up their belief in themselves" and concealed the "hate in their unconscious minds" (431), Billings argued that both their yearnings for the unaffordable pleasures of life and the restrictiveness of their beliefs were manifested through repressed sexual desires that surfaced during intense experiences of religious emotionalism. Asserting that "[t]here . . . can be no doubt even from mere observation alone that these church meetings provide vicarious outlets for pent-up sexual energies of some individuals," Billings theorized that these desires surfaced "with a certain degree of social sanction" during episodes of fervent emotionalism (432). Billings gave these accounts as evidence:

> I have the admission of a woman that when she was eighteen years of age and a member of a church quite similar to the one under discussion, she loved the preacher but dared not reveal her love. The libido was aroused especially when he talked and hence she started shouting every time he preached. During the shout she imagined herself with the object of her love and at the zenith of her shouting she experienced an orgasm and relief. (432)

Consider the author's interpretation of spirit possession of men from the United House of Prayer, a Pentecostal sect:

> In a similar manner the homosexuals have an opportunity to satisfy their cravings in a vicarious manner, thus avoiding the more stigmatized course usually followed. During these shouts they are able to be very close to men in the congregation while their actions are explained as but expressions of the ecstasy of religious fervor. This almost simulates the mechanism of masturbation in that the sexual appetite is appeased and yet the other possible actor in the act is present only in imagination. (432)

Middle-class blacks of a marginally lighter color sought compensation for white domination not in intense emotionalism but in a craving for social recognition. This craving, according to Billings, was satisfied through intense involvement in the organizational affairs of the church where members were "victims of a desire for social exhibition." These engaged church members—many of whom, Billings claimed, were "spinsters, childless women, and men grown impotent"—compensated for their feelings of inferiority by "doing things for the church, giving large sums of money, so that the membership may reward them with an office, such as a trustee or deacon" (1934, 435).

The black elite, in Billings's analysis, sought such compensation because of status prejudice from whites. The light complexion of the black elite, he contended, made them feel psychologically "closer to the white race than . . . to the dark part of that race with which they were identified." Their "inability to pass the [color] line embitters their lives," thus creating envy of whites and resentment against darker-complexioned blacks (1934, 438). Billings reasoned that racial prejudice against this class of blacks fostered internal conflicts, forcing them to "seek some relief, some solace, some method by which their troubled minds may be soothed"(439). They found this relief through their affiliations with mostly white Christian denominations where they could "escape" feelings of inferiority and even feel superior to other blacks. Billings explained: "To these people this class of churches offers an escape. . . . They can escape the company of the darker members of the race that is but an unpleasant and sharp reminder of their inferiority and they can enjoy the company of their like-colored fellow sufferers with whom they can share their sorrows even if they have no happiness to share" (440).

Beneath these Freudian and class interpretations, Billings subtly acknowledges the effect of religion on the self-worth of these different segments of the black communities he studied. Although Billings interpreted the psychological dynamics of religion as dysfunctional behavior deriving from social and economic inequalities, his own observations show how religion fostered self-esteem among socially and economically dominated individuals. If religion, for blacks, "bolstered up belief within," operated as a platform for "social exhibition," or served as a way of "soothing troubled minds," it may have cultivated feelings of self-worth and efficacy, which would, given opportunities for activism and strong feelings of racial solidarity, work for some as an empowering resource for political involvement.

The work of anthropologist Hortense Powdermaker echoes this possibility. In her study of religious emotionalism among blacks in Indianola, Mississippi, during the 1930s, she, like Billings, offered a Freudian interpretation. While Powdermaker did claim that ministers served as symbols of "erotic satisfaction" for black women and asserted that "[t]here is much to be said for the theory that the repressions caused by the inter-racial situation find relief in unrestrained religious behavior" ([1939] 1968, 273), she also emphasized that religious emotionalism provided more than an outlet for sexual repression. Although, like most scholars during this period, she did maintain that religion suppressed overt opposition to white domination, Powdermaker also insisted, unusually, that religion nurtured feelings of self-worth in black believers and thus subtly challenged ideas of white supremacy. She concluded that

> [i]n both its secular and its religious character, [religion] serves as an antidote, a palliative, an escape. . . . By helping the Negro to endure the status quo, this institution has been a conservative force, tending to relieve and counteract the discontents that make for rebellion. At the same time the equally vital function of maintaining the self-respect of the Negro individual is by no means a conservative one (285).

Instead of seeing religion as a "conservative force" that undermined "rebellion," critics of religion during the Jim Crow period might have considered that for people living under a rigid system of domination, opportunities for organized resistance are limited and risky. These scholars might have further explored the ways in which religion helped blacks to survive psychically—an all-too-subversive prospect in itself at that time. As James Scott implies (1985, 1990), dominated people use symbolic modes of resistance, challenging hegemonic ideals through cultural acts and beliefs. The fact that Christianity could preserve and nurture the self-worth of African Americans, despite a dominant ideology that devalued their humanity, attests to the positive psychological functions of religious belief.[3]

Religious Belief and Black Self-Worth

Mays and Nicholson's classic study of the black church during the 1930s ([1933] 1969) noted the empowering effects of Christianity among blacks. The authors concluded from their survey of 609 urban and 185 rural black churches that Christianity nurtured a sense of "somebodiness" in its congregants, buffering the negative psychological effects of white supremacy. Mays and Nicholson connected African Americans' sense of pride to their opportunities to participate in church affairs. Describing this aspect of African-American religious life as the "genius of the Negro church," Mays and Nicholson concluded that "the opportunity found in the Negro church to be recognized, and to be 'somebody,'" fostered feelings of self-esteem by "stimulat[ing] pride and preserv[ing] the self-respect of many Negroes who would have been entirely beaten by life and completely submerged" (281). Mays and Nicholson noted:

> A truck driver of average or more than ordinary qualities becomes the chairman of the Deacon board. A hotel man of some ability is the superintendent of the Sunday church school of a rather important church. A woman who would be hardly noticed, socially or otherwise, becomes a leading woman in the missionary society. A girl of little training . . . gets

the chance to become the leading soprano in the choir of a great church. These people receive little or no recognition on their daily job. There is nothing to make them feel they are "somebody." (281)

Acknowledging the role of church life in allowing congregants the opportunity to develop organizing and civic skills ([1933] 1969, 7–12), Mays and Nicholson also discovered how Christianity fostered self-esteem in African Americans. Church involvement, the authors noted, nurtured a sense of self-worth denied African-Americans outside the realm of their religious communities. However, Mays and Nicholson did not mention those aspects of Christianity that promote ideals of equality among all, which might, along with involvement in church activities, also have inspired feelings of personal efficacy and self-worth.

Although his writings emphasize the compensatory and otherworldly effects of Christianity, John Dollard also—apparently unconsciously—recognized its empowering possibilities during his observations of black Protestant church services in the deep South during the 1930s. He noted that these churches were "serviceable to whites," by—according to one informant in his study—allowing whites "to keep the status quo by offering an illusory consolation to the Negroes" ([1937] 1949 250). But Dollard also personally experienced the positive effects of religion through his participation in a religious service at a black church. When Dollard was asked by a minister to "say a few words" as "white guests usually are" invited to do, he took it upon himself in one instance to "take to the pulpit and expose myself to the congregation." "Not familiar enough with the Bible . . . I . . . spoke of the beauty of their land, and expressed my pleasure at being allowed to participate in their exercises" (243).

His account of the reaction from the congregation and the feelings he experienced during his "little talk" reveals the potential power of religion to inspire personal strength. Dollard reported that his spontaneous words were "[h]elped by appreciative murmurs which began slowly and softly and became louder and fuller" as he went on: "Well," "Hallelujah," and "Isn't that the truth?" The congregation's response *gave him* a "great sense of elation, an increased fluency, and a vastly expanded confidence in speaking." He summed up his feelings during his talk as follows: "[T]he crowd had enabled me to talk to them much more sincerely than I thought I knew how to do; the continuous surge of affirmation was a highly elating experience. . . . Here the audience was actually ahead of me, it had a performed affirmation ready for the person with the courage to say the significant word." ([1937] 1949, 243)

Dollard further revealed that he felt "a sense of loosing the limitations of self and of unconscious powers rising to meet the unbound, unconscious forces of the group" ([1937] 1949, 244). The performed affirmation from the congregation that sparked Dollard's feelings of "elation," "expanded confidence," and "unconscious powers" uncovered an aspect of religion that Dollard missed when he discussed Christianity's psychological impact on African Americans. The psychic nurturing of southern blacks under a rigid structure of white domination worked as a resource for their political mobilization later on, when they had more opportunities for activism. The idea that Dollard, a privileged, white, and "objective" Yale social scientist, experienced the benefits of participation in a black religious service during the Jim Crow South of the 1930s is an irony, given his conclusion that religion functioned as a means of social control by "keeping the peace" for southern whites, "not only in smothering revolts economically motivated, but in suppressing discontent with mores in general" ([1937] 1949, 249).

RELIGION AS THERAPY

Many pre–civil rights era social scientists thought that black religious belief undermined opposition. But after the civil rights movement, analysts of the psychological dynamics of religion came to regard Christianity as a therapeutic tool that helps blacks cope with social ills (Sata, Perry, and Cameron 1970; Griffith, English, and Mayfield 1980; Gilkes 1980). Most of the work on the therapeutic aspect of black religiosity focuses on the religious behavior of congregants from poor, nontraditional churches. These churches are characterized by the highly emotional rituals of testifying and spirit possession, in which congregants—most of whom are women—articulate their suffering, pinpoint their persecutors, and "act out" their frustrations. This process helps the believers to resolve personal suffering (Gilkes 1980). Referring to the process as a "collective therapeutic experience," Cheryl Townsend Gilkes argues that it nurtures the psychological strength of congregants against assaults of racial prejudice and economic marginality. Gilkes implies that this aspect of religion fosters the self-worth of religious blacks:

> To be able to know that their troubles are not the result of personal defects; that their inferiority is not a certified fact; and that people in certain positions in white society are actively persecuting them prevents for black [religious] people the disjuncture between personal experience and feelings and the realities with which they are coping, which for many other people renders them vulnerable to incarceration within institutions for the insane (1980, 42).

This religion-as-therapy perspective has at least two implications for assessing the psychological effects of religion on black political activism. On the one hand, Gilkes theorizes that intense religiosity among African Americans promotes feelings of self-esteem. Averting self-blame might allow people to attribute their problems to societal rather than personal causes. Blaming society might be associated with distrusting the government, which, when combined with group consciousness, is a significant component of black political activism (Shingles 1981). On the other hand, Gilkes's assertion that religiosity functions as a coping mechanism reinforces the compensatory and escapist perspective, undermining the idea that religion operates as a psychological source of political empowerment. As a coping mechanism, religion might actually undermine opposition by encouraging individuals to cope with, rather than act to change, their lot.

This dual dimension of religiosity's psychological aspect among African Americans is also implicit in the work of St. George and McNamara (1984). These authors found that private religious beliefs offered a greater boost to perceptions of psychological well-being among blacks than among whites. On measures of subjective feelings of happiness, excitement in life, satisfaction with community, family life, and friendships, intensely religious blacks were more likely to report satisfaction than were intensely religious whites.

The authors concluded that the compensatory perspective "seems unwarranted due to the fact that our findings hold up under controls for age, education, and income" and that religiosity "shows little sign of diminution as blacks improve their socioeconomic status in American society" (1984, 363). St. George and Mc-Namara are not entirely convincing here; given the economic and social inequalities between blacks and whites, the finding that religiosity has a greater effect on psychological well-being among blacks could actually reinforce the theory that black religiosity is compensatory. If religious blacks are collectively content with their lot in life, despite the social and economic inequalities of African Americans as a group, then religion might actually be operating as a panacea rather than as a call to overt resistance. Religion would then be thwarting incentives for African Americans to actively and collectively challenge the societal obstacles they face.

However, other studies reinforce the conclusions on self-worth and efficacy without suggesting that these feelings detract from the potential for political activity. In an ethnographic analysis of spirit possession among African Americans in New Haven, anthropologists Griffith, English, and Mayfield concluded, from their observations of mid-week prayer services of a black Pentecostal church, that religiosity fostered feelings of self-worth and personal efficacy:

> The sensation of being one of God's chosen and being pure enough to be a receptacle for the Holy Spirit was a crucial factor raising the self-esteem of these black people and convincing them that their lives were worth more than the outside society seemed to suggest. Many members of the church group constantly repeated that no other modality gave them power to overcome problems in living such as was given by the power of the Holy Ghost. (1980, 127)

The personal empowerment these prayer group members gained from their religious experience strengthened their determination to change their difficult lives. In observations much like those of Carter G. Woodson a generation ago, the authors note that those who attended the mid-week prayer services were experiencing personal crises where "the opportunity to pray, testify, and be possessed by the Holy Spirit would refresh them for the return to the daily struggle" (127).

If, for some African Americans, religious experience supports feelings of personal worth and perceived control over one's social environment, it may, also, for similar psychological reasons, foster feelings of internal political efficacy. In fact, some activists in the civil rights movement reported that religion did politically empower them, especially during episodes of risky protest.

RELIGIOUS FAITH AND POLITICAL EMPOWERMENT
IN THE CIVIL RIGHTS MOVEMENT

The feelings of self-worth and personal efficacy inspired by a commitment to religious faith served as a critical psychological resource for some blacks during the southern civil rights movement. Religion helped many activists face the threats of material and physical sanctions leveled against them by white supremacists. This psychological component of religion had effects even when church leaders discouraged their members' participation and resisted getting involved in the movement themselves (Payne 1990; MacLeod 1991).[4]

Recounting her involvement in a store boycott in Holmes County, Mississippi, Bee Jenkins described how she overcame her fear of the local law enforcement officers who confronted protesters with "big guns" (MacLeod 1991, 132–141). Leaving work to join the march, having been warned beforehand by her employer that "somebody gon' get killed" that day, Bee Jenkins "walked outta the house, looked up, said a prayer, and went and got in the marching." A feeling of divinely granted protection sustained her courage to march; "the law enforcements 'n' highway patrol was all gathered up there—you name 'em, they was there. I wasn't afraid. Because I know *I had somebody there who was on my side*. And that was Jesus; he was able to take care of me. *That who I can depend on and put my trust in*" (MacLeod 1991, 138, my emphasis).

Describing her participation in protests, including the march supporting the release of Fannie Lou Hamer from jail in Winona, Mississippi, and James Meredith's 1966 march through Mississippi, Leola Blackmon explained how her belief in Christ allayed her misgivings about becoming involved in the movement. She acknowledged the importance of self-esteem for activists by remarking "[Y]ou had to be somebody to stand up." She recalled how Christianity's tenets of equality nurtured her resistance to white domination, empowering her to get involved in the movement. Asked how she overcame her fear of participation in protest marches, she responded: "I tell you the truth: I never had no fear. . . . It was always brought up to me—I don't suppose to fear peoples. But one thing I learned young and that's *everything possible through Jesus Christ*. I don't feel like

I oughta have feared mens. The one I feared's Jesus Christ" (MacLeod 1991, 175, my emphasis).

Viola Winters also recounted how her belief in divine protection kept her strong during her involvement in the sit-ins aimed at integrating the waiting room of the local train station. Asked how she felt about participants being murdered for their involvement, she responded: "They sho' was [getting killed], but I still didn't get afraid. That didn't stop me. *I asked the Lord to take care of me* and just went on out there. I overcame fear by keep goin'. If I hadda stopped, I probably would've got afraid. But I kept it keepin' on" (MacLeod 1991, 84, my emphasis).

Asked whether he had ever considered violent retaliation for the cross-burnings and the destruction of personal and church property he had experienced, Reverend J. J. Russell replied that his Bible was "the best weapon of all times." He recalled:

When I get out, I pull [the Bible] up. The policeman starts tremblin'—he have his pistol—n' goes to shaking. When I go in the courthouse, we would go in and carry the Bible. And they'd be shaking. They never did stop me on the road; they'd stop everybody but me. But they followed us at night with their lights out, and I'd lay my Bible right on the dash [board of the car]. When they see that Bible, it just does something to them. *There's something about this Bible with you, you don't have to worry about anything.* Ain't nobody gonna bother you. (MacLeod 1991, 29, my emphasis)

Threatened with material and physical sanctions for leading the Montgomery bus boycott, Martin Luther King himself overcame his fear by calling upon feelings of divine protection. King recalled that in a critical moment during the initial phase of the Montgomery movement: "I got to the point that I couldn't take it any longer. I was weak. Something said to me, you can't call on Daddy now, he's up in Atlanta a hundred and seventy-five miles away. You can't even call on Mama now. You've got to *call on that something* in that person that your Daddy used to tell you about, *that power that can make a way out of no way*" (Garrow 1986, 58, my emphasis).

Praying for courage after receiving a threatening phone call, King, who had pastored a church in Montgomery for a year at that time, reaffirmed his commitment to Christianity.

I discovered then that religion had to become real to me, and I had to know God for myself. And I bowed down over that cup of coffee. I will never forget it . . . I prayed a prayer, and I prayed out loud that night. I said, "Lord, I'm down here trying to do what's right. I think the cause that we represent is right. But Lord I must confess that I'm weak now. I'm faltering. I'm losing my courage." . . . And *it seemed at that moment* that I could hear an inner voice saying to me, "Martin Luther, stand up for justice, stand up for truth. And lo I will be with you, even to the end of the world." . . . *I heard the voice of Jesus saying still to fight on.* He promised *never to leave me,* never to leave me alone. (Garrow 1986, 58, my emphasis)

Feelings of sacred protection even gave some people the courage to risk death. When attempting to integrate the University of Alabama in 1956, Autherine Lucy confronted an angry mob of white students who chased her with chants of "Let's kill her, let's kill her." Lucy, who was eventually expelled from the university because of student reaction to her presence, recalled:

I was very much afraid at this time. I sat there and tried to compose myself, and naturally the next thing that I thought of doing was *saying a prayer.* . . . I asked to be able to see the time when I would be able to complete my work on the campus, but that *if it was not the will of God* that I do this, that *He give me the courage* to accept the fact that I would lose my life there, and to help me to *accept it,* because this was a time when I felt then that I might not get out of it really alive. Of course, I wanted to, but I wanted the *courage to accept death,* at that point if it had to be that way. (Raines 1977, 325–326, my emphasis)

Civil rights activist Fannie Lou Hamer received death threats throughout her organizing efforts in Mississippi. At a mass meeting in Greenwood, Mississippi, in 1963, Hamer recounted how a divinely granted sense of security sustained her determination to persevere in face of such danger:

It's a funny thing since I started working for Christ—it's kinda like in the Twenty-third Psalm, He said, "Thou preparest a table before me in the presence of my enemies; thou anointeth my dead with oil; and my cup runnest over," and I have walked through the shadows of death, because it was on the tenth of September in 1962 when they shot sixteen times in [my] house—and it wasn't a foot over the bed where my head (usually) was—but that night, I wasn't there. *Don't you see what God can do?* Quit running around trying to dodge death, because this book says, "*He that seeketh to save his life is gonna lose it anyhow*" (Reagon 1990, 212, my emphasis)

These accounts illustrate how religious beliefs can inspire an internal sense of political efficacy during risky episodes of political action. Those beliefs can also influence routine acts of political engagement. Because personal self-esteem and the sense of personal efficacy usually promote the sense of political efficacy, and because the sense of political efficacy usually boosts political participation, taking one's religion seriously should indirectly promote political action among African-American activists.

Even among nonactivists, individuals who are deeply religious should exhibit high self-esteem and feelings of personal efficacy, which should in turn promote feelings of political efficacy, and thus political activities like voting. The data I have on the general population of blacks show only a modest link between these variables, probably because so many other variables have powerful effects on political action. The rich and subtle effects of religiously-inspired political efficacy detected in the narratives can only be imperfectly tested here with crude survey measures. These data do, however, demonstrate that religious belief does not today detract from participation in electoral forms of political action. They also demonstrate that privatized beliefs and practices can spur feelings of political empowerment by nurturing feelings of self-esteem and worth. Thus, these beliefs and practices provide a ready reservoir for the political mobilization of self-empowerment.

LINKING RELIGIOSITY, EFFICACY, AND ACTIVISM

Past research in political science demonstrates that feelings of personal strength (or personal efficacy) are positively linked to feelings of control over the political environment (or political efficacy), and that those feelings of control directly promote individual and collective political action (Campbell, Converse, Miller, and Stokes 1960). In his analysis of the psychological dimensions of political life, Robert Lane argued for a causal tie between personal and political efficacy. He found that "[m]en who have feelings of mastery and are endowed with ego strength tend to generalize these sentiments" in the political realm; they believe that "their votes are important, politicians respect them, and elections are, therefore, meaningful processes (1959, 149)." Thus Lane theorized that feelings of personal strength foster feelings of effectiveness in the political sphere. Lane's 1950s study dealt only with conventional forms of participation. More recent research, and my analysis of narratives from civil rights activists, shows that similar feelings of effectiveness support unconventional forms of activism as well (McAdam 1982).

In their classic study of voting behavior in the United States, Angus Campbell and his colleagues more conclusively established an empirical connection between feelings of personal and political effectiveness. As scores on their eight-item scale of personal efficacy increased, so did respondents' feelings of political efficacy. This relationship remained constant across educational categories, leading the authors to conclude that "both education and ego strength make independent contributions to the development of a sense of political efficacy" (1960, 518). In addition, they found that "ego strength," or a sense of personal efficacy, was, independently of political efficacy, positively associated with interest in political affairs and voter turnout (519).

Reexamining Herbert McClosky's 1955 survey of the "marginal believer," Paul Sniderman also established a link between the sense of personal and political efficacy. Individuals who felt unworthy and inferior also felt that they had little power to influence the government, whereas individuals who scored high on feelings of personal competence also felt more politically efficacious. As Sniderman argued, it is only logical that there should be a connection between senses of personal and political efficacy, for individuals who "lack . . . confidence in [their] capacity to master problems" are also likely to "see themselves as unable to exercise any influence in political affairs, believing that events in politics will continue to run the same course no matter what they want, say, or do" (1975, 80). Studies generally show that blacks feel less politically effective than whites (Abramson 1977), a factor that should have a negative effect on their political involvement. They are also less trusting of government than whites, which in some instances depresses and in others favors participation. But as black candidates have become elected to highly visible offices like mayor, blacks have developed a greater sense of political efficacy and trust in government (Bobo and Gilliam 1990).

None of the studies linking feelings of personal self-worth with feelings of political effectiveness consider religion as a psychological factor that—either directly or indirectly—promotes feelings of political empowerment. Yet because a sense of internal political efficacy comprises "that portion of a person's self-esteem which is perceived to stem from one's own internal strength and weaknesses" (Shingles 1981, 80), internal religiosity—or devotion to a perceived sacred force—should nurture one's feelings of ego strength, cultivating in some believers a sense of effectiveness in worldly affairs, including politics—the feeling I have described as a sense of religiously inspired efficacy.

Religion's psychological dimension could potentially empower individuals with a sense of competence and resilience, inspiring them to believe in their own ability, with the assistance of an acknowledged sacred force, to influence or affect governmental affairs, thus—in some instances—to act politically. The possibility that internal religiosity fosters such feelings of political efficacy, as it did among some activists during the civil rights movement, is significant, given that blacks in general feel less politically effective and more religiously devoted than whites.

Figure 5.1 illustrates how the links between internalized religious behavior and political activism might work. The diagram shows causal flows from internal religiosity to personal efficacy and self-esteem, which are intermediary psychological measures of an individuals' perceived ability to control their social environment and their feelings of self-worth. The model also theorizes that the more self-esteem one has, the more likely one is to feel personally efficacious. In turn, personal efficacy, as previous research has demonstrated, encourages feelings of

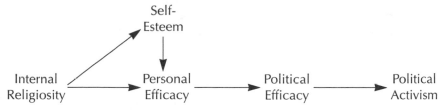

FIGURE 5.1. *Diagram of the Causal Linkages between Internal Religiosity and Political Activism.*

political empowerment, a psychological factor that directly promotes political activism.

These links are partially borne out by an analysis of the National Survey of Black Americans, a face-to-face cross-sectional survey of over two thousand African Americans that was conducted in 1979 and 1980 by the Survey Research Center at the University of Michigan. In addition to its large sample of black respondents, this survey also has the advantage of having included a battery of questions on religious behavior, self-esteem, feelings of personal efficacy, and political and social participation. Although the survey did not include questions about feelings of political efficacy, its data suggest that religiosity promotes feelings of personal self-esteem and personal efficacy, and that feelings of personal efficacy promote blacks' participation in neighborhood politics and (more weakly) political activism.

In this analysis internal religiosity, which measures the extent to which individuals engage in primarily private religious behavior, is composed of several indicators: frequency of praying, asking someone to pray for oneself, watching or listening to religious broadcasts, reading religious material, and attending religious services. Although church attendance is partially connected to the organizational aspects of religion, it has a psychological dimension as well. Like the other indicators of internal religiosity in this index, church attendance measures the extent to which a person is devoted to his or her religious beliefs, a feeling that is individually rather than collectively driven and is distinct from the institutional dynamics of religious life.

From the survey data, I created two measures of participation to assess the causal linkages between the feelings of internal religiosity, personal efficacy, and activism. Neighborhood activism measures one's involvement in neighborhood affairs by summing two questions on the number of neighborhood groups one belongs to and on whether one holds an office in such groups. Political activism, which measures activities linked to electoral politics, sums questions on whether one voted in the last presidential election (1976) and local and state elections, whether one has contacted an elected official about a problem, and whether one has worked for a political campaign. Both these modes of action demand from individuals time and commitment that could potentially conflict, for the most religiously devout, with their religious obligations (see appendix B for question wording on religious and political measures).

THE POSITIVE EFFECTS OF INTERNAL RELIGIOSITY

In this 1979–1980 survey, the magnitude of internal religiosity's hypothesized causal effects on measures of social and political participation are modest. Yet the data suggest that the psychological dynamics of religion foster rather than inhibit political and social activism. Specifically, internalized religious activities, measured by frequency of praying, asking someone to pray for one's self, watching or listening to religious broadcasts, reading religious material, and attending religious services seem to engender both feelings of self-esteem and perceived personal efficacy, both of which are usually linked to political efficacy (see appendix figures B.1 and B.2). These religious activities can be psychically mobilized, as we saw with activists during the civil rights movement, fostering feelings of political self-confidence and contributing to the self-empowerment side of micromobilization.

Indeed, these religious activities are directly linked to both neighborhood activism and conventional political activism. But just as important, I believe, they are also indirectly linked to both forms of political activism via feelings of personal efficacy, which foster people's strength in believing that they can affect the political process. Self-esteem, it seems, is positively related to feelings of personal efficacy; the greater a person's self-esteem, the more control the person feels over his or her own life. Personal efficacy is linked with blacks' participation in neighborhood activities and has a very small but significant connection to electoral political activities as well. These direct and indirect links strongly imply that religious practice probably has a positive effect on political activism; these links also provide a building block to explore more directly how religious beliefs foster feelings of political efficacy, a possibility that I take up in chapter 7. These findings challenge earlier views of religion's impact on black political activism; they suggest that for many African Americans today, religion is far from escapist or compensatory. Some combination of three explanations is possible. First, earlier scholarship on the psychological dynamics of religion may have overstated the opiate effects by not considering how religion may have contributed to the development and preservation of blacks' sense of self-esteem. Second, historical and demographic changes over time—for example, increases in education, the passing of an older generation who experienced Jim Crow, and the socializing effects of the civil rights and black power movements—may have diminished the otherworldly emphasis of religion among African Americans in the post–civil rights era (Lincoln 1974). Last, and probably most important, expanding opportunities for political engagement through black churches may have changed the effects of religion on black activism. Blacks who migrated to northern cities during the interwar and postwar period certainly mobilized religious resources in pursuit of political goals (Gosnell [1935] 1967; Johnson 1956; Bunche [1940] 1973; Drake and Cayton [1945] 1970).

The northern-southern differences in church engagement also suggest that southern blacks' lack of organized opposition to Jim Crow before the civil rights movement is best explained by the rigidity of the system of white domination under which they lived, and not—as some analysts have implied or argued—by their religious commitment. Some religious perspectives will, of course, undermine political action. Although fervent religious beliefs inspired feelings of efficacy among many civil rights activists, others did use religion to justify their withdrawal from the political sphere. However, in the contemporary era, these data of 1979–1980 suggest that the psychological dimensions of religion are salient components of contemporary black activism.

6

Rock in a Weary Land

Religious Institutions and African-American
Political Activism

> My God is a rock in a weary land,
> My God is a rock in a weary land,
> Shelter in a time of storm.
>
> African-American spiritual

DURING THE MODERN CIVIL RIGHTS movement, religious institu-
tions provided critical organizational resources for protest mobilization (McAdam
1982; Morris 1984). As Aldon Morris's extensive study of the southern civil rights
movement noted, the black church served as the organizational hub of black life,
providing the resources that—along with other indigenous groups and institutions—fostered collective protest against a system of white domination in the
South (1984).

In this chapter I survey the early history of the role of black religious institutions in electoral politics. I argue that, from Reconstruction to the present day,
black churches have served as a source of information, organizational skills, and
political stimuli. I will then show how black religious institutions operated under
different opportunity structures for participation during the Jim Crow period.
My analysis then turns to the present and shows, through participant observation,
primarily in Chicago churches, how politicians' explicit courtship of black
churchgoers brings those churchgoers both information and political stimuli, as
well as providing the politicians with an easily mobilizable constituency. Finally,
I take up the controversy over church-based political activism, concluding that
most black churchgoers approve of it so long as ministers do not explicitly endorse particular candidates.

Church-based activism predates the modern civil rights movement. Understanding the emergence of that movement and subsequent church involvement
in electoral activities requires that we understand the history of the black church.
As Adolph Reed asserts, "[a]ny rigorous analysis of the link between politics and
the black church must delineate the developmental context—and the trajectory
of actions and choices dictated by this context—through which the twentieth-
century black church evolved" (1986b, 45).

The following analysis does not argue, as many do, that religious institutions perform independently of mass mobilization or that black clerics act as "organic leaders" in African-American communities. Rather, I show that black churches are intricately connected to other sources of activism. Their communication networks, their capacity to promote social interaction, provide material resources, and give individuals the opportunity to learn organizing skills, and, perhaps most important, their sustainability over both time and physical space all combine to make them the only black institutions consistently promoting the collective resistance of African Americans. Black churches have performed these functions throughout several distinct historical periods, despite shifting political alliances and interests, and in vastly different contexts for activism.

Previous analyses have centered on the political acts of black religious leaders (Hamilton 1972, 110–145; Berenson, Elifson, and Tollerson, 1976; Childs 1980; Reed 1986b, 41–60; Lincoln and Mamiya 1990). Yet an exclusive focus on the political behavior of clerics presents a skewed view of religion and black political activism. Black ministers have championed but have also sometimes undermined mobilization efforts for racial integration, unionization, civil rights activism, and black electoral empowerment—as well as other black political interests (Reed 1986b; Marable 1983).

Black clerics both supported and subverted protest efforts during the boycott of segregated streetcars in the turn-of-the-century South. These boycotts, which emerged in Atlanta, Montgomery, Jacksonville, New Orleans, Richmond, and Nashville, were responses to city ordinances that were passed in the aftermath of the Supreme Court's *Plessy* decision on racial segregation. While black newspaper editors and prominent black business and professional men were leaders of the boycott, clerical leadership was less clear. Some clerics urged their congregation to stop riding the segregated trollies, while others undermined the boycott by ignoring it or by urging their members to ride the trollies. As Meier and Rudwick noted, "[i]t is true that often ministers were among the chief supporters of the streetcar protest. . . . Yet the individuals who stood out most prominently among the opponents of the boycotts were certain African Methodist Episcopal and especially Baptist ministers" (1969 769).

Similarly, black clerical leadership stood on both sides of African Americans' unionization efforts in the North during the interwar period. Union organizer A. Philip Randolph noted that although some black clerics assisted his efforts to unionize Pullman porters, many more resisted unionization. In an essay written during this period, he observed that in several cities Negro ministerial groups endorsed the union, but in many other places, clerical groups refused or withdrew their support. Randolph implied that many ministers' material interests deterred them from supporting unionization efforts. Commenting on the actions of a Baptist ministerial association in Chicago during 1926, he asserted that "[o]ne reason advanced for the refusal of the Baptist Alliance to come out for the Brotherhood is that the railroads who are interlocked with the Pullman Company give passes, through the President of the Baptist Convention, to preachers, which enable them to travel throughout the country at half-fare rates"([1929] 1990, 636).

In Detroit, too, during the interwar period, some black clerics opposed unionization. Describing black union-organizing efforts within the automobile industry in that city, Meier and Rudwick noted that several prominent black churches had financial ties to the Ford Motor Company, which recruited many black workers on the recommendation of local ministers (1979). This church-company alliance thwarted unionization efforts.

In the South during the civil rights movement, black clerics again both helped and hurt protest mobilization. Septima Clark noted how the naked self-interest of some black clerics frustrated her efforts when she was organizing citizenship schools for African Americans during the movement. Recounting the skepticism of Alabaman black ministers toward these schools, Clark maintained that the clerics "didn't want white people to know that we were teaching blacks to write their names, for then the merchants would stop giving the preachers their anniversary gifts." She added, "They wanted those gifts. Material things were more to them than human value things" (1986, 29). However, Clark also recognized the obstacles to clerical participation in organizing efforts:

> I understand those preachers. I know they were dependent on white people's approval. Even with their congregations' support, they could be run out of town if the white power structure decided they ought to go. Often they weren't against the Movement; they were just afraid to join it openly. It's simply a contradiction: so many preachers supported the Movement that we can say it was based in churches, yet many preachers couldn't take sides with it because they thought they had too much to lose. (69)

An emphasis on religious institutions rather than on clerical leadership provides a broader perspective on religion's effects on African-American political mobilization.

RELIGIOUS INSTITUTIONS AND AFRICAN-AMERICAN POLITICAL DEVELOPMENT

Historical circumstances help determine whether institutions will act as resources for political engagement. In his work on Italy, for example, Robert Putnam argues that the nature of communication networks within social organizations determines the availability of "social capital" needed for collective action. As Putnam theorizes, "Some . . . networks are primarily 'horizontal,' bring together agents of equivalent status and power. Others are primarily 'vertical,' linking unequal agents in asymmetric relations of hierarchy and dependence" (1993, 173). In Italy, the horizontal linkages are associated with broader civic competence and governmental performance. In the United States, as well, African Americans have gained social capital for civic engagement through the more horizontally structured Protestant denominations (Lincoln and Mamiya 1990; Washington 1985; Walker 1982; Verba et al. 1993).

After Emancipation, when newly freed black men had their first opportunities for open political engagement, religious institutions provided the organizational infrastructure for mass political mobilization (Foner 1988; Walker 1982). During Reconstruction, religious blacks organized autonomous Baptist denominations and joined the northern-based AME church, which fiercely competed with the independent Baptist churches for the religious loyalties of newly freed black people (Walker 1982).

White Protestant denominations in the South tended to exclude blacks, especially from clerical leadership. Combined with blacks' own desire for self-determination, this exclusion led ex-slaves to found and join mostly black-led denominations. The Baptist church commanded the loyalties of a majority of African Americans (Lincoln and Mamiya 1990). Few blacks joined racially separate branches of white Protestant groups like the United Methodist Church, South (Lincoln and Mamiya 1990). These separate black religious dominations were, and still are, the largest black organizations in the United States. Although northern black churches and religious leadership were an integral part of the abolitionist movement and the underground railroad before the Civil War, there were few other indigenous organizations for freed slaves.

Thus it was churches that provided meeting space for political gatherings, and church leadership and laity were elected to state political conventions and to state and local elected offices. Black clerics were particularly prominent in Reconstruction politics. Historian Eric Foner estimates that "[o]ver 100 Black ministers, from every denomination from AME to Primitive Baptist, [were] elected to legislative seats during Reconstruction." Ministers used their churches as a political launching point, and "among the lay majority of black politicians, many built a political base in the church"(1988, 93). Black religious institutions and organizations were strongest in the urban South. As Foner points out, "[p]olitical mobilization . . . proceeded apace in Southern cities, where the flourishing network of churches and fraternal societies provided a springboard for [political] organization"(110).

In his study of the AME church, historian Clarence E. Walker (1982) explains how the laity and hierarchy of that church met the organizational needs of the black male electorate. Church missionaries, presiding elders, ministers, and deacons served as delegates to state constitutional conventions as Republican presidential electors and were elected to congress, state legislators, and city councils. In some southern states, local AME congregations became the center of black political organizing.

Walker describes how the elaborate organizational infrastructure of the AME church politicized members:

Methodism, with its units of class, society, and band, provided ministers with an organization structure they could use for political purposes. This was particularly true of the class, which in some ways corresponded to the organization of a modern political party. These meetings and regular church services provided the minister-politicians with the arena for the dissemination of their political and religious ideals. (1892, 126)

With the end of Reconstruction, both religious and secular institutions "accommodated" to white domination in the South. As a result of the repeal of laws that legally protected black citizenship rights, black electoral mobilization came to a halt, leaving in its place severe sanctions against organized opposition. In the presidential election of 1876, the Republican party, the party of the freedmen and freedwomen, sabotaged black political development by promising to withdraw federal troops from the South in exchange for Republican control of the presidency (Logan 1968; Franklin 1980, 285). Thus, during the last decades of the nineteenth century, the consensus of both major political parties to allow the erosion of black citizenship rights effectively kept African Americans out of the American political party system. Within the Republican party, "lily-white" Republican factions cropped up throughout the South, while black Republican groups, now demobilized, were relegated to separate "black and tan" factions that competed with southern white Republicans on the national level for party patronage (Walton 1975). Historian Rayford W. Logan aptly describes this period as the "nadir" of race relations in the United States (Logan 1968; Higginbotham 1993). The growing exclusion of African Americans from voting and from party activity left a void that only black religious institutions could fill. In the South, whites promoted their political interests through the Democratic party, which, in many states, restricted participation to whites only. African Americans could participate in the American polity only through an ineffectual Republican party.

Although in the North, after the Great Migration, urban party machines attempted to include black migrants along with European immigrants, in the South such interracial coalition was rare. The populist agrarian revolt of the 1890s saw one such moment—both blacks and poor whites in the South mobilized against the economic domination of Bourbons and northern industrialists. But even then, the resulting Populist party was organized around racially separate rural organizations. Historian Lawrence Goodwyn notes of black mobilization during the agrarian revolt that "white supremacy prevented black farmers from performing the kinds of collective public acts essential to the creation of an authentic movement culture" (1978, 122–123). After the Populist party's electoral defeat in 1896, one of its most prominent leaders, Georgia Populist Tom Watson, abandoned his ideals of interracial cooperation and became a defender of white supremacy (Franklin 1980, 260–263; Goodwyn 1978). These events and policies intensified the development of racially separate political spheres, forcing African Americans to cultivate their own organizational resources for political mobilization. One of the most crucial of these was the black church.

RIGID SANCTIONS AND DIMINISHING OPPORTUNITY STRUCTURES

As a result of intensified legal barriers and physical and economic sanctions against black political mobilization in the South, black religious institutions became, in E. Franklin Frazier's phrase, a "nation within a nation" ([1963] 1974). Frazier argued that black interests in politics increasingly turned to the internal politics of religious institutions and organizations to compensate for the exclusion of African Americans from the American polity. Although Frazier did not recognize the significance of African Americans developing organizational and civic skills within their religious institutions, he did see one role for the internal politics of black churches. He observed that after Reconstruction "[a]s the result of the elimination of Negroes from the political life of the American community, the Negro church became the arena of their political activities" where "the struggle for power and the thirst for power could be satisfied" (48).

Mays and Nicholson's extensive work on the black church during the Jim Crow epoch provides a more detailed perspective on how the elaborate church structures of the mainstream black denominations continued to nurture the civic and organizing skills of African Americans during a period of dim prospects for mass mobilization against white supremacy. Writing in the early 1930s, the authors acknowledged how black institutions developed political skills even though these skills could not be practiced in the secular sphere of politics.

> The Negro's political life is still largely found in the Negro church. . . . The great importance attached to the political maneuvering at the National Baptist Convention, or at the General Methodist Conference, can be explained in part by the fact that the Negro is largely cut off from the body politic. The local churches, associations, conventions and conferences become the Negro's Democratic and Republican conventions, his Legislature and his Senate and House of Representatives. ([1933] 1969, 9)

The political skills that Mays and Nicholson observed during this period were not exclusively confined to the internal politics of religious organizations. As Evelyn Higginbotham's groundbreaking work on the history of black Baptist women indicates, the institutional resources of black churches enabled women to challenge racial and gender domination during the Jim Crow epoch of white hegemony. Higginbotham argues that African American religious institutions functioned for both black women and men as a "public sphere" in which "values and issues were aired, debated and disseminated throughout the larger black community" (1933, 7).

Higginbotham also points out that the reform-oriented women's club movement among African Americans drew its early leadership and membership from
black women's religious groups. As she explains, "[t]he club movement among
black women owed its very existence to the groundwork of organizational skill
and leadership training gained through women's church societies. . . .
[M]issionary societies had early on brought together women with little knowledge
of each other and created bonds of sisterly cooperation at the city and state levels"
(1993, 11).

By facilitating the development of politically relevant organizing skills, indigenous leadership, and the dissemination of information through church-affiliated
networks and religious publications, religious institutions directly contributed to
the political mobilization of women in the South during a period of diminishing
opportunities for, and rigid sanctions against, their participation in the secular
realm. These networks were particularly relevant to the political development of
women who—now as well as then—represent the majority of African American
churchgoers, although clerical leadership has been, and still continues to be, predominantly male.

CHURCHES AND BLACK ELECTORAL
MOBILIZATION IN THE NORTH

During the interwar period and after World War II, mass migration of African
Americans to northern cities opened up opportunities for black political engagement. Churches worked with political parties and civil rights organizations like
the NAACP and Urban League to forge resources for electoral and protest mobilization. Gosnell noted of Chicago during the interwar period: "It is not uncommon on a Sunday morning during a primary or [general] election campaign
to see a number of white candidates on the platform ready to present their claims
for support at the polls as soon as the regular service is over and before the
congregation is disbanded. . . . The church is an institution which plays an important role in their social life and they look to it for advice on political matters"
([1935] 1967, 96).

Candidates' visits to churches may have informed parishioners about elections
and encouraged them to vote. Gosnell also pointed out that many black ministers
were a part of a patron-client relationship that characterized party machine politics. The machine gave ministers fees, loans, and gifts in exchange for allowing
candidates to speak to their congregations: "Sometimes Negro ministers [sought]
campaign funds outright in return for the delivery of a block of votes." The
practice appeared to be so widespread that it drew editorial criticism from several
contemporary black newspapers in Chicago (Gosnell [1935] 1967, 96–97).

However, Gosnell observed that "[n]ot every colored minister permits candidates to address his congregation and there have been occasions when the

Negro clergymen as a group protested against political interference" ([1935] 1967, 97). Negro churches, he noted, furnish opportunities for the development of leadership within the group (98).

In research compiled for Gunnar Myrdal's *American Dilemma*, political scientist Ralph Bunche's mammoth and largely overlooked study ([1940] 1973) of black mobilization during the interwar period provides insight into how different structures for participation among African Americans in the North and in the South affected overt activism.[1] Bunche described the quietude of southern black churches and the ties between urban machines and black clerics in northern cities in the mid–twentieth century. In Atlanta, Bunche wrote, the lack of social, economic, and political progress among blacks was largely "the fault of the ministers, who direct the social thinking of so a large part of the population"(490). In Memphis, black ministers "avoided social questions" altogether. In Bunche's words, "[t]hey have preached thunder and lightning, fire and brimstone, and Moses out of the bulrushes, but about the economic and political exploitation of local blacks they have remained silent" (501).

By contrast, in the same period, black churches in northern cities were engaged in electoral mobilization, although its nature and intensity varied from city to city and often depended on the strategy of political parties. In St. Louis, for instance, blacks held the balance of voter power between Republicans and Democrats. Both political parties consequently targeted churches to mobilize the black electorate. Bunche contended that electoral engagement by black churches was motivated by the self-interest of black clerics; he commented that "[g]enerally the Negro preacher's interest in procuring the vote for his congregation varies in direct proportion to his own pecuniary interests" ([1940] 1973, 592). He added that the Democratic party in the city exploited the "smaller churches of the store-front variety" and that the Republican machine in that city "had been running the Negro preachers, along with everything else in the town, and had on occasion paid fifty or sixty dollars for their help" (592–593). Bunche further noted that:

> In New York City, Harlem became "politically-minded" when these Southern Negroes migrated. This is accounted for in large measure by Protestant churches, inasmuch as Baptist, Methodist, and "store-front" preachers have been politicians of one kind or another since Negro churches appeared on the American scene. In fact, if a "political machine" is defined as a "deliverable vote," the church is the only effective, disciplined machine that Negroes have developed. (599)

In the postwar period Ruby Johnson also contrasts the community involvement of black Protestant churches in the North and South (1956). On the basis of her analysis of churches in South Carolina, Johnson noted that southern black ministers were "hesitant" to engage in "practical action" to improve their communities—mainly, she implied, because whites imposed harsh sanctions against politically involved blacks. She wrote: "Fear of the threat of application of sanctions to the disadvantage of the person or group which seeks to institute change restrains action. This consideration is important with reference to a comparison of church programs of southern and northern clerical leaders" (189).

In South Carolina, Johnson discovered churches working cooperatively in self-help community social services efforts, but she also reported some organized opposition to the existing political structure within black churches. She noted that for several years some black clerics had been involved in the NAACP—"holding executive positions, making individual contributions, urging their congregations to contribute to this organization, and . . . carrying the organization directly into the church in spite of opposition from many members." Moreover, Johnson observed that "ministerial action was conspicuously tremendous" during 1947 and 1948, when "[p]reachers were active in actually executing the increase of teachers' salaries, in educating Negroes for citizenship by conducting classes and speeches, and in urging them to qualify to vote" (1956, 193). The "conspicuously tremendous" church-based activism that Johnson noted from 1947 to 1948 in South Carolina probably derived from the expanding opportunities for black mobilization kindled by a 1947 federal court decision—successfully argued by NAACP attorney Thurgood Marshall—upholding the right of blacks to vote in the state's Democratic primary (Bergman 1969, 514). The surge in black activism may have also derived from black opposition against the anti–civil rights presidential campaign of South Carolina's governor, Strom Thurmond. In 1948, Thurmond ran for president under the "Dixiecrat" party ticket after the Democratic party included a pro-civil rights plank on the party's convention platform (Key 1949, 317–344). The activity of the NAACP was severely curtailed throughout the South after the Supreme Court's *Brown* decision, and the organization was outlawed in several southern states. Johnson's observation of church-based political activism—six years before the *Brown* decision and eight years before the Montgomery bus boycott—provides further evidence that, on the eve of the southern civil rights movement, some churches operated as organizational resources for protest mobilization (Morris 1984).[2]

In contrast to the limited church-based activism of African Americans in South Carolina, in Boston Johnson found thriving religious institutions engaged in a variety of community efforts, including electoral and interest group politics. Johnson reported of the black churches in Boston during the mid-fifties:

[M]ost of the [Negro] pastors of Boston churches manifest some form of political action. The extent of activity varies as other phases of group life. Some churches act in a passive capacity, while others actively campaign and support certain candidates for public office. Most ministers impress upon audiences the importance of voting, making wise use of the ballot, and taking advantage of the opportunity to vote. Some present information on candidates for office and discuss various platforms in relation to the community. Some tell their congregation whom to support, while others do not. Some clergymen permit candidates for office to speak in their churches. ... Some clergymen seek to be elected to public office. (1956, 203)

POLITICAL PARTIES, CHURCHES, AND
BLACK POLITICAL DEVELOPMENT

The church-based political activism in the urban North during the interwar and postwar periods demonstrates how opportunity structures for participation affected black mobilization. As Martin Kilson has observed, none of the several stages of black electoral engagement during the interwar period contributed significantly to the long-term political development of African Americans. Much of this period of black electoral politics was characterized by patron-client relationships between urban machines and black leaders, which worked through "a small group of blacks who fashioned personalized links with influential whites, becoming clients of the whites for a variety of sociopolitical purposes" (1971, 171).

Kilson points out that the exclusionary practices of the northern political machines undermined black political development. The machine leaders, for the most part, effectively incorporated European immigrants into party politics yet treated African Americans as a guaranteed bloc of votes rather than as partners within the machine apparatus. Kilson explains that "in the years 1900–1940 the goal of white-dominated city machines toward Negroes was to neutralize and thus minimize the political clout of the Negro urban community and not infrequently even to distort that community's social and political modernization." He argues that this strategy on the part of white party organizers "emanated largely from the racist perspective of the American social system" (1971, 17–18).[3]

Black realignment during the New Deal, the Democratic party's support of civil rights issues on the national level in the 1960s, party reform initiatives in the sixties and early seventies, and the election of thousands of black elected officials within the Democratic party during the seventies and eighties have gradually integrated African Americans into the Democratic party apparatus. These events have occurred, however, along with the declining mobilization capacity of political parties and the advent of personality- and media-centered politics.

As an indigenous institution that has survived Reconstruction, Jim Crow, the Great Migration, urbanization, the depression, machine politics, partisan realignments, and a host of other social and political movements throughout the late nineteenth and much of the twentieth century, black churches continue to operate as an organizational resource for black mobilization. Churches have given many blacks their only experience with public speaking, planning meetings, managing finances, and making group democratic decisions—all skills necessary for collective action. Thus we see on the eve of the 1970s explosion of black electoral activism, shortly after the passage of the 1965 Voting Rights Act, a candidate for justice of the peace in rural Mississippi offering her leadership experience to voters:

> I, Mrs. Thelma L. Berry am a native Mississippian. Born March 11, 1911, in Moorehead, Mississippi Sunflower County Mississippi. United with the St. Luke Church of God In Christ in August, 1939. Have served as a Sunday School teacher, Prayer and Bible Band teacher and President of the Home and Foreign Mission Band, also presently serving as President of the Mother's Board. Reared and educated five children in this community. Became a midwife in this county in December, 1932. Became a registered voter in 1965.[4]

The rest of this chapter will examine how, today, black Americans learn their organizing skills through religious institutions, find out about politics through religious networks, and gain motivation for political participation from political stimuli in church. It will demonstrate how churches promote political activism and will report how people feel about this kind of church involvement in political activity.

LEARNING ORGANIZING SKILLS

The organizational structures of predominantly black denominations, as well as those of majority black congregations affiliated with majority white religious groups, give blacks the opportunity to learn organizing and civic skills through their participation in church work. These organizing and civic skills are derived from participation in groups such as the trustee and deacons' boards; in spiritually focused organizations like prayer bands, choirs, deaconess boards, praise and worship teams; in service-oriented groups like missionary societies, ushers boards, nurses' guilds, and pastor's aide clubs; and in support groups such as singles' ministries and fellowship groups. Through Sunday school, Vacation Bible school, and church-run youth groups, children and young adults gain organizing skills that are likely to enable their participation in secular politics when they become adults.

Organizing skills are also cultivated through lay participation in denominational bodies. For instance, the AME church holds jurisdictional elections for lay delegates to its General Conference, which is held every four years (the same year of the U.S. presidential elections). Delegates attend the General Conference and vote to elect ministerial candidates to the board of bishops, as well as to other offices. The National Baptist Convention meets annually, and its delegates vote for convention officers, including the president. Candidates for denominational offices campaign for delegate votes by holding rallies, dispensing campaign literature and buttons, writing position papers, and giving campaign speeches (see figures 6.1 and 6.2).

In his study of the political behavior of black ministers in the early 1970s, Charles Hamilton recognized the role of African-American religious institutions in developing organizing skills. "Many blacks," he noted, "learned about organizations, acquired political skills and developed an ability to work with and lead people through the institution of the church" (1972, 117).[5] Mays and Nicholson had observed the same pattern during the 1930s, and E. Franklin Frazier had commented on it during the 1950s.

Confirming that this phenomenon retains its strength today, Sidney Verba and his colleagues report from their recent extensive survey of volunteerism in the United States that many individuals learn civic skills through their religious institutions. The researchers asked their respondents if they had written a letter, gone to a meeting where they took part in a decision, planned or chaired a meeting, or given a presentation or a speech. They report that although over two-thirds of individuals in the United States have learned civic and organizing skills at their place of employment and about two-fifths practice such skills through nonpolitical organizations, nearly one-third reported practicing such skills at their place of worship (1993, 477).

The Verba study also found considerable variation by racial/ethnic groups and by religious orientation. Members of Protestant congregations report practicing political skills at their churches more than members of Catholic parishes. For African Americans, religious institutions are a particularly important place to develop politically relevant skills. Nearly 40 percent of African Americans practice organizing skills at their place of worship, compared to only 20 percent of Latinos and 28 percent of Anglo-whites (1993, 477). Similarly, African Americans (38 percent) are slightly more likely than Anglo-whites (35 percent) and substantially more likely than Latinos (16 percent) to hear political messages at their place of worship (table 4, 485). The study concludes that "[f]or several reasons, African-Americans derive more participatory benefit from their churches." This benefit derives from African Americans being more likely than Anglo-whites and Latinos to be a member of a church, be affiliated with Protestant rather than Catholic churches, and to be exposed to politically relevant stimuli at their place of worship (491–492).

Protestant churches are more congregationally organized than Catholic churches, allowing churchgoers more participation in lay activities. The overwhelming majority of African Americans are Protestant. As a consequence, the ability of African Americans to learn civic skills within church settings may somewhat offset the socioeconomic disadvantages they experience as a group. (Verba et al. 1993, 491). The politically relevant organizational skills learned at church combine with political stimuli provided at church to increase the likelihood of a churchgoer's becoming politically activated.

AN OPEN LETTER

TO THE ADMINISTRATION

WHY?

AND

WHAT IS THE DEAL,

AND WHERE IS OUR MONEY?

The National Baptist Convention, USA, Inc.

FIGURE 6.1. *Position paper, 114th Session of the National Baptist Convention, USA, New Orleans, Louisiana, September 1994.*

WHY?
AND
WHAT IS THE DEAL AND WHERE IS OUR MONEY?

1. WHY? Has this administration refused to present or publish a Budget for OUR Convention in the past 12 years? We have not been presented with or adopted a Convention Budget in 12 years!

2. WHY? Has this administration refused to annually provide the Convention with a detailed report of income and expenses? How much money from all sources has the Convention received and how much has been spent?

3. WHY? Has this administration not shared with the Convention the full details of our arrangements with Delta airlines? How much free travel is provided and who is allowed to travel free?

4. WHY? Did this administration give the highest award of OUR convention, the "Cross and Crown Award" to boxing promoter and convicted felon DON KING?

5. WHY? Did this administration loan comedian Dick Gregory $80,000.00 in Convention funds when many of our churches are in desperate need?

6. WHY? Did this administration initiate an ill-conceived "pension plan" that resulted in trouble with the Federal Securities and Exchange Commission, the quick shut-down of the plan, enormous legal fees and disappointment to those who trusted the convention administration.

7. WHY? Has this administration refused to tell us the whole truth about the World Center? How much did it really cost?

8. WHY? Has this administration refused to tell us how much it cost to maintain and staff the Office of the President and the Office of the Secretary?

10. WHY? Has this administration continually inflated the costs of hotel rooms for delegates, while refusing to account for the rebates the Convention has received from hotels? How much money has the Convention received in rebates from hotels in the past 12 years and where did it go?

11. WHY? Did this administration borrow six-million dollars without Convention approval?

12. For the past 12 years, what was the Deal and where is OUR Money?

FIGURE 6.2. *Campaign pamphlets, 114th Session of the National Baptist Convention, USA, New Orleans, Louisiana, September 1994.*

DISSEMINATING INFORMATION

The dissemination of information on political matters can occur within several church-based venues, offering congregants facts about political and social issues and giving them the opportunity to hear several points of view regarding candidates and issues. For instance, at the Second Baptist Church of Evanston, Illinois, a Sunday bulletin encouraged members to attend a rally for a candidate running for county office for the 1990 primary election.[6] The candidate, a "guest speaker" for the church's black history month program that Sunday, told congregants during his talk about the county-wide office for which he was running; his opponents; and his reasons for running for that office. A flyer with a photograph and professional resume of the candidate was stuffed inside the bulletins, and alongside the regular announcements was what could be interpreted as an endorsement of the candidate:

> JUDGE R. EUGENE PINCHAM will be our Guest Speaker today, at both worship services. At 3:00 p.m. this afternoon . . . there will be a "RALLY" for those in support of the candidacy of JUDGE R. EUGENE PINCHAM, FOR THE PRESIDENT OF THE COOK COUNTY BOARD. Do join us! JUDGE PINCHAM, the man who will run the County Government to serve ALL THE PEOPLE!

Sermons also disseminate political information to congregants. Ministers can support their preferred candidate during regular worship services primarily by opposing that candidate's opponent. When Reverend Charles Adams of Detroit's mostly middle-class Hartford Memorial Baptist Church criticized the record of 1992 Republican presidential candidate George Bush during a sermon the Sunday before the Tuesday general election, he made known his preference for Democratic presidential nominee Bill Clinton without ever mentioning the candidate's name.[7] Telling the congregation "When you wake up Tuesday morning, say your prayers, but then let your prayers get in your hands and in your feet" and "go [to the polls] and vote," Reverend Adams assailed Bush's record as president and the Republican party's conservative Christian supporters: "Some of us are trying to make this election a referendum on God. . . . As if God belongs to Bush and his party and his ideology. Well, I don't believe that's true. He slammed the Democrats for leaving God out of their platform. They were just being honest. I don't like it when folk lie and put God's name in their political aspirations just to win an election."

Reverend Adams then questioned the incumbent's belief in Christianity and criticized the Bush administration's involvement with the Iran-Contra sandal, Bush's opposition to pending civil rights legislation, and his nomination of Clarence Thomas, a conservative black Republican, to the Supreme Court: "Bush doesn't even know God. If Bush knew God he wouldn't have lied about Iran-Contra. If Bush knew God, he wouldn't have failed to sign the civil rights bill in 1990. If Bush knew God, he wouldn't have put a handkerchief head on the Supreme Court. If Bush knew God, he wouldn't destroy and oppress the people of this United States."

Candidates themselves give out information to congregants through their visits to worship services. Many speak from the pulpit to present their stands on issues, and they sometimes use the opportunity to criticize their opponents. During a campaign stop the Sunday before the 1994 Democratic gubernatorial primary election in Illinois, gubernatorial candidate Roland Burris told congregants at the Corinthian Temple Church of God in Christ on Chicago's West Side what ballot numbers to punch for him and his running mate. After he had been introduced by a member of the church who told the congregation and the church's live radio broadcast audience that "we need an effective Christian leader on our side in government . . . Roland Burris is that leader," Burris made these remarks from the pulpit: "We're talking about two punch numbers, two punch numbers. Number three and number six. So once you punch three, just double it and you'll give us your vote. You'll get double your money because we are going to create jobs in the state so that we can put people back to work."

The candidate then became more partisan in his remarks, specifically questioning his leading opponent's prospects for winning against the Republican incumbent: "I'm the only one who can make a change in Springfield and go out and stand toe-to-toe with [the Republican incumbent]. . . . And if the head of the Democratic ticket is a tax-and-spend Democrat who's soft on crime, the Republicans will not only win the governorship, they may even win the state House of Representatives." (These remarks were made during the Sunday morning worship service at Corinthian Temple Church of God on March 13.)

Other church-based venues for disseminating political information are not as partisan. Church-sponsored political forums, for instance, allow several candidates to present their points of view and permit congregants to question candidates and public officials about their policy positions. In the strongly contested 1983 mayoral race in Chicago, several religious groups sponsored candidate forums. For example, on January 29, 1983, Reverend W. L. Upshire of the Prince of Peace M.B. Church wrote to Harold Washington that the West Side Ministers' Coalition and West Side Baptist Ministers' Conference sponsored a forum "for scrutiny of candidates in the Mayoral race," in which candidates were sent fourteen questions "posed by various Ministers and their Parishioners" that would be covered during the event (Harold Washington Papers). The questions covered issues as diverse as affirmative action, neighborhood redevelopment, funding for education, election fraud, and support for lower utility rates.[8]

FACILITATING POLITICAL ACTION

While religious institutions operate as a means for congregants to make judgements about political issues and candidates, they can also facilitate political participation by directly appealing to congregants. These appeals, made in church bulletins, by clerics, or by political entrepreneurs themselves, foster direct involvement in both electoral politics and community organizing efforts in African-American communities. The Sunday bulletin of Chicago's Progressive Community Church, for instance, included this announcement about voter registration for the upcoming 1990 November general election:

VOTER REGISTRATION

IMMEDIATELY FOLLOWING OUR MORNING WORSHIP SERVICE IN THE LOWER LEVEL OF THE CHURCH, THERE WILL BE VOTER REGISTRARS SET-UP. . . . TUESDAY, OCTOBER 9TH IS OUR LAST CHANCE TO REGISTER AFTER TO-DAY. . . . *DO IT TODAY—DON'T WAIT!*

After the scripture reading and the recognition of visitors, the minister emphasized the voter registration and encouraged members who are not registered to do so because, as he told the congregation, voting was their "civic duty as good Christians."[9]

Recruiting workers for political campaigns not only helps politicians, as I show in the next section, it also helps to facilitate the congregants' own actions. In the 1994 Illinois Democratic primary race for governor, Reverend J. L. Miller of Mt.

Vernon Baptist Church on Chicago's West Side endorsed gubernatorial candidate Roland Burris and asked congregants to assist with the church's effort in getting out the vote and passing out flyers in support of the candidate.[10] Criticizing polls that showed the candidate's support slipping and media predictions of a low voter turnout, the minister solicited the congregation for support:

> Now I need you to use your car, telephone, and your fingers to push door bells. Tomorrow—those of you [who are] not working, we're walking.... The flyers are out, the [copying] machine is still working, we will be running off some additional flyers. We're going to make certain that everybody knows the polling place if it's been changed. We're going to make certain that everybody knows the direction and route to take on Tuesday morning. We're going to make it happen in this political process.

Churches may also facilitate participation by asking congregants to contribute financially to political campaigns. Evidence from the campaign records of Harold Washington's 1983 mayoral campaign suggests that African-American religious institutions are a significant source of money for black candidates. Even before Jesse Jackson's 1984 presidential campaign, which raised a considerable amount of money from church-based sources (Cavanagh and Foster 1984), similar fund raising took place during Washington's campaign.

For example, the middle-class congregation of Park Manor Christian Church requested Washington, in a letter written to him by E. Toy Fletcher on February 28, 1983, to appear at a church-sponsored rally at the end of a Sunday service, "at which time we are asking members to make a financial contribution to help support the campaign" (Harold Washington Papers). A Dr. Royce D. Cornelius, writing to Washington requesting his appearance at a Sunday evening rally, said that "the Pastor and members of Mount Pleasant Missionary Baptist Church are interested in our continued efforts to raise funds for you as a Mayoral candidate" (Harold Washington Papers). Church-based contributions during Washington's campaign ranged from as little as one hundred fifty dollars from Allen Temple CME Church to as much as thirty-four hundred dollars from South Park Baptist Church.[11]

RESOURCES FOR POLITICAL ENTREPRENEURS

In addition to serving as sources of information and facilitating political action among churchgoers, churches may also serve as resources for political entrepreneurs. These entrepreneurs often nurture ties with black clerics to solicit black support for their political goals. For instance, Democratic congressional candidate Bobby Rush, who in his previous campaigns for alderman received the endorsement of several clergy in his Chicago ward,[12] solicited the support of ministers in his congressional district for the party's efforts in the 1990 general election.

With a letter written on campaign stationery, the candidate invited clerics in his district to attend a breakfast with Ron Brown, then chairman of the National Democratic Party:

> Dear Reverend—
> As you are well aware, the November . . . General Election provides all of us with the opportunity to utilize our votes to help bring about much-needed changes in state and federal government. Chairman Brown will be in Chicago to present the Democratic Party's plans for the future. Your participation in this pivotal gathering is indeed vital.[13]

Some political entrepreneurs cultivate ties with black clerics well ahead of an election. One candidate who lost in the 1992 Democratic primary for U.S. Senate in Illinois attempted to extend his relationships with ministers after his defeat in the primary. These contacts may have provided him with a wider church network when he successfully ran for the Democratic party's nomination for state attorney general a year and a half later. Writing about six months after his defeat in the Senate race and looking ahead to future political aspirations, Al Hofeld wrote this letter seeking clerical support:

> You may remember me, I was the candidate for the United States Senate in the most recent Democratic primary campaign. I am now doing everything within my power to see that Carol Moseley Braun is elected as our next United States Senator. . . . Since the primary, I have been out in the community and seen for myself some of the hardships that exist. . . . I would like to come out and meet with you or fellowship as a parishioner at your Church sometime in the near future.[14]

Recognizing the organizing skills of churchgoers, some political candidates recruit workers for their campaigns through church networks. One candidate in New York City, for instance, advertised jobs for her re-election campaign through the church bulletin of Harlem's Abyssinian Baptist Church: "Manhattan Boro President Ruth Messinger is seeking a number of organizers to join her grassroots reelection campaign. The ability to work with a wide range of people, personal organization and commitment to progressive politics are among the qualities they are looking for, and a sense of humor wouldn't hurt. Specific requirements are listed with each job description."[15]

Some political entrepreneurs contribute money to churches or religious organizations directly from their political campaign funds. Others are known to give cash contributions to ministers under the table.[16] For instance, Chicago mayor Richard Daley contributed, as reported from the itemized expenditures of his campaign committee, to several black churches and religious institutions from 1990 to 1993. These expenditures, reported as "donations," range from two hundred to fifty-five hundred dollars.[17] In the closely contested 1993 New Jersey gubernatorial race, Republican Christine Todd Whitman's campaign consultant Ed Rollins bragged about giving black ministers "street money" to suppress black voter turnout. In order to hold down the vote of Democratic candidate Jim Florio, Rollins alleged that the campaign "went into black churches and . . . said to black ministers who endorsed Florio, 'Do you have a special project?' " He then said that he urged ministers not to "get up on the Sunday pulpit and preach . . . and say its your moral obligation that you go on Tuesday to vote for Jim Florio." Rollins later recanted his comments.[18]

THE CONTROVERSY OVER CHURCH-BASED ELECTORAL ACTIVISM

The degree to which black churches ought to be involved in electoral politics has been contested within black communities for several generations. While there appears to be a consensus on the importance of church-based networks as a source of information for congregants, African Americans differ on the question of ministers' explicit support of political candidates. During the interwar period in Chicago, for instance, editorials in black newspapers criticized the practice of political candidates making campaign visits at black churches during Sunday worship services. They also criticized the practice of ministers accepting financial contributions for such visits. The *Chicago Defender* wrote in the spring of 1920:

> The ministers excuse these things on the grounds that it is their duty to direct their congregations in matters political as well as spiritual. . . . One scarcely, if ever, hears of a white church being used for such purposes. . . . There is generally some sinister reason for this action. The white politicians know how susceptible some of our people are to the urgings of the pulpit. . . . The ministers are aware of this attitude on the part of the political powers and take advantage of it to turn a handy penny for themselves. (Gosnell [1935] 1967, 97)

More than half a century later and in another city, an editorial in Cleveland's black newspaper, *Call and Post*, on September 20, 1978, expressed remarkably similar sentiments. Entitled "Churches and Political Prostitution," the editorial noted that "many black and white politicians have seized every opportunity to use the black church as a base for political operations." Acknowledging the importance of black churches as vehicles for the dissemination of political information and as a means to encourage civic activities, the editorial agreed that ministers should "in their church bulletins, during pastoral comments, through other means, persuade their parishioners to register, vote, and endorse issues." It added that the church should "use its influence, clout, and facilities to educate minorities in the political process." On the other hand, the editorial argued, involvement in electoral politics should not involve visits by political candidates during worship services. "The legitimate entry by the church into political affairs has been prostituted to the point that politicians walk in and out of our pulpits on Sundays, allowed to campaign during church services and make vicious attacks on opponents in political races. White politicians in particular have abused this privilege granted to them by some ministers."

Noting that such practices were usually not allowed at white churches or synagogues, the editorial asserted: "Some ministers try to rationalize and justify these abuses by allowing both Democrats and Republicans to appear and thus claim the church is non-partisan. . . . To accept the trivial donations given in the collection plate by these politicians is almost sinful in itself if it is given to influence voting. . . . [R]eligious services should be that and no more."

The direct involvement of black clerics in electoral politics continues today. Candidate or party endorsements by black clerics usually occur during Sunday worship services on the eve of local, state, or national elections. For instance, Bishop David L. Ellis of Detroit's Greater Grace Church overtly endorsed both local candidates and Democratic presidential candidate Bill Clinton the Sunday before the 1992 general election.[19] During the church's live radio broadcast, Bishop Ellis introduced three local judicial candidates he described as "personal friends" and "very fine people" and told the congregation: "[W]e are supporting all of them on Tuesday." Bishop Ellis then proclaimed—using the campaign slogan of the Clinton-Gore team—"[w]e are going to vote for a change."

Outspokenly defensive about his public support of these candidates and giving biblical legitimacy to his engagement in political activities, Bishop Ellis defended his endorsements by saying: "We preachers are highly criticized because we talk like this. . . . Every one that knows the sound of my voice, you ought to vote for a change. . . . Just pull that Democratic switch. Punch that Democratic button."

Proclaiming "I don't know who your candidate is but as of today, your candidate is the Clinton-Gore ticket, the Democratic ticket all the way," Bishop Ellis assured the congregation and the radio audience of his independence: "We ain't being paid a dime to talk about something political." To further legitimize his support of these candidates, Bishop Ellis referred to himself as a "community leader." He also promised transportation to voters who needed assistance on election day. Referencing a 1988 Bush campaign slogan and citing a negative stereotype often leveled against blacks by whites, he insisted:

I'm just here as a guide and as a leader in this community to tell you it's time for a change. . . . Read my lips, its time for a change!. . . . Let's get our lazy selves up tomorrow morning and get out there, amen! Get to the polls. If you ain't got a way, call here. . . . We'll send somebody to pick you up. I'll bring the van myself. I'll take you to the poll, amen! You say, "I can't write." I'll guide your hand, I'm serious about this. Time for a change.

Most clerical candidate and party endorsements are not as direct as that of Bishop Ellis. Earlier that Sunday in Cincinnati, Ohio, Bill Clinton visited the Tryed Stone Missionary Baptist Church. Although the presidential candidate did not speak during the service and the minister did not ask members to vote for him, the service expressed support for Clinton symbolically in other ways. When asking the congregation for contributions to Thanksgiving baskets for poor families in the city during pastoral announcements, Reverend Culbreath told the congregation, "There's a candidate out there that says there needs to be a change, and he speaks that because the economic situation is so grave, we want to give a helping hand again this year."[20]

During the congregational prayer, after reading names of about two dozen members of the congregation who requested prayer from the minister, Reverend Culbreath announced, "I've got a note here that the governor would like a spiritual prayer before he leaves." With applause from the congregation, the minister intoned: "Saints, let's pray." With the choir singing a gospel standard, "I Don't Feel No Ways Tired," the minister requested divine assistance in Clinton's behalf.

In return for their endorsements, ministers may urge their views of morality on potential candidates. For instance, during the 1983 mayoral campaign in Chicago, a group of black ministers called Prophets for People expressed concerns over Harold Washington's views on abortion and homosexuality. Writing to Washington's secretary, Velma Wilson, on January 19, 1983, about an upcoming meeting between the ministers' group and the mayoral candidate, Reverend Clarence Hilliard, the executive director of Prophets for People, noted:

> [The ministers] are interested in sharing our views and interacting with our future mayor on two moral issues that are of grave concern to us. . . . One is the question of homosexuality or the "Gay Rights Movement," and the other is the question of abortion or the "Right to Life" vs. "abortion on demand" controversy. It is our belief that we can come to a satisfactory agreement so that as we engage in the serious business of this campaign we may not unwittingly prove to be an embarrassment to each other. (Harold Washington Papers)

Reverend Hilliard would later recount how Washington agreed during the meeting that he would "not do anything to initiate legislation in regard to gay rights."[21]

Some ministers, believing that politics and religion should be separate, abstain altogether from overt support of political candidates, even when their own congregants express support for such activity. For example, Paul and Nancy Littleton, a married couple, members of an interracial and multicultural church on Chicago's North Side, wrote to Harold Washington on March 1, 1983, after his victory in the 1983 Democratic mayoral primary:

In the service immediately following your nomination, our pastor, Al Smith, told us that specific demonic powers rule individual cities. . . . [I]n Daniel 10 Gabriel has to wrestle for 21 days with the "Prince of Persia" to get a message through Daniel. [Our minister] stated that the demonic forces enslaving this city have had their physical manifestation in the "Machine" that runs City Hall. Excitedly, he shared that your successful breach of the visible "Machine" means that the invisible "Prince of Chicago" has sustained a mortal blow, too. (Harold Washington Papers)

In a second letter, on March 10, the same couple invited Washington to address about one thousand church members at a prayer breakfast, asserting that "we're confident that the People of Faith Temple will offer you a very sympathetic forum" (Harold Washington Papers). On March 17, however, Faith Tabernacle's minister, Al Smith, wrote to Washington to revoke the invitation:

I have been informed that a member of our congregation . . . has invited you to address the members of Faith Temple on Sunday . . . and at our Prayer Breakfast. . . . Please be advised that [our member] was not acting on behalf of the leadership of Faith Tabernacle and was not authorized to extend an invitation to you as a candidate or to any other candidate. You are most welcome to attend these functions, but in keeping with our policy of remaining apolitical, you will not be allowed or asked to speak. (Harold Washington Papers)

CONGREGANTS' ATTITUDES TOWARD CHURCH-BASED ACTIVISM

Concerns about the influence of clerics over the black electorate may be exaggerated. Although the 1991 Chicago Area Survey showed that among black church members, more than half reported candidate visits at their churches, a 1980 NBC/Associated Press poll suggests that few ministers, black or white, specifically endorse political candidates. Ninety-seven percent of whites (N = 2098) and 92 percent of blacks (N = 178) reported that they had not been asked by a religious leader to vote for a specific candidate in that year's Fall election. An overwhelming majority of respondents (more than 80 percent of both blacks and whites) also felt that an endorsement of a candidate by a religious leader would have no effect on their choice of candidates.

On the other hand, both black parishioners and political entrepreneurs view black clerics as indigenous leaders. A 1984 *USA Today* survey asked: "A variety of groups and people occupy leadership roles within the black community. For each person or groups I mention, please tell me how effective you think [they] are as leaders—very effective, somewhat effective, or not very effective?" Figure 6.3 shows the "very effective" responses for six leadership categories mentioned

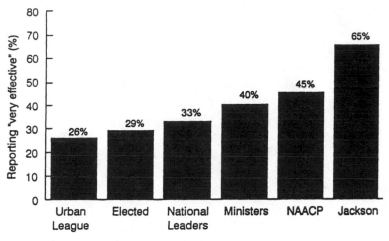

FIGURE 6.3. *Perceived Efficacy of Black Leadership as Community Leaders—Groups and Individuals (N = 280). Source: 1984 USA Today Survey of Registered Voters.*

in this order: local black officeholders, national political leaders, the NAACP, the Urban League, black ministers and clergy, and Jesse Jackson. Jesse Jackson, a minister-politician, ranked first (65 percent), and black ministers (40 percent) as a group ranked second to the NAACP (45 percent) as the most effective leaders. Black ministers were perceived as more effective than national black political leaders (33 percent), local black elected officials (29 percent), and the National Urban League (26 percent), a civil rights organization. The clerical leadership category even rivals the oldest and most prominent civil rights organization for African Americans, the NAACP.

Although some commentators criticize the appropriateness of black clerics as representatives of black interests in the American polity (Reed 1986b), political entrepreneurs certainly woo the activist clergy within black communities as a means to legitimize and garner support for their political goals. Moreover, Lincoln and Mamiya's survey of over two thousand black clergy between 1978 and 1984 reveals that black ministers of the various mainstream black denominations overwhelmingly approve of an activist ministry (1990, 223). Over 90 percent of black ministers, independent of age, education, and denominational affiliation, supported clerical involvement in civil rights demonstrations and clerics expressing their views on social and political issues (table 26, 225). Lincoln and Mamiya also cite findings from a Gallup survey on a similar question in 1968 that showed nonwhites more supportive than whites of ministers speaking out on social and political issues. Finally, they found in a later 1986 survey of AME church leaders that nearly 90 percent supported clerical involvement in social issues, while only 3 percent agreed that churches should keep out of political matters altogether

(226). Lincoln and Mamiya conclude from these surveys that "there is broad support and consensus in the black community, both within and without the church, among clergy and laity, for a social prophecy role for black churches. . . . The attitude is pervasive that churches should be involved in and express their views on everyday social and political issues." They further conclude: "[I]t is also clear that black people generally support a much more activist role for their churches than do whites" (226).

Although Lincoln and Mamiya's extensive survey reveals a consensus among black clerics in the post–civil rights period, they may overstate the case by extending this consensus to African Americans as a whole. Two surveys at approximately this time measured popular attitudes toward church-based political activism. A NBC/Associated Press survey of two thousand four hundred respondents in October 1980 asked two questions: "Should the churches and members of the clergy express their views on day-to-day social questions, or should they keep out of social matters?" and "What about politics? Do you think the churches and members of clergy should be involved in politics, like backing a candidate for public office, or don't you think so?"[22] The September 1984 *USA Today* poll of over one thousand two hundred registered voters also asked: "In general, do you think it is right or wrong for religious leaders to promote a particular political point of view during religious services?"

Figure 6.4 shows affirmative responses to all three questions by race. Blacks and whites equally approved of churches and clergy expressing their views on social issues, although blacks approved slightly more than whites (57 percent compared to 55 percent, with about a third of both black and white respondents stating that churches and clergy should not express their views on social issues). However, blacks and whites differed more dramatically in regard to the explicit involvement of religious institutions in politics. While less than a third of whites thought that churches or clergy should be able to back political candidates (28 percent) and that religious leaders had a right to promote a particular point of view during religious services (29 percent), more than two-fifths (43 percent) of blacks approved of such involvement, and half (50 percent) approved of clerics promoting a political point of view during religious services.

THE EFFECTS OF CHURCH-BASED STIMULI
ON POLITICAL PARTICIPATION

The black-white differences in approval of church-based political activism may simply reflect racial differences in the incidence of that activism. Those differences in approval may also reflect racial differences in the actual effect of church-based stimuli on political participation.

The 1984 *USA Today* poll also asked about the frequency of political discussions during religious services: "How often does your (minister/priest/rabbi) dis-

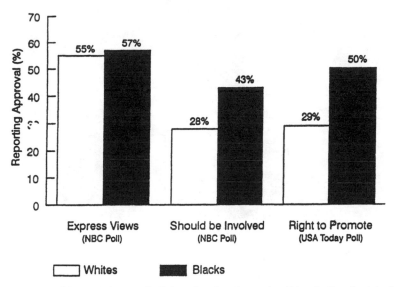

FIGURE 6.4. *Public Opinion on Religious Leaders Becoming Directly Involved in Political Matters, by Race. Sources: 1980 NBC/Associated Press Survey and the 1984 USA Today Survey of Registered Voters.*

cuss political issues as part of the service?" Figure 6.5 reveals striking racial variations among churchgoers. Blacks were three times more likely (28 percent) than whites (8 percent) to report that their religious leaders discussed politics all the time or frequently. They were also more likely than whites (31 percent compared to 21 percent) to report that such discussions took place "sometimes." Nearly three-fourths, or 71 percent, of whites reported that their clerics seldom or never discussed political issues during religious services, compared to only two-fifths (40 percent) of black respondents.

Given the historical importance of black religious institutions in black political mobilization, we might predict from the quantitative data that clerical discussion of politics would have a greater effect on the political participation of blacks than on whites. In fact, the 1984 *USA Today* poll also revealed racial differences in the effects of clerical political discussion in church on the political participation of churchgoers. Figure 6.6 displays the average rate of campaign participation as related to the reported frequency of clerics' political discussions during church services for both black and white churchgoers. The campaign participation rate is a cumulative index of questions that asked if respondents distributed literature for a candidate, went to a political meeting or rally, gave money to a candidate, called on the telephone in behalf of a candidate, or helped to register voters.[23]

Among churchgoers, registered voters who reported that their religious leaders never discussed political issues during religious services, the rate of participation

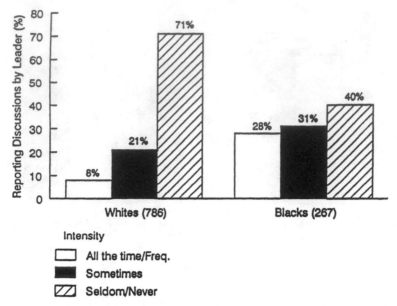

FIGURE 6.5. *Frequency of Clerical Discussion of Politics, by Race, 1984. Source: 1984 USA Today Survey of Registered Voters.*

in campaign activities is about the same for both blacks and for whites. However, as clerical discussions increase in frequency, the rate of participation diverges between the two groups. Among blacks, the average rate of campaign activity gradually increases as respondents reported that their religious leaders "seldom," "sometimes," "frequently," or talked "all the time" about politics.

Discussion of politics in church also raises the participation rate of whites, but more slowly and not as much. We see no increase between "never" and "seldom," and only a small increase when leaders discuss politics "sometimes" in religious services. The white participation rate does not exceed the population average until respondents report that their minister, priest, or rabbi discusses political issues "frequently" as part of the service. The rate of participation returns to below the average level among whites exposed to clerical discussion of politics "all the time," but this decline is probably an artifact of the small number of white respondents in that category.

Among churchgoing registered black voters, the link between campaign activity and the frequency of clerical discussion of politics reveals a linear pattern. As political discussions increase in frequency, so does the level of campaign activity. The average rate of campaign activity is 0.94 for blacks who reported that their leaders "seldom" discussed politics; it jumps to 1.43 for those blacks who reported that their church leaders discussed politics "all the time."

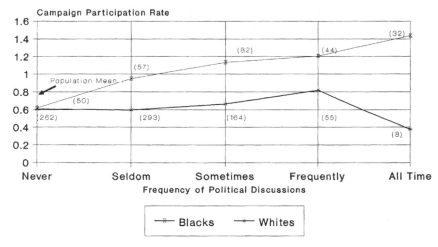

FIGURE 6.6. *Mean Campaign Activity, by Reported Frequency of Clerical Discussion at Place of Worship, Blacks and Whites. Figures in parentheses represent the number of respondents in each category. Source: 1984 USA Today Survey of Registered Voters.*

Using the 1984 *USA Today Poll*, table 6.1 shows the ordinary least square (OLS) estimates of the effects of race and the frequency of church-based political discussions on campaign activism. Controlling for demographic factors, one model shows the results of the independent effects of clerical discussion of politics on campaign activity; the second model shows the interactive effects of race and the frequency of clerical discussion of politics. Controlling for SES, demographic factors, and the effects of church attendance as a civic-oriented resource for electoral participation,[24] it becomes clear that the frequency of clerical discussions has a positive independent effect on campaign participation.

The extent of clerical discussion of politics rivaled income and exceeded church attendance as a predictor of campaign activism, although being black and education were, among these churchgoers, stronger predictors. The strong impact of race on campaign activism among churchgoers in 1984 is probably attributable specifically to Jesse Jackson's presidential election campaign in 1984 (Table 1991, 1993) and generally to the contextual effects of black office-seeking and black representation on black mobilization in this period (Kleppner 1985; Bobo and Gilliam 1990; Tate 1993).

As the second OLS model demonstrates, being black and hearing frequent political discussions by one's religious leader diminished the independent effect of clerical discussions on campaign activism. The interactive model suggests that—independent of personal SES and demographic factors—religious institu-

Table 6.1 Effects of Race and Clerical Discussions on Campaign Activism
(Ordinary Least Squares Estimates)

	Independent Model		Interactive Model	
	b	(SE)	b	(SE)
Demographic factors				
Education	.16***	(.03)	.15***	(.04)
Gender (male)	−.01	(.07)	.02	(.08)
Urban	−.01	(.07)	.02	(.08)
Age	.14***	(.04)	.11**	(.05)
South	.05	(.08)	.02	(.06)
Income	.07*	(.04)	.05	(.05)
Race (black)	.42***	(.09)	−.67	(.62)
Religious resources				
Church attendance	.08**	(.03)	.08*	(.04)
Clerical discussion	.11***	(.03)	.04	(.04)
Attendance × black			.02	(.04)
Discussion × black			.18**	(.07)
Total cases	1,029		1,021	
Adjusted R²	.08		.09	

Source: 1984 *USA Today* Survey of Registered Voters.
Note: Entries are unstandardized regression coefficients with standard errors in parentheses.
Total sample = 1,271.
*p < .05.
**p < .01.
***p < .001.

tions were a potent force for black electoral mobilization in 1984. The combined effects of race and the frequency of clerical discussion of politics suggests that black religious institutions were, as several analysts have demonstrated and speculated, critical resources for mobilizing campaign activity during the 1984 elections.

The 1984 *USA Today* survey therefore suggests both that clerical discussion of political matters are relatively infrequent among whites compared to blacks and that such discussions among whites appear not to stimulate political participation greatly. However, church attendance, a religiously based resource for civic participation, positively predicts campaign activity for both blacks and whites. For today's African Americans, religious institutions may serve as an indigenous source of political information and stimulation that competes favorably with mainstream sources of political information.

Table 6.2 The Intensity of Church-Based Political Activism among African Americans

	Yes (%)
Has a member of the clergy or someone in an official position talked about the need for people to become more involved in politics?	63
In the last year, have you heard any discussions of politics at your church or place of worship?	61
Has any local or national leader spoken at a regular religious service?	48
Have you talked to people about political matters at your church or place of worship?	44
Has a member of the clergy or someone in an official position ever suggested that you vote for or against certain candidates in an election?	29

N = 1,206
Source: 1993 National Black Politics Study.

COMPARING WHITE AND BLACK CHURCH-BASED POLITICAL ACTIVISM

Findings from the 1993 National Black Politics Study (NBPS) indicate that religious institutions are an important organizational resource for disseminating information about elections, encouraging church members to get involved in politics, providing a space for them to talk about politics, and exposing them to local and national leaders. Table 6.2 shows that these modes of church-based political activism varied in intensity, ranging from 63 percent of African Americans reporting that a cleric or official at their church talked about the need for people to become involved in politics to 29 percent reporting that a church official urged them to vote for or against a political candidate. Although these findings confirm the enduring significance of religious institutions as a resource base for black electoral mobilization,[25] we cannot judge from the NBPS how these modes of activism compare with those in other ethnic and religious groups.

Questions on church-based political activism from the 1991 Chicago Area Survey provide a snapshot of various modes of church-based activism and the ways these modes differ in intensity by race and ethnicity, religious orientation, and social class.[26] The questions asked church members how often their religious leaders discussed politics, if their place of worship encouraged members to vote, how often candidates for public office made visits, and whether their place of worship had ever taken up a collection for a political candidate. About 83 percent

Table 6.3 Church-Based Political Activism by Race/Ethnicity in Metro Chicago (Percentage of Church Members Who Participate)

	Blacks	Whites	Latinos
Discuss politics			
Nearly all the time	6	2	8
Frequently	15	7	10
Sometimes	30	30	18
Rarely	30	42	46
Never	19	20	18
Encourage members to vote			
Yes	65	30	36
No	35	70	64
Host candidate visits			
Frequently	14	2	10
Only sometimes	43	10	19
Basically never	43	88	71
Take up a collection			
Yes	10	1	3
No	90	99	97
Number of cases	145	463	22

Source: Northwestern University, 1991 Chicago Area Survey. Total sample = 1,027.

of the 1,027 respondents reported that they were members of a religious institution. Using this group as a base, table 6.3 reports the frequency of responses from questions measuring church-based activism for African Americans, Anglo-whites, and Latinos.

For each of the four modes of church-based activism, African Americans reported more involvement than Anglo-whites and Latinos in this survey.[27] The modes of church-based activism varied in intensity for each act. More than a third of all respondents reported being encouraged to vote at their place of worship; 20 percent reported that political candidates visit their place of worship "frequently" or "only sometimes"; about 10 percent reported that their religious leader discussed politics during religious services "nearly all the time" or "frequently"; and 3 percent stated that their place of worship had taken up a financial collection for a political candidate.

As in the 1984 *USA Today* survey, the intensity of church-based activism varied by race and ethnicity. African Americans were more than twice as likely as Anglo-whites to hear frequent discussions of politics from their clerics and to be encouraged to vote. They were more than twice as likely to receive visits from political candidates and to have had a collection taken up for a candidate at their place of worship. For Latinos, the intensity of church-based activism may be greater than Anglo-whites but less than African Americans.

Table 6.4 shows that church-based political activism also varied by religious orientation. Catholics reported less political activism at their place of worship than either Jews or Protestants. Jewish respondents reported that their leaders discussed politics more than Protestants; and candidate visits at synagogues were reported as frequently as at Protestant churches. On the other hand, Protestants, more than Jews, reported being encouraged to vote and collections being taken for candidates at their place of worship. However, given the small number of Jewish respondents in this survey who reported affiliating with a synagogue (N = 33), these estimates should be read with caution.

Like the findings of Verba and his colleagues, results from the Chicago Area Survey indicate that church-based political activism varies by race/ethnicity and religious orientations. African Americans are more likely to receive political stimuli at their place of worship than Anglo-whites and Latinos, and Jews and Protestants are more likely to receive such stimuli than Catholics.

EDUCATION AND CHURCH-BASED ACTIVISM

In addition to variations by race and ethnicity, exposure to church-based political stimuli varies considerably by education and religious orientation. Figure 6.7 reports from the 1991 Chicago Area Survey the average rate of political activism within religious institutions by education for blacks, whites, and for white Protestants and white Catholics. The sample size of Jews and Latinos, as well as for African-American Catholics, was too small for a comparison over educational categories.[28]

As figure 6.7 demonstrates, the intensity and direction of church-based political activism varies between the educational categories of blacks and whites. The average rate of church-based activism for blacks with less than a high school education is about one standard deviation above the mean, while for blacks with a high school education, the average rate of activism is about three-quarters of a standard deviation above the mean. In contrast, blacks with some college and with a full college education are less likely to report political activism at their place of worship than blacks with less education. The average activism scores of both college-educated groups hovered around one-half of a standard deviation above the mean for the population as a whole. These findings indicate that for African Americans at churches in the Chicago area, church-based political activism may mediate the socioeconomic disadvantages of blacks in the political arena.

For whites, the average rate of church-based activism also changes by education and religious orientation, but in the opposite direction. Whites of all three educational categories are less likely to be exposed to church-based activism than blacks. Protestant and Catholic whites with less than a high school education and

Table 6.4 Church-Based Political Activism by Religious Orientation in Metro Chicago (Percentage Who Participate)

	Catholic	Jewish	Protestant
Discuss politics			
Nearly all the time	0	15	3
Frequently	7	15	11
Sometimes	26	51	30
Rarely	44	18	37
Never	22	0	18
Encourage members to vote			
Yes	25	42	54
No	75	58	46
Host candidate visits			
Frequently	2	3	7
Only sometimes	12	28	24
Basically never	85	69	69
Take up a collection			
Yes	2	0	5
No	98	100	95
Number of cases	333	33	270

Source: Northwestern University, 1991 Chicago Area Survey. Total sample = 1,027.

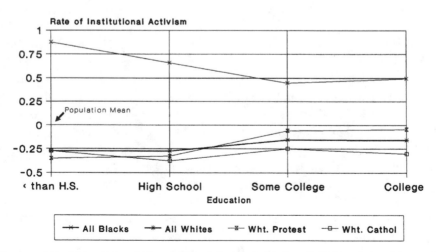

FIGURE 6.7. *Mean Rate of Church-Based Activism, by Race/Religious Orientation and Education. Source: Northwestern University, 1991 Chicago Area Survey.*

with a high school education receive on average fewer political stimuli in church than their counterparts with some college or more. However, within the two highest educational categories among college-educated whites, there are noticeable differences. While the average rate of activism among white Catholics dips to below one-quarter of a standard deviation below the mean, the average rate for college-educated white Protestants nudges toward the population mean.

PERSONAL DETERMINANTS OF INSTITUTIONALLY BASED ACTIVISM

Table 6.5 shows OLS estimates of personal determinants of church-based political activism in the 1991 Chicago Area Survey. Demographically, socioeconomic advantages have a negative effect or no effect at all on being exposed to political stimuli at church. The greater one's income, the less likely one is to be so exposed. The relationship between being exposed to church-based political stimuli and

Table 6.5 Personal Determinants of Church-Based Political Activism (Ordinary Least Squares Estimates)

	b	(SE)
Demographic factors		
Education	.04	(.04)
Gender (male)	−.03	(.14)
Age	−7.04	(8.66)
Income	−.12**	(.06)
African American	1.51***	(.19)
Latino	.42	(.31)
Religious orientation		
Catholic	−.49***	(.18)
Protestant	.01	(.20)
Born-again Protestant	.80***	(.20)
Jewish	.62*	(.35)
Total cases = 826		
Adjusted R^2 = .16		

Source: Northwestern University, 1991 Chicago Area Survey.
Entries are unstandardized regression coefficients with standard errors in parentheses.
*$p < .10$.
**$p < .01$.
***$p < .001$.
Total sample = 1,027.

education is statistically insignificant. In this OLS model, the strongest predictor of being exposed to political stimuli at one's place of worship is race. Being African American is positively related to receiving political stimuli at one's place of worship, while being Latino has no effect (here, as in the rest of this analysis, the small number of Latino cases makes interpretation difficult).

In addition, the model provides estimates of the effect of one's religious orientation on exposure to church-based political activism. A question on this survey asked respondents who claimed a Protestant affiliation: "Some people have had deep religious experiences which have transformed their lives. These experiences are sometimes described as 'being born again in one's faith' or 'discovering Jesus Christ in one's life.' There are deeply religious people who have not had an experience of this sort. How about you—have *you* had such an experience?" Twenty percent of Protestants in the survey answered positively. I will call this group "born-again" Christians.

Table 6.5 shows that both being Jewish and being a born-again Christian are positively associated with exposure to political stimuli at one's place of worship. In contrast, being Catholic is negatively associated with exposure to church-based political activism. The differences between Catholics and Protestants in 1991 in Chicago are similar to the findings of other researchers on religious institutions and political participation (Verba et al. 1993). They provide further evidence on how the internal structure of institutions may promote or undermine civic action.[29] Congregationally organized religious institutions such as many Protestant churches seem more likely to promote political action than hierarchically structured institutions such as Catholic churches.

Religious institutions within African-American communities are important resources for black political mobilization. These resources include clerical appeals, candidate contacts at religious services, church-sponsored political forums and rallies, group endorsements by ministers and religious groups, and fundraising for political candidates. These sources of information and activism have deep historical roots. Black religious institutions also serve as resources for political entrepreneurs by providing campaign funds and workers and a mobilizable source of voters. Although the direct involvement of black religious institutions produces some ambivalence in the black population, by and large black clerics have a strong commitment to political activism, and black churchgoers generally approve of that commitment. Their approval may well be related to the stronger positive effect of religious institutions on black than on white political activism. Both quantitative and qualitative data indicate that black religious institutions have a potent effect on black political activism by providing information about politics and by facilitating political mobilization.

7

Ties That Bind

Linking Religion and Intermediary Resources to Political Action

When we asunder part, it gives us inward pain
But we shall be joined in heart, and hope to meet again.

John Fawcett, "Blest Be the Tie That Binds," 1782

THIS BRIEF CHAPTER PROVIDES A statistical conclusion to my quantitative analyses in chapters 5 and 6 by examining the combined effects of religion's macro and micro resources on black political mobilization. I consider here the multidimensionality of religious beliefs and practices and estimate not only the direct effects of different religious factors on political action but their indirect impact—through intermediary resources that are psychological and organizational in nature.[1] Intermediary resources, like participation in social organizations and feelings of political empowerment, foster political participation by linking individuals to political action.

Three themes are covered in this chapter. First, I present a causal model of how religion operates through organizational and psychological resources for political action. The model shows how religion's macro and micro resources contribute to intermediary resources for participation. Second, results from the causal analysis allow us to consider changes and continuities in religion's effects on black political activism since the 1960s. Using survey data from the 1980s, the results make it possible to examine, for instance, whether deeply felt religious feelings among blacks continue to undermine demanding modes of political activism or whether church attendance and participation in church work remains a positive force for black participation in the post–civil rights era. Finally, differences in religion's organizational and psychological impact on political participation are examined for blacks and whites. Differences in religion's effects on the participation of blacks and whites shed light not only on religion's multidimensional character but also on its capacity to function differently across social groups.

Figure 7.1 illustrates the causal relationships I hypothesize between the organizational and psychological aspects of religion and political action. Religion, in its diverse forms, affects political action both directly and indirectly. As figure 7.1 shows, religious beliefs and practices create and promote psychological and or-

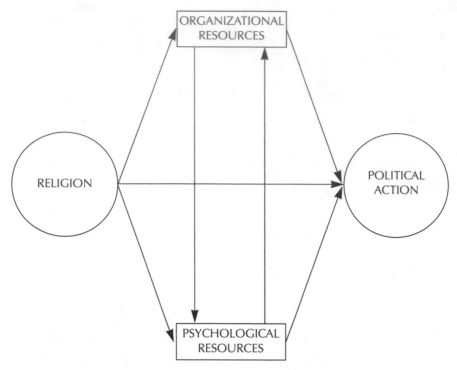

FIGURE 7.1. *Causal Model of Religion and Political Action.*

ganizational resources for participation, both of which directly foster individual and collective action. Religion should affect psychological resources for participation, given the relationship of religion to belief systems and efficacy (Gilkes 1980; St. George and McNamara 1984; McGuire 1983; Hughes and Demo 1989; Allen, Dawson, and Brown 1989). As I have discussed throughout, involvement in church activities, a macro resource for political action, nurtures skills that can be used in political action. Religious factors might also encourage political participation directly, mobilizing deeply committed adherents who are politically motivated by their religious worldviews. Figure 7.1 also illustrates the potential reciprocal relationships between organizational and psychological resources for political action. Church visits by political candidates, for instance, might provide congregants with more knowledge of political affairs, while the sense of religiously inspired political efficacy might inspire congregants to engage in civic activities through church groups that are engaged in community activities.

A causal, quantitative approach allows us to examine not only religion's direct impact on political action but also its indirect effects on intermediary resources for political action, such as interest in political matters, the sense of political efficacy, knowledge of political affairs, and organizational participation. In chapter

5 I investigated the role of psychological resources in some detail. Here I will combine similar measures of psychological resources with some detailed measures of organizational resources.

Previous research and my own observations led me to hypothesize that organizational involvement in church activities, church attendance, and internal religious behavior would have different effects on individual and collective political action, as well as on the intermediary resources for participation that directly promote participation. As we have already seen, participation in church work promotes modes that require a high degree of self-initiative, while church attendance promotes voter participation, a mode of participation that requires relatively less self-initiative. Privatized religious beliefs, on the other hand, in data examined from the civil rights movement, discouraged participation in high-initiative modes of political action like campaigning for political candidates and protesting. The patterns show that religious behaviors should have different effects on voting, a relatively easy and more individualistic mode of political participation, than on collective action–oriented participation, which is more demanding and requires interpersonal cooperation.

This analysis uses data from the 1987 General Social Survey (GSS), a representative, cross-sectional survey on political and social attitudes taken by the National Opinion Research Center (NORC) at the University of Chicago.[2] In this analysis, I have used several indicators of religious activity and commitment that measure macro and micro resources: frequency of church attendance; membership in a church-affiliated group; active involvement in a church group; active participation in a church group that works on community problems; being more active in a church group than in other organizations; frequency of prayer; feelings of closeness to God; and strength of religious affiliation.[3] These indicators clustered around two broadly defined measures of religious behavior. The first was church group activism—intensive and extensive organizational involvement in church life; participation in church life encourages political participation. The second was internal religiosity—private, internalized religious behavior. A third factor, church attendance, may reflect both public and private commitment to religion, affirming the distinctiveness of church attendance as a factor separate from either strictly organizational or psychological religious behavior.

Measures for political participation, as well as for intermediary resources for participation, are partially replicated from Verba and Nie's *Participation in America* (1972). I use two measures of political participation, voting and collective action behavior. Collective action behavior is partially replicated from Verba and Nie's description of "communal-cooperative activity": working for change, focusing on "the broader social issues in the community or society" by working with others to solve community problems (69). Including a measure on community-based activities is important, since black clergy and churches participate politically in ways that go beyond the realm of electoral and protest politics; their involvement also entails "community organizing and community building" (Lincoln and Mamiya 1990, 243).

An index of membership in secular, nonpolitical organizations is included in the analysis so that the independent effects of church activism can be measured against those of general involvement in organizational life. Secular organizational involvement also functions, within this model, as an intermediary resource for participation.[4] I used path analysis to estimate the direct and indirect effects of religiously based resources for participation on the frequency of both voting and communal collective action behavior among African Americans.[5] In addition to these hypothesized causal links, this analysis also posits that religiously based resources for political action will have different effects on the participation of black and white Americans. As a group with fewer conventional forms of resources, blacks in the American political system rely on extrapolitical and nontraditional resources for political action. Given the dominant role of religion in African-American life, certain religious factors should have a greater effect on blacks' political involvement than on that of whites.[6] This research will assess how religiously based resources for participation might interact with race.[7]

Since previous research on social participation has reported higher levels of organizational participation among blacks than among whites when SES factors are controlled (Babchuk and Thompson 1962; Orum 1966), we should expect church activism to affect blacks' voting and communal collective action behavior more than it affects that of whites. In this sample as in others (Gallup and Castelli 1989), blacks are more likely than whites to show an internal relationship to religion. If this is accompanied by an otherworldly orientation, then internalized religion should have a greater negative effect on voting and collective action behavior among blacks than among whites.

PATH ANALYSIS

Figure 7.2, representing the empirical data and deriving from a variation of the model in figure 7.1, shows the most plausible model describing the hypothesized causal relationships between the religious factors, intermediary resources, and frequency of voting among African Americans. The standardized regression estimates are presented with education, income, gender, age, and region controlled. Only statistically significant relationships are presented in the model. The relationships between internal religiosity and the two intermediary psychological resources for participation empirically confirm the idea of the sense of religiously inspired political efficacy and counters the belief that deep psychological commitments to one's religion undermine interests in politics. These findings provide more evidence against the opiate theory. As the causal model indicates, the more

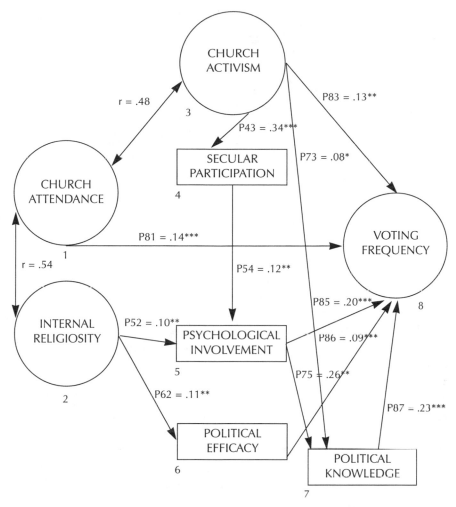

FIGURE 7.2. *Path Model of the Effects of Religion on Frequency of Voting among African Americans. Paths from exogenous variables are controlled for education, income, gender, age, and region;* ***p < .001; **p < .01; *p < .10; Adjusted R^2 = 31.

blacks are psychologically devoted to their religion, the more they think about politics and feel politically empowered. Internal religiosity, measured by praying, feeling close to God, and considering oneself a "strong" member of one's denomination, has a weak and insignificant negative link to voter participation among blacks, suggesting that being deeply committed to religion acts as a drag on black voter activity. However, to make this conclusion would misinterpret the relationship, since internal religiosity promotes black voter activity through psychological resources for participation.

Interviews of black churchgoers in Chicago also suggest an indirect link between internal religiosity and political participation. Some congregants referred to the empowering effects of religion on their lives while at the same time expressing neutral attitudes toward religion's role in political life. Others referred to religion's empowering effects and thought about politics through their religious worldviews. When asked in what ways, if any, does religion provide personal guidance, one woman from a Pentecostal church articulated religion's empowering influence: "It gives me strength that I need, it comforts me in times of distress, it lifts my spirit when I'm depressed, it becomes a part of my whole life being." Asked next whether her religious views have any influence on her political views, she responded: "With me, I don't try to mix politicians with religion, I don't think the two should be mixed." Another woman from the same church also expressed the empowerment she received from her religious beliefs: "It's so hard dealing with obstacles in our lives, but by having religion and God in our lives we can always look to that for guidance. When I get weak and want to stray, or when I want to get mad and hurt somebody or cry, or just give up, you can just reach out for that rope. That rope is there and you just hold on."

When asked whether her religious views influenced her political views, she noted that "as we vote, we want someone who is for the people, and hopefully they are of sound mind and they will just do right. We have to pray for our politicians because even though we vote them in we don't know what they really are going to do what's right. They may have other motives. We have to pray behind them."[8]

In contrast to internal religiosity, participation in church work directly and indirectly promotes black voter participation. The results show a direct link between activism in church work and voter participation. Church work also encourages voter participation through its link with participation in secular activities, demonstrating, as I have discussed throughout, how participation in church work encourages participation in civic activities.[9]

The model also shows how activism in church work—through its connection to intermediary resources for participation—has both psychological and organizational consequences for political action. Activism in church work has a positive, though weak, association with knowledge of political affairs, while participation in secular, nonpolitical organizations, an organizational resource with a strong association with church activism, is positively linked to psychological involvement in politics.[10] Thus, the more blacks are active in church work, the more likely they are to be knowledgeable about public affairs; similarly, the more they are active in church groups, the more they are active in secular groups, which, in turn, supports their interests in political affairs. As table 7.1 shows, the indirect effects of church activism are 0.034, contributing to a total causal effect of 0.161. This total effect accounts for 66 percent of the "original" or total correlation between church activism and frequency of voting, indicating the relatively strong association of church activism with black voter participation.

As previous studies on religion and voter participation have found, and as we discovered from our analysis of survey data from the civil rights movement, church attendance has a positive and direct effect on frequency of voting. The more blacks attend church services, the more they are likely to vote. Figure 7.3 outlines the causal linkages between the religious factors and a more demanding mode of political action—participation in community-based collective action.

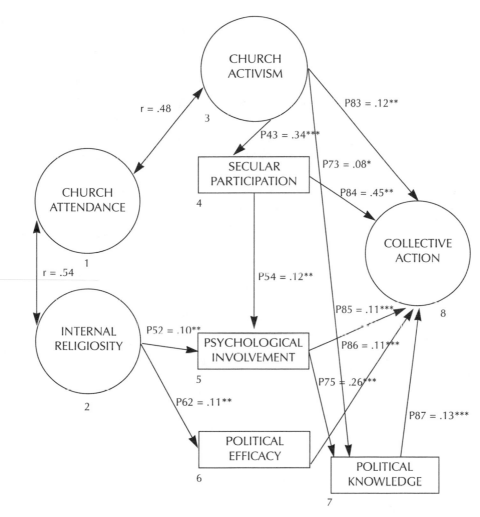

FIGURE 7.3. *Path Model of the Effects of Religion on Collective Action Behavior among African Americans. Paths from exogenous variables are controlled for education, income, gender, age, and region;* ***p < .001; **p < .01; *p < .10; adjusted R² = .46.*

Table 7.1 Direct and Indirect Effects of Religiously Based Resources on Voting among African Americans

	Total effect	Direct effect	Indirect effects through political resources	Total causal
Church activism	.240	.127	.034	.161
Church attendance	.240	.135	—	.135
Internal religiosity	.162	−.047	.034	−.013

Activism in church work, independent of participation in secular, nonpolitical organizations, is positively and significantly linked to community-based collective activities, as is participation in secular organizations. The indirect estimated effect of church activism on communal activities through organizational and psychological resources is 0.168, for a total causal effect of 0.287. Neither church attendance nor internal religiosity has a significant effect on community-oriented collective action. However, as table 7.2 shows, internal religiosity has an indirect estimated effect on collective action behavior through psychological involvement in politics, internal sense of political efficacy, and political knowledge. As indicated by voter participation, the direct negative impact of internal religiosity on collective action behavior among African Americans is diminished by its estimated indirect effects. As I have demonstrated through the analysis of survey data on black participation during the civil rights movement (chapter 4), religion's effects on political action are determined by the multidimensionality of both religion and political action.

How Religious Resources Interact with Race

Tables 7.3 and 7.4 report the interaction effects of race and religion on voter participation and community-based collective activities. These effects are reported

Table 7.2 Direct and Indirect Effects of Religiously Based Resources on Collective Action

	Total effect	Direct effect	Indirect effects through political resources	Total causal
Church activism	.330	.119	.168	.287
Church attendance	.127	.029	—	−.029
Internal religiosity	.068	−.005	.016	.011

Table 7.3 Regression on Voting and the Interaction Effects of Race and Religion

Independent variables	Standardized	Tolerance
Religious dimensions		
Internal religiosity	−.02	.5409
Church attendance	.19***	.5163
Church activism	9.272E-04	.5393
Organizational resources		
Secular participation	.06**	.6556
Cognitive resources		
Political efficacy	.06**	.7177
Interest in politics	.18***	.7015
Political knowledge	.24***	.7253
SES and demographics		
Education	.12***	.5537
Income	.02	.9750
Age	.23***	.6688
Region—South	−.08***	.7918
Gender—male	−.03	.7978
Race—black	.15	.0097
Interaction effects		
Internal religiosity × black	−.00	.4491
Church attendance × black	−.14*	.0913
Church activism × black	.10***	.2992
Adjusted R^2	.33	
N	1,185	

Interaction estimates for other predictors are not reported in model.

*$p < .10$.

**$p < .05$.

***$p < .01$.

with their component parts, along with the impact of demographic, SES, and political resource variables.[11]

As tables 7.3 and 7.4 report, in the wider population the impact of internal religiosity, church attendance, and church activism depends on the mode of political action. While internal religiosity has an insignificant impact on frequency of voting, it has a positive and significant impact on communal collective action. In contrast to the casual model from the all-black sample, it appears that the more Americans are internally religious, the more they are likely to participate in community-based cooperative activities. In the opposite direction, church attendance positively predicts frequency of voting, while its impact on community-oriented collective action is negative. Activism in church work has no indepen-

Table 7.4 Regression on Voting and the Interaction Effects of Race and Religion

Independent variables	Standardized	Tolerance
Religious dimensions		
Internal religiosity	.06**	.5423
Church attendance	−.07***	.5206
Church activism	.14***	.5606
Organizational resources		
Secular participation	.48***	.6701
Cognitive resources		
Political efficacy	.13***	.7328
Interest in politics	.14***	.7012
Political knowledge	.09***	.7346
SES and demographics		
Education	.16***	.5821
Income	−.00	.9756
Age	.11***	.6764
Region—South	.05**	.8122
Gender—male	−.01	.8018
Race—black	.20	.0126
Interaction effects		
Internal religiosity × black	−.05**	.4833
Church attendance × black	.03	.1057
Church activism × black	.01	.3957
Adjusted R^2	.50	
N	1,386	

Interaction estimates for other predictors are not reported in model.
*$p < .10$.
**$p < .05$.
***$p < .01$.

dent effect on voting but positively predicts cooperative participation in community activities.

The interaction effects of race and religion explain some of the differences in religious behavior and political action. These results support the view that for both whites and blacks, religion serves as a resource for political action, but in different ways. Internal religiosity provides psychological resources for participation. Specifically, an individual's private devotion to religion promotes feelings of political effectiveness, as well as interest in political matters. It might be that internal religiosity fosters political efficaciousness through a belief in divine inspiration, while the relationship of internal religiosity to interest in politics might be associated with interest in morally defined political issues or with racial identity and consciousness, factors that are strongly related to religiosity (Dawson, Brown, and Allen 1990) and promote political involvement (Verba and Nie 1972).

Another important finding is the direct positive effect of church attendance on voting between both blacks and whites. Those who attend worship services regularly are likely to be faithful voters. (Both could be explained by a third variable, a general sense of duty, not measured in the GSS). As table 7.3 indicates, church attendance has a greater impact on voting than even education, the factor generally considered being the most important predictor of voter participation (Wolfinger and Rosenstone 1980). However, the effect of church attendance on voting is more significant for whites than for blacks; whites who regularly attend worship services are more likely than blacks to vote frequently. For whites, church attendance might promote civic attitudes that are important to voter participation. Civic attitudes are generally less important to black voter participation than factors such as group identity and consciousness.

Nonetheless, blacks who are active in church work are more likely to be committed to voting than white church activists. In fact, the interaction of race and church activism is such a powerful predictor of regular participation in elections that, when it is taken into consideration, the independent effect of church activism on voting is insignificant. This greater impact of church activism among blacks is attributed to the level of political activity in black churches. Black church activists—indeed, black church members in general—receive more political messages at their places of worship than white churchgoers do; these political messages directly inspire political activity. As Verba and Nie maintain, the combination of organizational activity and "politically relevant stimuli" promotes political participation: "manifestly non-political organizations appear to have an impact on the political participation rate of their members, providing that the [two] internal processes . . . take place within them" (1972, 191). The positive effect of church participation on black voter participation at the time of this survey points to a partial continuity of this effect since the civil rights movement, when, as shown in the analysis of survey data from the 1960s, participation in church work also increased blacks' participation in campaign activities.

Religious beliefs and practices appear to have a mixed impact on communal collective action. Internal religiosity and church activism encourage community-oriented collective action, while church attendance, a reliable predictor of voter activity, is, when other factors are controlled, negatively associated with participation in community-oriented collective action.

Activism in church work, independently of SES and demographic factors, as well as participation in nonpolitical secular organizations, predicts community-oriented collective action, which suggests that churches have an important role to play in community organizing. The positive impact of private religious devotion on communal collective action, while small, nevertheless challenges the belief that strong religious commitment erodes incentives for political participation. Those who score high on internal religiosity are likely to be engaged in community organizing activities through their church.

As table 7.4 shows, the impact of private religious behavior on collective action is greater among whites than among blacks. For internally religious whites, especially fundamentalists, issues like abortion and pornography might inspire collective action efforts on morally defined political issues. Although black and white fundamentalists share similar attitudes about such morality issues, black fundamentalists as a group have been less visible than their white counterparts in mobilizing around such issues (Wald 1987; Calhoun-Brown 1998).

Unlike internal religiosity and church activism, church attendance, which encourages voting, actually discourages communal collective action once it is entered into a model with all the other forms of religious feelings and participation controlled. This finding is puzzling, given that a "churchlike" religious orientation has been found (among blacks) to promote political participation (Hunt and Hunt 1977). This finding probably reflects the difference between those who simply attend church and those who are actively involved in church life; the latter group's activism positively correlates with community-based collective action. Those whose involvement in church life extends beyond the regular weekly service may cultivate and nurture organizational skills that they can channel into community organizing as well as other forms of political activism.[12] There is no significant interaction between the effects of race and church activism on community-oriented collective action or between those of race and church attendance. For blacks and for whites, church activism appears to encourage collective action, while for both blacks and whites, frequent church attendance (with all other forms of religious participation controlled) discourages community-based collective action. Except for church attendance per se, both organizational and psychological resources of religion promote black political participation.

8

The Last Shall Be First

Religion, Oppositional Culture, and African-American Political Mobilization

I know thy works, and charity, and service, and faith, and thy patience, and thy works; and the last to be more than the first.

Revelation 2:19

I heard a loud noise in the heavens, and the Spirit instantly appeared to me and said the Serpent was loosen, and Christ had laid down the yoke he had borne for the sins of men, and I should take it on and fight against the Serpent, for the time was fast approaching when the first would be last and the last should be first.

The Confessions of Nat Turner, 1831

From the fourth chapter of St. Luke, beginning at the eighteenth verse: "The Spirit of the Lord is upon me because he hath anointed me to preach the gospel to the poor; he hath sent me to heal the broken hearted, to preach deliverance to the captives, and recovering of sight to the blind, to set at liberty them who are bruised, to preach the acceptable day of the Lord."

Fannie Lou Hamer, speaking at a mass
meeting in Hattiesburg, Mississippi, 1963

THOUGH GENERATIONS APART, NAT TURNER'S apocalyptic vision of a bloody slave insurrection and Fannie Lou Hamer's use of a sacred passage to explain her commitment to the modern civil rights movement both exemplify the enduring, empowering effect of religious culture on black political mobilization. Initially imposed on African slaves as a means of social control, Christianity has emerged in the post–civil rights era as a catalyst for black activism by serving as an organizational and psychological resource. However, the impact of religion on black activism stretches beyond its institutional and psychological influences. As this analysis demonstrates, and as analysts of American political behavior are beginning to recognize, "culture counts" significantly as a mobilizing force behind political activism (Leege, Lieske, and Wald 1991).

Scholarship on black political mobilization has, however, largely neglected the effects of culture, particularly black religious culture. With a few notable exceptions regarding political behavior in general (Edelman 1985; Kertzer 1988; Laitin 1988) and African-American political behavior in particular (Henry 1990), most scholarly work on culture and political action supports the civic culture perspective, viewing culture as a mediating factor indirectly promoting participation by inculcating democratic values that support the existing social order (Almond and Verba 1989).

This literature neglects the independent contribution of culture to action. Although institutions clearly do play an important role in socializing citizens into supporting the system, when one considers the diverse functions of culture in societies, the civic culture perspective falls short in several ways. Specifically, it does not tell us much about how or why popular culture directly promotes political activism, nor does it speak to how culture works politically for dominated groups in democratic societies.

Broadening the resource mobilization perspective, I posit that culture and, by extension religious culture functions as a micro resource for political mobilization by shaping the way activists frame strategies. Culture helps in at least two ways. As David Laitin explains, culture functions politically in a "Janus-faced" fashion: "people are both guided by the symbols of their culture and instrumental in using culture to gain wealth and power" (1988, 81).

Merging anthropological theories of culture with the theoretical richness of the resource mobilization perspective, I argue that the indigenous culture of politicized groups facilitates the construction of meaning for action. Expressed through symbols and performed through rituals, religion among African Americans inspires action by (re)inventing meaning for targeted goals.

Drawing on historical accounts, primary sources, and material collected from my own participant observations at churches and political events, I argue that the religious culture of African Americans is a preexisting resource for mobilization that is autonomous from, yet complementary to, psychological and organizational resources for mobilization. A qualitative approach to the study of religion and political mobilization unearths cultural elements of activism that are difficult to tap through quantitative approaches. As David Laitin correctly points out, qualitative methods are crucial to a sufficient understanding of the link between culture and political action:

> Surveys . . . have inherent limits. The claim that culture provides guidance
> for political action implies that symbols frame and rituals sustain a particular political vision. Part of the power of culture is that its members are

not fully conscious of the sources of their visions and, even if honest, would not necessarily provide the relevant data to survey researchers. Participant observation and the other tools of ethnography are therefore crucial in making connections between worldview and political action. (1988, 592)

Interpreting the religious symbols and rituals used by political entrepreneurs to guide mobilization allows us to uncover the overt and subtle power of culture to influence political activism. As this analysis of religiously based strategies of political action reveals, the religious culture of African Americans not only stimulates mobilization by serving as a guide for interpreting political goals but, just as important, it also provides sacredly ordained legitimacy to political action.

RELIGION, DOMINATION, AND BLACK OPPOSITIONAL CULTURE

Scholars have long viewed the cultures of dominated groups as forces undermining their political engagement. The often fervently emotional religious practices of African Americans have historically been disparaged by many intellectuals, who have seen them as a way for blacks to vent their earthly frustrations while continuing to submit to domination, in the name of a divine authority.

This perspective underestimates the ways that the cultural practices of subordinated groups, often subtly, and at times overtly, promote resistance to domination. Cultural practices that have traditionally been viewed as instruments of acquiescence may actually serve as disguised forms of resistance (Scott 1990). Stressing the role of religious culture in understanding African-American political thought and action, Cornel West points out that "any political consciousness of an oppressed group is shaped and molded by the group's cultural resources and resiliency as perceived by individuals in it," noting further that "the extent to which resources and resiliency are romanticized, rejected, or accepted will deeply influence the kind of political consciousness that individuals possess" (1982, 71).

Critics of popular culture and religion often fail to recognize that opposition to domination can occur within the prevailing ideological framework. Peck reminds us that the culture of oppressed groups should not be understood simply as the result of racial or class domination. Instead "culture implies praxis," activating "forces through which human beings produce their modes of existence and give meaning to their lives under historically-specific conditions." To understand these forces, Peck urges cultural analysts to "look beyond obvious appearances to more subtle, liberating tendencies residing beneath the surface" (1982, 161).

Culture further enhances the political resources of dominated groups by shaping political reality and being shaped by it (Geertz 1973a, 93). Thus, when opportunities for activism arise, people can, by actively resisting domination and

adapting the symbols available to them, draw on cultural perspectives and practices that are lodged in the oppositional tendencies of their own cultural group.

Many of the cultural resources through which blacks shape oppositional
worldviews evolve from their religions (Thurman 1981; Genovese 1974; Raboteau
1978; Cone 1969; Cone 1972; Cone 1986; Levine 1977). The use of religious language
and icons in the political discourse of the former Democratic candidate, the
Reverend Jesse Jackson, served as a valuable cultural resource for the mobilization
of black voters during his 1984 and 1988 candidacies (Henry 1990; Barker 1988;
Washington 1985; Wills 1990). Similarly, Martin Luther King and other civil rights
movement activists used religious language and art to articulate views and motivate participants (Branch 1988; Raines 1977; Walker 1979; Washington 1986).

As Cheryl Townsend Gilkes observes, indigenously expressed forms of African-
American Christianity like sermons and testimony "speak directly to the structures of oppression which cause black suffering" (1980, 36). This collective
perspective on racial domination appears in other cultural forms of the African-
American religious experience as well, particularly in music. As Wyatt T. Walker
theorizes, African-American religious music operates in at least two ways. It cre-
ates an oppositional space for political reflection by "locat[ing] the people's
strength of heritage, their roots, where they are and where they want to go." It
also "mobilizes and strengthens the resolve for struggle," functioning as an agent
of oppositional consciousness by serving as a "primary reservoir of . . . Black people's historical context" and performing as an "important factor in the process
of social change" (1979, 181).

Thus African-American religious symbols, carved from the experience of white
domination, promote a collective perspective of opposition in American society,
which in turn fosters psychological resources for political participation such as
group consciousness and feelings of political efficacy. Culture operates as a resource for mobilization by serving as a means for interpreting and legitimizing
political goals.

Culture and the Construction of Collective Action Frames

Why or how political actors construct meaning for individual and collective action is often overlooked in the literature on political mobilization. With this
analysis I hope to illustrate that mass response to mobilization is more complex
than the psychologically and organizationally centered models of activism convey.
When mobilized, individuals do not detach themselves from their cultural milieu.
Rather, actors make sense of political goals by developing indigenously constructed meanings drawn from shared worldviews, language, religion, experience,
and history.

The construction of meaning for political goals occurs in the context of what some scholars of social movements have called collective action frames, a term that refers to the way actors create "purposely constructed guides to action" (Tarrow 1992). Specifically, collective action frames "organize experience and guide action" and are a "necessary condition for movement participation, whatever its nature or intensity" (Snow et al. 1986). As Sidney Tarrow points out, action frames operate within the culture of politicized groups, providing "leaders with a reservoir of symbols with which to construct a cognitive frame for collective action" (1992, 177).

As the diagram in figure 8.1 illustrates, culture and political goals work in tandem to influence the construction of action frames. Culture influences the goals or "preferences" of groups that emerge from "points of concern" (Laitin 1988). Group preferences evolve from the interaction of material interests with cultural ties that bind individuals into groups. Culture as well as material interests make certain preferences "obvious and important" to the members of a collectivity and thus endogenous to collective action. Without such stated goals or preferences, there can be no targeted action.

Culture also supplies material for the production of action frames. During the process of mobilization, stated objectives alone might not be sufficient for gaining an understanding of a targeted action. Instead, potential activists must, in order to reduce uncertainty about their articulated goals, make sense of these goals. Political entrepreneurs must clarify goals to potential actors by conveying them through familiar language and images.

Responding to value-centered approaches that link culture to action, sociologist Ann Swidler implicitly argues that the construction of action frames through culture is critical to mobilization. More than a mechanism that inculcates participatory values to actors, culture acts as a "tool kit" for constructing "strategies of action" that are indigenous to a group's culture. As Swidler explains, "[p]eople do not build lines of action from scratch." Instead they "construct chains of action beginning with at least some pre-fabricated links," where "[c]ulture influences action through the shape and the organization of those links, not by determining the ends to which they are put" (1986, 277).

Thus, by such "linking" or "framing" of action through culture, goals are readily communicated to targeted groups, according legitimacy and certainty to action, and in turn, mobilizing. Conferring legitimacy to political action is, as Murry Edelman argues, crucial because, through symbols, actors are able to construct diverse meanings for political events that "[shape] support for causes and that [legitimize] value allocations" to actors (1985, 195). Movements that lack an existing, easily grasped, and mutually important cultural framework through which to communicate meaning will find group-based mobilization a far greater challenge.

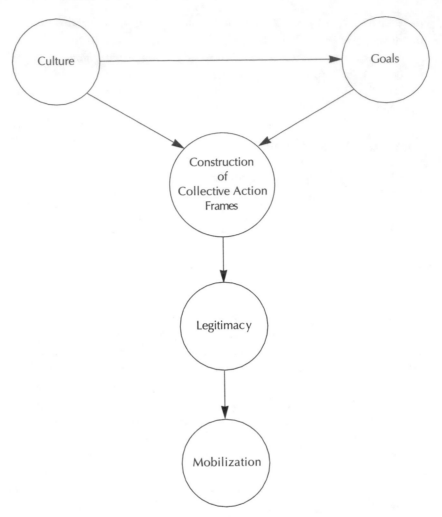

FIGURE 8.1. *Diagram of the Sources and Effects of Collective Action Frames.*

UNCERTAINTY, SACRED SYMBOLS, AND ACTION FRAMES

Sacred symbols, like secular ones, may be used to clarify and legitimize political goals. Culture traffics in symbols that give meaning to reality and experience. Culture is performed through ritual, a means of inventing and sustaining symbols. For those with whom sacred symbols resonate, such symbols might be more persuasive vehicles for political meaning than their secular equivalents. Sacred symbols have, as Geertz points out, a "peculiar power" that comes from "their presumed ability to identity fact with value at the most fundamental level, to give what is otherwise merely actual, a comprehensive normative import" (1973b, 127).

By reducing the abstract to the familiar, sacred symbols and rituals provide meaning to articulated goals, reducing uncertainty about political action and conferring upon it a sacredly-ordained legitimacy. As David Kertzer argues,

> [t]he world out there confronts each individual with an infinite number of stimuli, yet no one can deal with all of them. We must be selective in our perceptions, and those aspects of the world that are selected must be further reduced and reordered in terms of some system of simplification (categorization) that allows us to make sense of them. This order is largely provided by the symbols system we learn as members of our culture, a system that allows for both social creativity and idiosyncrasy. (1988, 4)

If people are inherently "symbolizing, conceptualizing, meaning-seeking animal(s)" (Geertz 1973b, 140), rituals and symbols should act as culturally based resources for mobilization by constructing frames of action through religious meaning. Sacred symbols do not work in isolation from secular ones; in many situations they complement one another, working together to strengthen frames of action.

POLITICIZED RITUALS AND SYMBOLS IN HISTORICAL PERSPECTIVE

Religious rituals and symbols were used for black political mobilization in the modern civil rights movement (Morris 1984; Branch 1988; Raines 1977) and the 1984 and 1988 presidential campaigns of Jesse Jackson (Henry 1990; Barker 1988; Washington 1985; Wills 1990, 193–256). Former civil rights activist Andrew Young comments here on organizing in the Mississippi Delta (Hamilton 1972, 132–133):

> Nobody could have ever argued segregation and integration and gotten people convinced to do anything about that. But when Martin [Luther King] would talk about leaving the slavery of Egypt and wandering into a promised land, somehow that made sense to folks. And they may not have understood it; it was nobody else's political theory, but it was their grass roots ideology. It was their faith; it was the thing they had been nurtured on. And when they heard that language, they responded. You could go into Mississippi and tell people they needed to get themselves together and get organized. And that didn't make much sense. But if you started preaching to them about dry bones rising again, everybody had sung about dry bones. Everybody knew the language.
>   I think it was that cultural milieu, when people were really united with the real meaning of that cultural heritage, and when they saw in their faith also a liberation struggle that they could identify with, then you kinda had

'em boxed. They all wanted to be religious. And when you finally helped them to see that religion meant involvement in action, you kinda had 'em hooked then. You had a ready framework around which you could organize people. You had people in churches. And usually in the smallest country town, you had people in those churches. And that was what, I guess, gave us kind of [a] key to the first organizing phases.

Yet the influence of religious culture on black mobilization predates the modern civil rights movement. As we have seen, and as Eric Foner's analysis of black mobilization during Reconstruction notes, throughout that period "religious convictions profoundly affected the way blacks understood the momentous events around them," in that the religious language they used "expressed aspirations for justice and autonomy" (1988, 3). Black political entrepreneurs then as now were keenly aware of the political importance of religious culture; they drew on shared symbols and rituals that made meaning out of actors' immediate situations. These meanings were often constructed from sacred texts; for indigenous political actors "the Bible—the one book with which they could assume familiarity among their largely illiterate constituents—served as a point of reference for understanding public events" (94). Rather than creating a worldview entirely divorced from their experience as slaves, blacks during Reconstruction constructed one that resisted white supremacy, drawing on Christianity as a source for political meaning, and thus creating an oppositional space that challenged their domination within the framework of a religion that overtly legitimized black servitude.

Some years later and in an entirely different context, religious rituals and symbols became an integral part of Marcus Garvey's post–World War I black nationalist movement. Under the banner of "One God! One Aim! One Destiny!" Garvey's Universal Negro Improvement Association (UNIA), perhaps the largest social movement of African Americans in the twentieth century, fused Christianity with a black nationalist ideology that advocated black separatism from the United States and espoused the "redemption" of Africa from European colonial rule. The oppositional culture of racial separatism was thus grounded, ironically, in two Eurocentric value systems—nationalism and institutional versions of Christianity.

Garvey's nationalist ideology was steeped in the images and language of Christianity. Often speaking of Africa as the "Promised Land" and people throughout the African diaspora as God's "chosen people" (Burkett 1978), Garvey's goal of "redemption" served for his followers as a symbol of an African version of Zion. Psalm 68:31, "Princes shall come forth from Egypt; Ethiopia shall stretch forth her hand to God," was used in UNIA events to confer sacredly ordained legitimacy upon Garvey's goal of black nationhood. In fact, the scripture was reconstructed into a politicized ritual by serving as a catechism for UNIA members (Burkett 1978, 34):

Q. What prediction made in the 68th Psalm and the 31st verse is now being filled?

A. "Princes shall come out of Egypt; Ethiopia shall soon stretch forth her hands unto God."

Q. What does this verse prove?

A. That Negroes will set up their own government in Africa, with rulers of their own race.

Through such rituals and symbols, Garvey and his religious advisors renegotiated Eurocentric ideas of Christianity by transforming biblical icons from white to black and by reconstructing anthems, liturgies, and catechisms of the Catholic and Protestant churches to fit the aims of the UNIA. As Randall Burkett implies in his history of the religious elements of Garveyism, Garvey built "grass roots support" for the movement by recognizing that "the beliefs and rituals [of the UNIA] grew out of a shared experience of oppression and were predicated on the solid foundation of the religious faith of black folk" (1978, 8).

The use of religious culture for black activism was not limited to electoral mobilization during Reconstruction, or to Garvey's black nationalist movement; it also played a significant part in black radical organizing during the depression era. Robin Kelley's history of Alabama Communists (1990) details how Christianity supported a "rich source of oppositional culture" for black party organizers by providing them with a ready framework for conveying meaning. Independent of the clerical leadership, who mostly played a counter productive role in both unionization efforts and Communist party activity, black organizers of the Alabama Communist party relied on the "prophetic tradition of Christianity" to give meaning to class struggle (107). Unpredictably, participants in this struggle appeared to learn more about class exploitation and domination from Christianity than from Marxist ideology.

Christianity, Kelley reported, was a "major factor in drawing blacks into the Communist Party and its mass organizations" (1990, 107). These activists' "grassroots understanding of exploitation" was "based . . . on scripture" (107) far more than on Karl Marx's *Communist Manifesto*. The indigenous religion-centered culture of African Americans granted conviction and legitimacy to class struggle. Sacred songs were transformed into political anthems as they were during the Garvey movement and the modern civil rights movement; both opposition and allies were symbolized by biblical figures. Thus was forged a Christian-influenced oppositional culture for radical mobilization during the 1930s.

During the Great Migration of southern blacks in the interwar period and after World War II, religious culture also supported black electoral mobilization. Incorporated into the urban machines of northern cities, this mobilization relied on the institutional resources of the black church and on its cherished ritual and symbols. Harold Gosnell's analysis of black politics in Chicago during this period details how religious culture served to motivate voters, reporting that "[b]iblical and religious references [were] common even in the mouths of speakers who are known to be non-church members," and ministers were "frequently part of the program of meetings" and were "expected to introduce some of the atmosphere of a revival" ([1935] 1967, 184). Gosnell's casual observations of political rallies in Chicago's Black Belt during the 1930s reveal the continuity and variability of religious culture's effects on black activism.

As these examples have demonstrated, religious symbols and rituals have served as resources for black mobilization in a variety of historical settings and political contexts. As a guide to mass mobilization and a tool for political entrepreneurs, religious culture assisted the building of action frames for mobilization efforts, ranging from Reconstruction-era electoral mobilization efforts, to the urban machine politics of the interwar period, to Marcus Garvey's black nationalist movement, to the radical class politics of the 1930s, and to the modern civil rights movement. These varied illustrations suggest that religious ritual and symbols can be (re)constructed to fit almost any political interest of concern to African Americans. Often contradictory and at times used out of context, religious symbols and rituals have nonetheless, for blacks, historically served as a guide to mobilization and as a means of conferring legitimacy upon active engagement.

MANIPULATORS AND MOBILIZERS: STRATEGIC USES OF RITUALS AND SYMBOLS

In the post–civil rights era, religious culture continues to assist black mobilization. Its current use among black political elites reveals that it is often pressed into use to serve both group and individual political interests. Political entrepreneurs strategically employ religious rituals and symbols to enhance their own legitimacy and mobilize voters behind their candidacies. The use of symbols and rituals is often subtle, as in the case of one political entrepreneur who politicized the religious ritual of "testifying" as a means of bestowing legitimacy to his election to public office. Traditionally, by testifying or "bearing witness," the converted publicly affirm their faith through expressions of appreciation and acknowledgement of God's guidance and protection.

This political use of testimony appeared, perhaps unnoticed, in Chicago, during a community program commemorating Martin Luther King's birthday.[1] A cleric had, moments before, admonished politicians present for "belonging to nobody's church" but "[running] . . . in and out of our churches during election time." Roland Burris, the state's attorney general, responded immediately—perhaps unconsciously—by "testifying." To distance himself from other politicians who might indeed attend church services only during election time, thus using religion for their own selfish needs, Burris publicly affirmed his belief in Christianity and simultaneously justified his church campaigning:

> You can call my pastor, the Dr. William A. Johnson at the St. John's Baptist Church, the friendly church by the library on Forty-eighth and Michigan Boulevard. Reverend Johnson has been there for fifty-one years, and I've been there for twenty-eight years serving my own little people of St. John, serving the Lord, the people of Chicago, the people of Cook County, the people of Illinois. So I am a politician that could stand anywhere, any church, anytime, and say that I don't run in and out [of a church] to give a political speech.

Amid shouts of affirmation from the audience, Burris continued, insisting that his election to public office had been divinely directed:

> I'm in there every day working with the people because that's what the Lord has directed me. Can you all imagine a young, black kid in Centralia, Illinois, at the age of sixteen saying he wanted to do two things? One, to be a lawyer and the other, to be a statewide elected official. Reflect on this, my Christian friends. There weren't even that many black lawyers in 1953, let alone any black politicians in 1953. That wasn't me, that was the Lord! As the thirty-ninth attorney general of the sixth largest state in America, that's the Lord's work.

At the same event, Margaret Smith shared her fond memories of Martin Luther King, then asked for divine intervention in her campaign for re-election to the state senate. Concerned about running in a recently redrawn legislative district that diluted her voter base, Senator Smith asked the audience to pray for her electoral success and to mobilize the community on her behalf. Saying that "the only way to serve people is love people," Smith then made this request:

> I'm asking you to go and pray with me that the Lord will step in. . . . I'm in the race of my life. . . . I love my job, and they're trying to take me out, but I'm a role model and I could go anywhere and I'm well respected in the legislative circle. But I am asking you, please, get our people together and fire them up and tell them that you must go to the polls and vote this year, for all of us. . . . You can be heard loud and clear with your vote. . . . You can be heard loud and clear if you keep that dream alive. So this is our challenge and all, flowing responsibility, to save our humanity. God is on our side. Let Him use you now, while the time is still here.

The "I" in Senator Smith's request for prayer is subtly transformed into a collective and divinely sanctioned entity. Making "a difference" by voting "for all of us . . . while the time is still here," suggests service to God before His imminent return—a compelling exhortation to Christian citizens to engage actively in the worldly affairs of politics.

Biblical symbols also legitimize electoral campaigns for public office. Eugene Pincham, a Democratic party primary candidate for president of the Cook County Board, strategically selected verses from the book of Joshua to justify his decision to run for that office at a Sunday morning church service.[2] Describing his candidacy as "filling a void" for the electoral coalition that had divided after the death of Chicago's first black mayor, Harold Washington, Pincham wove a narrative that likened Washington's coalition to the Israelites, God's chosen people, and himself to Joshua, who, after the death of Moses, became the spiritual and military leader of the Israelites in their quest for the promised land. In Pincham's words:

> I went to a book called Joshua, the first chapter. Now that book reads in the first verse: "Now after the death of Moses, the servant of the Lord had came to pass. Let the Lord speak onto Joshua, the son of Nan, Moses' minister saying, 'Moses, my servant, is dead. Now therefore rise. Go over this Jordan. Thou allow all His people unto the land which I do give to them, even to the children of Israel. There shall not allow any man to be able to stand before thee, all the days of our lives.'" Let me read that again to you. "'There shall not allow any man to be able to stand before thee, all the days of our lives. As I was with Moses, so will I be with thee. I will not fail thee, nor forsake thee. Be strong and have good courage, for onto this people shall thou divide for inheritance of the land, which I swear onto their fathers to give them.'"

Pincham, self-symbolized as the Joshua of the divided Washington coalition, implicitly emphasized his opponent's vulnerability by twice repeating the passage "There shall not allow any man to be able to stand before thee." He then interpreted these passages as divine providence for his candidacy: "A decision had to be made. Moses was dead. The land was to be given us, and just as we were fighting for survival, I believe that God has given us another chance for political empowerment."

A year later, during the Chicago mayoral election, Pincham, now a candidate for the newly created Harold Washington party, compared himself not to Joshua but to Moses—perhaps unaware of the contradiction in the sequence of biblical leaders he had evoked in each of his failed campaigns.[3]

Entrepreneurs can appropriate biblical symbols to convey meaning to just about any political predicament. Giving a political speech at the Omega Missionary Baptist Church the Sunday before the Tuesday election, Danny Davis, a mayoral candidate for the 1991 Democratic primary, likened his own unpopularity, as reflected by his weak support in public opinion polls, to that of Jesus before the crucifixion.[4] As if he were giving a sermon rather than a stump speech, each breath Davis took was punctuated by a call-and-response chord from the church organist. He wove together, into a narrative intended to mobilize support for his candidacy, both a passage from Matthew 16:13 that describes an exchange between Jesus and His disciple Peter regarding divine identity ("Whom do men say that I the Son of Man am?") and a line from a slave spiritual proclaiming the birth of Christ. That narrative was also meant to inspire confidence in his prospects for victory by convincing potential activists and voters that with their support he could prevail over incumbent mayor Richard Daley just as the historical Jesus had triumphed over adversity:

> So I ask you to come out on Tuesday, tell a neighbor, tell a friend, tell everybody that you run into, run and tell it on the mountain and let them know that no matter what the polls are saying, see it's not the polls, we make the polls. Because you remember when Jesus asks Peter, "Say Peter, who do they say I am?" Peter said, "Some of them say you are John the Baptist, some say you are Elijah." Jesus says to Peter, "I know all about the polls, I've been reading the same newspaper you've been reading. I've been watching the same television you've been watching. I want to know who do you say I am?" All that we have to know is, Who do we say? What do we say? If we go to the polls and vote on Tuesday, Danny Davis becomes the next mayor of the city of Chicago.

Ritual and Symbols in a Religious Culture of Opposition

A close look at the biblical ritual and symbols that black politicians have appropriated to promote their political goals reveals those rituals and symbols to be permeated with the language of resistance.[5] These evocations draw primarily on the Old Testament, especially the language of Exodus, with its stress on the oppression of the chosen people, their material weakness, and their need to rely on God's help in the imbalance of power within which they find themselves. The language also stresses the need for collective action and community vision against individualist apathy and the other individual incentives that might lead voters to stay home and indulge themselves rather than contribute money to a candidate and get out to vote on election day.

Held at the Bethel AME Church, a church on Chicago's South Side that frequently hosted voter mobilization rallies during former mayor Harold Washington's campaigns, the gathering officially started with public prayer that combined the sacred with the political.[6]

With the church pulpit and choir stand packed with political activists and elected officials, Reverend Cornelius Haynes, the pastor of the church, began the rally by calling the audience to attention. Proclaiming that "if we put our hearts and our resources together, success will be ours," the minister then asked a fellow cleric to offer a prayer, requesting divine guidance and revelation regarding the mayoral campaign. The prayer, spoken in poetic cadence, began with a biblical scripture from the Book of Proverbs (29:18). On this occasion the scripture's symbolism was clear; the group was looking toward the upcoming campaign. With bowed head, the minister began to speak in words that could easily have had no political content:

> As our Bible says,
> where there is no vision, the people will perish.
> Oh Lord this day we ask Thy blessings,
> and that Thou will reveal to us
> these things that are to come forth.
> Oh Lord, Thy people suffer from a lack of knowledge.
> Father God we stand, But Lord we thank You for Your amazing grace,
> and for Your power.

Invoking biblical figures known for their personal strength and divinely granted wisdom, the minister then made requests on behalf of the candidate as well as those attending the rally. The prayer conferred legitimacy upon the candidate and the activity of the assembled, reaffirming the goals of the gathering:

> Father God we ask that Thou will anoint for us
> the head of our brother Danny K. Davis
> that Thou will give him the wisdom
> of a Solomon and the strength of Samson, Lord.
> And father God bless all of your people
> who are here, for we must choose
> between chaos or community.
> Our Lord, our Savior, our Redeemer
> bless us, keep us, strengthen us,
> guide us. Amen.

Shortly afterward, a political activist introduced the various politicians present at the rally and described the process through which Davis had been chosen as the mayoral candidate. A minister in the pulpit then led the audience in a modified version of the spiritual "Everybody Say Amen," transforming the last verse of the sacred melody into "Everybody say Danny." Soon after that performance, audience members were asked to remain standing and sing the first stanza of the "National Black Anthem," more commonly known as "Lift Every Voice and Sing"; they did this with clenched right fists, a symbol of black resistance used during the black power movement of the late 1960s and early 1970s.

After more speeches, two little girls performed another sacred tune. Although its lyrics might appear to have no connection to a mayoral campaign, they demonstrate how religion is ingrained into African Americans' oppositional culture. The slave spiritual "Oh Mary Don't You Weep" was, in this performance, performed in a steady, bluesy tempo with two-part harmony. The sacred tune symbolized opposition through both the Old Testament account of the Exodus and a reconstructed New Testament description of God's comforting Mary and her sister Martha after the crucifixion of Christ. The lyrics were sung as follows:

> Oh Mary don't you weep, tell Martha not to moan.
> Oh Mary don't you weep, tell Martha not to moan.
> Pharaoh's army drowned in the Red Sea;
> Oh Mary don't you weep, tell Martha not to moan.
> If I could, I surely would
> Stand on the rock where Moses stood.
> Pharaoh's army drowned in the Red Sea;
> Oh Mary don't you weep, tell Martha not to moan.

Although the comparison was not explicitly articulated, Davis could easily be personified as Moses, the incumbent Richard Daley and supporters as Pharaoh and his army. The sacred symbols were integrated into politics so easily that the process appeared routine to those involved. Mary and Martha, like southern blacks in slavery and, arguably, black voters as a 12 percent minority in an 80 percent Anglo-white world, were in a position of relative powerlessness, as were the Jews in their flight out of Egypt. This spiritual and the larger ritual reminded participants at the political rally that in all these cases God's help allowed the objectively weaker to prevail.

A final example derives from an entirely sacred setting, in which Bishop Paul Morton, a politically active minister in New Orleans who pastors a charismatic congregation called the Greater St. Stephen Full Gospel Baptist Church, mobilized opposition against the gubernatorial candidacy of David Duke. In a televised sermon the Sunday before the election, Morton selected passages from both the Old and New Testaments to explain the meaning of Duke's rise as a credible candidate, why he had supporters, what was required of both black and white Christians to oppose him, and what would occur if Duke was elected.[7] Gradually, Morton constructed an oppositional action frame by going, as he said, "to [the] word of God to see what the Lord [had] to say" regarding the campaign.

Morton began reinterpreting David Duke's candidacy by drawing on the New Testament language of Romans 28:1, which discusses the people's rejection of God during biblical times and warns of the societal consequences of such rejection. Morton read the scripture as follows: "And even as they did not like to retain God in their knowledge, God gave them over to reprobate minds to do those things which are not convenient."

In Bishop Morton's exegesis, it was immorality, not racism or economic dislocation, that accounted for Duke's rise. He explained further:

Our major problem is, we are ignoring the voice of God. How do we ignore the voice of God? Well, when we fail to acknowledge God, to recognize God for who He is, in what His word is saying to us. When we fail to retain Him in our knowledge, and I just do what I want to do and whatever suits me is all right, you're headed for a problem. We took prayer out of schools. Our schools are a mess, because schools did not want to retain God in their knowledge. We have become so depressed over our economy that it doesn't matter what God says as it relates to what He has for our lives, and how we should get and how we should receive.

From outside the culture of black religion, Morton's morally centered explanation for Duke's rise might seem ahistorical. Neither prayer in schools nor a healthy economy has ever eliminated white domination in the United States. One could argue that Morton's statements promoted hegemonic values by advocating moral conservatism and legitimizing the economic status quo. Yet his use of biblical symbols subtly builds the inspiration for communal action by denigrating individual selfishness ("what I want to do and what ever suits me") and by focusing on the New Testament depiction of hate. Invoking the first chapter of Romans, Morton explicitly identified those supporting Duke as being of "reprobate mind." He explained: "A reprobate, the Bible says, that he would rather walk in darkness than in light and we're seeing today, my brothers and sisters, people are laying aside their rules and their principles and what's disturbing me, is that they're doing it to vote for a man who hates. Now you have to see the true picture, my brothers and sisters, because talk is cheap."

Morton then cited from Luke 6:44 a parable spoken by Jesus that reads: "For every tree is known for its fruit." As Jesus gave His disciples a way to identify good in others, so could Morton's parishioners recognize the fruits or falsities of Duke's newfound Christianity. Pointing out the contradictions between Duke's present statements and his past ties to the Ku Klux Klan, Morton (re)wove the parable, asserting: "Anybody can say that 'I love, and I don't hate,' but the Bible says, 'By your fruit, you shall know them.' Now that's God's word. If you plant an apple seed, you ought to see some apples. If you say that you love, there ought to be some examples of love. And what is happening, my brothers and sisters, you can take the [Ku Klux Klan] hood off, but if your speech is the same, you have not changed."

Probably unaware of the biblical contradictions to his opposition to Duke, just seven verses away—"Judge not, and ye shall not be judged; condemn not, and ye shall not be condemned; forgive and ye shall be forgiven" (Luke 6:37)—Morton soon broadened his criticism by painting a picture of Duke as Satan personified:

Let me tell you something about the devil. You have to know the devil; the devil deceives. The devil looks like he cares; he doesn't care. You see deceit

is cunning. Making someone believe that you're something that you're not.
. . . The Antichrist in the last day is going to be a human being that is going
to impress the world; people are going to be running to the Antichrist to
receive from the Antichrist. Now what's going to happen, people are going
to be so impressed, so down and so disturbed, that the Antichrist is going
to appeal to the emotion, to their self-consciousness, not to the spiritual
man, not to the God consciousness within them.

Morton further demonized Duke by indicating that the "end of time" was
approaching and, as predicted in the Book of Revelation, people would take from
the Antichrist the "mark of the Beast" (Revelation 14:9) in the "last days." Morton insinuated that Duke's followers were really following the Antichrist, saying
that "people . . . are going to be in line, [saying] 'I want the mark of the beast.'
And all the time, the devil is going to be laughing. And that number that will be
pressed in your hand or that number on your forehead, help me Holy Ghost.
. . . People standing in line, like a voting booth. Standing in line that have just
lost all principles and who don't care anymore." Morton then directly challenged
Duke's white supremacist ideology, asserting that because of the history of whites'
domination over blacks, God had provided a "special place" for African Americans as the end of time approached. Referencing Matthew 19:30, which has a
special meaning for African Americans, Morton declared:

I'm here to tell you that God has not sent David Duke to put African
Americans in their place. The reason why I know this is not true [is] because God has already put us in our place. Now some of you don't know
your place, but I know my place. I know my purpose, and I know what
God has told me in the last days. And He told me what would happen,
and He told me what my place would be in the last days, What is my place?
What is your place? Listen to what the Bible says: "The last shall be first
and the first shall be last." Now I didn't make that up. That's what God
said in the last days. And He's trying to tell white brothers and white sisters,
Wake up! You've been first a long time. We've been in slavery, we didn't
have education, we were saying "yes ma'am" and "no sir," but God is
saying it's time to take our place.

As the Hebrew Seder reminds the Jews of their past oppression, so Morton
adapts to this election God's promise of power reversal. Taking a more this-
worldly note and warning that "black militants [will] be coming from all over
this county" to say "we ain't going back," Morton predicted that Louisiana would
be "cursed" with violence if Duke were elected. Demonstrating at once both the
oppositional and system-supportive tendencies of African-American Christianity,
which I have described as an oppositional civic culture, Morton proclaimed that

righteous [black] Christians would nonviolently oppose Duke if he were elected governor:

> [T]he Christian is not going to be sitting by either. No, we are not going to be out there with guns, but Christians are going to be making a stand also. You see, because we know where the Lord has brought us from. And I'm just not going back. I'm here to tell you—you might as well call me Paul "Mandela" Morton, because I'm not going backwards. . . . As long as I am here and David Duke is in the State House, ain't gon' be no peace in the state of Louisiana, because there are some things God doesn't stand for. And God says that when it's not like Him, it doesn't have to be.

The Lord having brought black Americans from slavery, it is now up to them to support God and not to go back. Nearing the end of his sermon, Morton justified blacks' active opposition to Duke's candidacy by quoting Joshua 17:17–18, an Old Testament scripture that details the post-Exodus promises of the territory awaiting the Israelites when they reach the promised land.[8] The passage goes as follows: "And Joshua spake unto the house of Joseph, even to Ephraim and to Manasseh: saying, Thou art a great people, and hast great power: thou shalt not have one lot only: But the mountains shall be thine for it is a wood; and thou shall cut it down: and the outgoings of it shall be thine: for thou shall drive out the Canaanites, though they have iron chariots, and though they be strong."

Proclaiming that "this is what God is saying to African Americans," Morton then reinterpreted the verse "Thou art a great people and hast great power" as a call to direct action. This reinterpretation simultaneously promoted a sense of group efficacy and racial consciousness, both psychological resources for black mobilization. Morton proclaimed: "Black man, black woman, black child, you are great in God's sight. Thou art a great people and hast great power. We got to learn more and more to begin to help one another because our world is waxing colder and colder and colder."

As God promised the Israelites rewards for keeping His commandments, Morton said that God has not only "one lot" for African Americans but many earthy material benefits. He insisted:

> We have great power, but look, "Thou shalt not have one lot only." Don't be happy with one lot. God has got so many blessings out there for you. Don't be satisfied with one lot. He wants to multiply, and you've got to see that in the spirit. You got to see many blessings coming your way. Your Bible says, "He'll open up the windows." That means more than one lot, because every time a window in Heaven opens, that's another lot. So you shall have more than one lot. But look at verse eighteen . . . "But the mountain shall be thine." The high places shall be yours. Don't worry about it.

God said He's getting ready to bless you. In these last days, He's pouring out his blessings upon all of his people. He wants to do it for you.

Some analysts might see Morton's promises of blessings from God here as a form of material incentive for political participation, appealing to members' self-interest. Others might view his counsel "Don't worry about it" as a call for passivity and inaction. But this text reveals the complexity of religion's effects on black political mobilization. As Michael Dawson argues from his work on African-American political behavior, it is group-based heuristics—rather than individually based ones—that most influence the political decision-making processes of African Americans (1994a). Dawson and Wilson explain that blacks' shared experience of racial domination in the United States allows "individuals' decision-making, choice processes and utility maximization [to be] greatly economized by using the status of the group as a proxy for individual status in making social decisions" (1991, 212).

The earthly and otherworldly rewards that Morton claimed God has promised African Americans are part of the mix of factors that might inspire political action among blacks. This complexity was further demonstrated as Morton called the congregation to action: "In these last days, He's pouring out his blessings upon all of His people. He wants to do it for you. He wants to give you higher places, but look, He says you got to do something: 'For it is a wood, and thou shall cut it down.' You see, the lot is there, but you got to work to get the lot. You got to cut down the trees. There is a forest that's in the way. And you got to cut down the trees, help me Holy Ghost."

Morton's call for direct action in the campaign simultaneously evoked a negative stereotype that whites often use against blacks:

And when you cut down the forest and when you begin to work, and that's what we got to do on November 16, we got to go to the polls. There's gonna be work. Don't lay in your bed lazy. . . . If you're sick, call me to pray for you, and God will heal you right there, and get up and go to the polls. You have got to work. If we are going to claim what's rightly ours, we got to work. And the outgoings of it shall be fine. We will have victory on November 16 if we do our part.

Phrases like "in these last days," "He's pouring out blessings," "you have to work," and "claiming what's rightly ours," demonstrate how incentives for action can be articulated in terms of both this-worldly and otherworldly interests and how calls to action are articulated in both individualistic and collective terms. Likewise, as Morton explicitly said, religious faith is not antithetical to engaged action. Rather than praying Duke away, Morton used religiously assembled meanings to inspire this-worldly action.

Finally, symbolizing Duke supporters as "Canaanites," a corrupt tribal group in the Old Testament that was driven away by the Israelites so that they might claim God's promise, Morton again legitimized and urged active opposition to Duke with a biblical reference, this time from James 2:26: "Faith without work is dead! Faith without work is dead! You could have all the things that you want, but God says you got to work! And look, here's the promise: 'Thou shall drive out the Canaanites.' In this day and time, thou shall drive out Duke aiders. How are you going to drive out Duke aiders? By praying and going to the polls. By praying and going to the polls . . . You will drive them out."

Another verse, from Joshua 7, instilled the congregation with feelings of group efficacy in spite of their numerical weakness and granted divine legitimacy to the possibility of a Christian-oriented, interracial coalition opposing Duke:

> Look what it says: "Though they have armed chariots and though they be strong." I'm not going to tell you that when you look at the polls and it says it's mighty close, so it means that they're strong and all the [black] registered voters in the state of Louisiana is 28 percent. I mean they look strong, but I got some news for you. You see, everybody out there don't hate, thank God. There are some white brothers and sisters who love God's plan, who are listening to God's voice today, and what God will do is he'll take our 28 percent and he's got some white brothers and sisters who are saying "No Duke," because you are not going to destroy what God has sent to Louisiana. And God will touch white brothers and white sisters in the body of Christ, and there's enough white Christians out there, help me Holy Ghost, because if you say you love Jesus you better hear what God is saying to you today.

Morton ended his sermon by claiming that he had been personally guided by God to stop Duke, even before Duke's rise to prominence. Warning whites who might be watching the broadcast, he instructed them:

> Wake up and hear what God is saying! Yes, you are hearing it from a black man today, but you're hearing it from a Holy Ghost–filled black man who's giving to you what God has said. God saw this day when I was in Windsor, Ontario, Canada. He knew that a David Duke was gonna rise up. But He shipped me here all the way from Windsor, Ontario, Canada, and He said, "I got a preacher who's not ashamed to stand up to David Duke. Who's not ashamed to stand up to hate and tell people there is victory!"

These excerpts from Bishop Morton's sermon shed light on how religiously constructed action frames are assembled for black political mobilization. The sermon lent religious legitimization to Duke's opposition. It also provided a mechanism for interpreting his ascendancy, while promoting the identity, group consciousness, and sense of efficacy of the congregants. All of these factors encourage political mobilization. God Himself is politicized as a force opposing Duke's candidacy.

As I have emphasized throughout this analysis, activists use cultural material to construct frames of action, which inspire confidence in their goals by conveying information in familiar images and language. Simply put, culture figures considerably in the process of mobilization. In the case of African-American politics, sacred symbols and rituals provide the material from which to construct an action frame, giving sacredly ordained legitimacy to political goals. Given the perceived infallibility of the sacred, the impact of religious culture on mass activism could be far greater than that of secular culture.

9

In My Father's House

Religion and Gender in African-American Political Life

Let your women keep silent in the churches: for it is not permitted unto them to speak.

I Corinthians 14:34

I wanted to preach a great sermon about colored women sitting on high, but there wasn't no pulpit for me.

Zora Neale Hurston, *Their Eyes Were Watching God*

The general run of church women do not challenge or resent male domination in the pulpit. They accept their place in a church pattern where the shepherds of the sheep are men.

St. Clair Drake and Horace Cayton

A lot of our brothers don't mind women cleaning up in front of the pulpit, cleaning up the pulpit, but don't believe you can stand in the pulpit. If God can use Balaam's jackass to preach His word, can use a man to preach His word, God can use a woman to preach His word.

Reverend Frederick Haynes, III,
"When Black Women Wake Up"

IN THE OLD TESTAMENT STORY of the Exodus, Balaam, a pagan priest who tries to curse God's people, is steered away from evil-doing by the voice of a donkey. Seeing an angel who appears to warn Balaam of his misdeeds, the donkey balks and is punished by Balaam for refusing to move forward. The donkey says to Balaam: "What have I done to you, that you have struck me these three times?" Balaam responds: "Because you made sport of me. I wish I had a sword in my hand, for then I would kill you." The donkey responds: "Am I not your ass, upon which you have ridden all your life long to this day? Was I ever accustomed to do so to you?" (Numbers 22:21–35).

In her novel *Their Eyes Were Watching God*, Zora Neale Hurston refers to southern black women as the "mules of the world." As laborers, caretakers of their families, and sustainers of community life, black women filled many roles that needed to be filled. Their role as "doers" and "carriers" in African-American life is particularly evident in their unfailing devotion to black churches. Though Saint Paul instructed women to keep silent in the business affairs of the church, ministers like Reverend Haynes, who support the right of women to preach, remind their hearers that if God can speak through Balaam's donkey then He can also inspire women to preach. The irony of using a donkey to symbolize women's worth—an analogy I have heard used by several male ministers who *support* women clerics—is not lost when we consider the complicated and paradoxical roles black women play in black churches. As institutions that are central to black civil society, black churches are led by a male-dominated clergy yet sustained by a membership that is, on average, 70 percent female (Lincoln and Mamiya 1990).

This gender inequality in church leadership and participation presents a paradox. On the one hand, black women contribute to the upkeep of black churches through activities in which they learn and sharpen skills that facilitate their participation in electoral and community politics. On the other hand, black women's exclusion from clerical leadership and key decision-making processes in their congregations—and the biblical and doctrinal justifications for that exclusion—sanctions with sacred text the ideas and practices of male authority.

The civic and organizing skills black church women gain from their involvement in religious institutions evolve from their activities in church auxiliaries. Missionary societies, usher boards, pastor aid groups, choirs, Sunday schools, nurseries, youth groups, guilds, beautifying committees, and fundraising clubs are all mostly organized by church women. Some church auxiliaries, such as the deaconess board of the Baptist church and the stewardess board of the Methodist church, are designed specifically for women. These women-only groups almost always have less formal power and authority in deciding church policy than their male counterparts, the deacon and steward's boards. These two male dominated groups are the most powerful lay organizations in Baptist and Methodist congregations, responsible for both the financial and governing functions of congregations. The members of the deaconess and stewardess boards are usually the wives of deacons or stewards, and their leadership roles are strictly in the spiritual domain of congregations—although more women today are becoming deacons and stewards.

In his history of black churches in Brooklyn during the interwar years, Clarence Taylor documents the paradox in black women's church participation. In

Brooklyn, as in other black communities throughout the nation, black women were confined to gender-specific roles in their churches. However, these gendered roles provided a separate sphere that encouraged church-based civic action. Church women established temperance leagues, suffrage groups, missionary societies, and other voluntary associations, creating an alternative space that simultaneously provided service to black communities while giving black church women an arena to hone their leadership skills (Taylor 1994).

Yet, as Clarence Taylor shows through his analysis of church leadership patterns by gender, this alternative sphere of women's work excluded black women from the governing bodies of churches. Indeed, Taylor's observation of black churches in interwar Brooklyn can be applied across time and beyond the boundaries of Brooklyn: "Besides being barred from entering the ministry, women have had difficultly gaining positions as deacons and stewards or on the trustee boards, where financial affairs, selection of personnel, and other administrative concerns are commonly discussed and determined." He adds that black women's leadership positions have been "outside of the administrative and decision-making branches" of local congregations (1994, 168).

Today, a striking gender inequality in power and authority continues to exist in local congregations and denominational bodies. It is most glaring in the largest black religious denomination in the nation—the National Baptist Convention, Incorporated—although dramatic gender inequalities in church leadership can also be found in the all-male bishoprics of the AME, AME Zion, CME, and the COGIC churches. The governing body of the National Baptist Convention has only a handful of women. Although Baptist women established their own "Women's Convention" at the turn of the century, that convention operates as a "department" of a denomination whose membership is over two-thirds female. The president, secretary, treasurer, and six vice-presidents of the National Baptist Convention are all male; the supervisor of the denomination's Sunday school publishing board and the two representatives of the Women's Convention are female. Even in church activities where women clearly dominate—such as the foreign and home mission boards—male ministers chair the convention's committees.[1]

Whether women consent to formal and informal exclusion in church governance or fight for their inclusion, the existence of an autonomous space for women has both an empowering and a restraining effect on black women's religious and political leadership. Some scholars, such as Cheryl Townsend Gilkes, note the benefits of autonomous spaces for church women. She argues that black women's gender roles in churches do not reflect sexism, since "Euro-American modes of sexual oppression are not totally reproduced in the public affairs of Afro-American life" (1997, 370). Other scholars, such as Dolores Williams, recognize at least implicitly the shortcomings of these spaces, commenting: "[T]oo long have black women in the churches taken a back seat and not pushed ahead for female leadership to be visible in the major and financially benefiting roles in the churches" (1993, 219).

When Balaam's donkey—with God's direction—rescues Balaam from danger, the angel tells Balaam that if the donkey (a female), "had not turned aside from me surely just now I would have *slain you and let her live*" (Numbers 22:33: my emphasis). This act symbolizes the idea of a common bond between black women and black men. That the faithful donkey redeems Balaam by putting his interests first, despite his dominion over her, is an allegory of the way race often overrides gender in the political preferences of black women.[2] The religious thrust behind the "redemption" of black men—including political leaders such as Marion Barry, entertainers like Mike Tyson and O. J. Simpson, and religious leaders like Henry Lyons of the National Baptist Convention—allows us to ask whether black women's socialization in an institution that legitimizes male authority may lead them to see black men's concerns as preeminent over those of black women.

The question of whether gender or race predominantly affects the lives of black women has been extensively debated by feminist scholars. But religious perspectives and experiences with racism have made black women suspicious of the feminist movement, a movement that has been dominated by middle-class white women. Writing during the height of mobilization for the Equal Rights Amendment, Dr. Ethel M. Gordon, in her book celebrating the seventy-fifth year of the women's auxiliary to the National Baptist Convention, explicitly endorsed the importance of race over gender in the lives of black women and the religious justifications behind black women's race loyalty:

> I am not optimistic about full equality [for women], nor do I champion it on all occasions and dimensions. Man and woman are meant to share the earth as complements to God's unchanging plan—Not always equals—Not antagonists—Particularly not so for us who are black and have witnessed the demoralizing impact of this world's dominance on our men. . . . Black sisters, we must support our men and bolster their morale, for the "lib" that liberates us from any of the cherished connections to earthy or Heavenly relation is no "lib" at all, but slavery thinly veiled. (1976, 74)

This chapter explores the effects of religion on gender politics in African-American life. First, it examines Afro-Christianity's impact on black civic culture. It argues that although Afro-Christianity has provided ideological and material resources to resist racial domination, it has also privileged patriarchy, another form of human domination that affects the lives of black women. Patriarchy has operated through religiously sanctioned rules that exclude women from sharing power and authority *with* men, a practice that became especially entrenched in mainstream black religious institutions just as black men were excluded from the nation's political sphere in the late nineteenth century.

Second, I examine support for women's participation in the most powerful position in churches—the clergy. To assess attitudes toward gender equality in the religious sphere, I compare ministers' and church members' attitudes on the idea of women being members of the clergy. I then compare black women who are the most active in their churches with those who are the least active, looking at their support for women in both religious and political leadership. Third, I look at both how ideas about manhood shape black discourse about black men's lack of participation in churches and how those ideas serve as a magnet for black men's interests in the Black Muslim sect the Nation of Islam. Finally, by comparing black women's participation in church life with the participation of black men, white women, and white men, I show the enormous benefit that black women gain politically from their extensive participation in church life.

PATRIARCHAL NORMS IN A CIVIC CULTURE OF OPPOSITION

As I have argued throughout, the culture and institutions of Afro-Christianity serve dual purposes in African-American political activism. The institutions, feelings of self-empowerment, and sacred rituals and symbols of Afro-Christianity both reinforce the reigning values of the dominant society and oppose the ideas and practices of racial domination. Yet while opposing racial domination, this civic culture of opposition has had less influence in challenging the sexism black women face in black communities and throughout American society. Dolores Williams, following other black feminist theorists, explains that "black women . . . must realize that black men may disagree with and fight white men over racism, but far too many black men and white men (preachers included) are throughly bonded in their affirmation of the subordination of women" (1993, 214). Because black women are affected by their race, gender, and class positions in American society, they experience what many black feminist scholars have termed triple jeopardy, a situation in which black women are affected by the "interlocking systems" of race, class, and gender subordination.

These multiple categories of subordination have not led to the formation of an oppositional consciousness that challenges these three forms of oppression at once. For African Americans—men and women, poor and affluent—a political consciousness that counters the ideas and practices of white supremacy has been the dominant mode of organized resistance, in spite of the dehumanizing effects of sexism and classism in the lives of black women. The predominance of race is not surprising. "One system of domination may in fact enjoy a position of privilege and power in the next" form of human domination (Morris 1992, 364). While an ideology of linked fate with all blacks might bind the political interests of black men and women against racial domination, the norms and structures of male authority that operate in Afro-Christianity continue to enjoy a privileged position in African-American political life. Because "oppositional consciousness is often locked in a reactive stance," as Morris further explains, "it usually does not reject all the viewpoints and interests embraced by a hegemonic consciousness, but only those that are repugnant to the perceived interests of a particular oppressed group" (363).

Patriarchy is embedded in the structure of nearly all religions. In a historical review of women's participation in black churches, Dolores C. Carpenter points out that male members of the clergy have used the Bible both to challenge racist ideas and practices in American society and to restrict women's leadership in church and denominational affairs (1990–1991).

Black and white male clerics do not differ in the biblical justifications they give for women's exclusion from the clergy. Women, they say, should not preach because they were not among the twelve disciples (Matthew 10:2–4); Eve was responsible for man's downfall (Genesis 2:18); women were created by God to assist men as "helpmates," and thus should not attempt to undermine men's God-given authority over women (Genesis 2:18); God made man head of women, as God is head of the church (I Corinthians 11:3); and Paul instructed the church of Corinth to command women to keep silent in the business affairs of the church (I Corinthians 14:34), a charge reinforced in the private sphere of the home, where wives are instructed to submit to their husband's authority (Ephesians 5:22).[3] Except in the Methodist denominations, which dropped their restrictions against women clergy around the time of World War II, male clergy have used these and other biblical justifications to exclude women from the ministry as well as from the decision-making bodies of local churches and denominational bodies.

BLACK CHURCHES, PATRIARCHAL STRUCTURES, AND AFRICAN-AMERICAN POLITICAL DEVELOPMENT

The mass inclusion of African American men in the nation's political sphere during the mid–nineteenth century occurred during the period when black denominational bodies were building or solidifying their institutional base. Institution-building accompanied the development of the gendered organizational structures that today remain a part of the practices of local congregations and denominational bodies. Norms and rules restricting women's participation in religious institutions became especially rigid at the close of the century when black men were being stripped of their voting rights. Responding to the imposition of rules excluding their involvement in the business affairs of the church, black church women created "alternative models of power, authority, and leadership" in local churches and denominational bodies (Gilkes 1994, 85). As we have seen, auxiliary groups like the Women's Convention of the National Baptist Convention, the missionary societies of the AME church, and the Women's Department of the Church of God in Christ allowed church women to govern their own programs, a development that helped foster black women's participation in community organizing and, when opportunities availed themselves, in electoral politics.

Whether separate religious spheres are a reflection of patriarchal practices or a part of African-American religious traditions that are "benignly patriarchal" is the question at the center of the controversy about black women's participation in religious institutions. Some scholars argue that gendered norms and structures should not be viewed as a device to perpetuate male domination while others point out that Afro-Christianity furthers the ideas of patriarchy. Dolores Williams, who challenges the patriarchy in Afro-Christianity, argues that the gendered leadership arrangements in mainstream black churches are a reflection of the dominant society's sexism with regard to all women (Williams 1993).

Cheryl Townsend Gilkes brings a different interpretation to the gendered norms and practices of Afro-Christianity, arguing that black churches exhibit an "ambivalent patriarchy." She argues that the gendered norms and structures in black churches reflect the "dual sex" political system that blacks derived from their West African heritage. "The West African women who came to the New World," Gilkes explains, "came with a highly developed sense of their importance to a polity and an economy. Slavery, then, was a loss of authority for women as well as men. Any struggle to gain autonomy and retain authority over their lives, from an African perspective, was a struggle for both female and male authority" (1994, 89).

Gilkes explains that the informal power and authority that black women have in local congregations and denominational bodies are key to understanding the "dual-sex system." Though church women may not have formal authority and power, many church women function informally as a "bridge between the women's world and men's world" of Afro-Christianity (1997, 370). Gilkes points to the "church mother," an honorific and informal position usually bestowed upon the most senior woman of a congregation, as an example of black women's informal power in churches. This position, which comes with no formal role or authority, exists only in black Protestant churches. The institutional memory of these women, and the respect in which they are held by male leaders and congregants alike allow church mothers to give, as Gilkes explains, "advice, warnings, and cautions" to male church leaders:

> Occasionally, the church mother performs the role of a stage manager or a director of public worship. Where tension exists concerning certain practices, her opinion may prevail. In one Baptist congregation, the insistence of a church mother that "this is not a Sanctified church!" moved the deacon board to call an emergency meeting with the pastor in order to persuade him to withdraw his permission for drums to be used during the morning service: the church mother prevailed. Other members of the congregation

may walk out when they disagree with the pastor, but their actions will be ignored. The church mother is never ignored. (1994, 92–93)

Although Gilkes recognizes the importance of informal norms in shaping black women's leadership, her explanations for the evolution of those norms raise more questions than they answer. The emergence of structures and norms of women's exclusion occurred after Emancipation, a fact that challenges the theory of an unbroken link to the dual-sex norms of leadership in West African societies. Although the music and spirituality of Afro-Christianity do exhibit traces of West African culture, it is less clear how the institutional dynamics of West African societies survived several generations of slavery and were *then* incorporated into the institutional design of local congregations and denominational bodies at the end of the nineteenth century. In fact, as Gilkes herself recognizes, the alternative spheres of women's religious life appeared to be less prominent in slave communities than in black communities after slavery. The evidence we have indicates that, with the exception of slave preachers (selected by plantation owners), religious practices tended to be more egalitarian regarding gender during the slave era than *after* slavery (1994, 90–91).

Moreover, the alternative spheres for church women and the development of informal roles of power and authority did not emerge in the Catholic and Protestant churches of African-derived populations in the Caribbean, Latin America, and South America (except, perhaps, in the American-based AME churches in those societies). Nor is it clear from Gilkes's argument which norms and structures were derived from West African societies and which from "the imposition of Euro-American patriarchy" (1994, 84), since gendered patterns of leadership also exist in the predominately white Baptist and Methodist denominations. The historical record suggests that gendered institutional arrangements in Afro-Christianity occurred just as the National Baptist Convention and the predominately-black Methodist denominations developed into full-fledged national bodies.

Lincoln and Mamiya present the counter-theory to that of Gilkes—that the patriarchal values of the larger mainstream and of Christianity itself were responsible for the sexism in black churches: "As the invisible, underground religion of the slave churches merged into the visible, institutional black churches of Baptist and Methodist persuasion, the freedmen and the former slaves who founded these churches often accepted in toto the rules, beliefs, hierarchy, structure, and patriarchal conventions of their white counterparts from whose churches they were now separated" (1990, 278).

In her work on black women's political activism in the aftermath of the Civil War, Elsa Barkley Brown documents how practices excluding women from the decision-making arenas of black political and social life were less pronounced right after Emancipation than they were toward the end of the nineteenth century.

Although black women were denied the right to vote in the American polity, she argues that in the immediate post-Emancipation period the newly freed men, women, and children all understood the franchise as a collective good, not the exclusive preserve of male voters. This collective understanding of the vote for freedmen changed when black male leaders began to embrace the dominant society's views and practices toward women. Thus, Brown argues, the creation of alternative spheres for women's work (both religious and secular) in the late nineteenth century evolved not from the dual sex practices of West African societies but because black women were seeking "not a new authority but rather a lost authority, one that they now often sought to justify on a distinctively female basis" (1994, 108).

The emergence of a new authority for women at the turn of the century opened "free spaces" for the development of a proto-feminist consciousness among black women that interacted with their feelings of racial solidarity. In an informative history of the founding of the Women's Convention of the National Baptist Convention, Evelyn Brooks Higginbotham shows how black Baptist women resisted their exclusion from positions of power, forming a separate all-female auxiliary to the ministerially led National Baptist Convention. As Higginbotham explains, the Women's Convention developed both during the "women's era," an intensive period of women's activism around social reform and suffrage, and the "nadir," the lowest point of blacks' civil rights since slavery. The Women's Convention addressed the concerns of women and "the race." Although black Baptist women did not challenge men's exclusive right to the pulpit, activist church women nonetheless resisted the patriarchal views of male church leaders by developing from biblical texts a "feminist theology" that contested women's subordinated roles in church polity. Higginbotham explains that black Baptist women "working within the orthodoxy of the church turned to the Bible to argue their rights—thus holding men accountable to the same text that authenticated their arguments for racial equality. In drawing upon the Bible—the most respected source within their community—they found spiritual precedents for expanding women's rights" (1993, 120).

THE POLITICAL CONSEQUENCES OF GENDERED SPHERES

This early formation of an alternative sphere for women's work in the churches has complicated black women's leadership in politics. As black women began to assert themselves in the decision-making realms of male-dominated political organizations, they met resistance from male leaders. Scholars of black life often do not make a connection between the gendered practices in black churches and men's resistance to women's political leadership outside the church. Feminist writer Patricia Hill Collins, for instance, commends church women's alternative spheres of influence but at the same time praises women political activists for rejecting sexism in political organizations. Noting that black women's roles in churches are "far more complex than that proposed by traditional models arguing that female 'followers' obey orders of male 'leaders,' " Collins, like Gilkes, argues that "men and women exert different types of leadership within black church communities" (1991, 152). But when she discusses black women's *political* leadership, she praises women activists—like Ella Baker and Septima Clark—for their ability to "routinely reject modes of authority based on hierarchial power relations (157)."

Yet the ideology behind women's alternative spheres in the church probably contributed to male resistance to women's leadership in politics. Women activists like Baker and Clark were challenging the SCLC, an organization that operated on the basis of the gendered, hierarchial practices of the Baptist church and was, as Aldon Morris puts it, the"decentralized political arm of the black church" (1984, 77). Its organizational structure and decision-making process reflected Baptist norms and practices. The founders of the SCLC were mostly Baptist ministers, and the group's executive board operated like a deacon's board, with ultimate decision-making powers vested in Martin Luther King. His charismatic leadership held the group together in the same way that a pastor secures his leadership over a local congregation.

Given the SCLC's links to the norms and the practices of the Baptist church, it is not surprising that women activists like Baker and Clark met resistance from this all-male black clergy. Accustomed to an alternative sphere of women's work, where women assisted men but did not intrude in the administrative and policy-making decisions of churches, the ministerially led SCLC expected the women in their organization to follow that model. Baker, who was committed to a group-centered approach to decision-making and leadership (a style antithetical to the norms of the Baptist-influenced SCLC), explains how these religious norms undermined her leadership in the SCLC:

> There would never be any role for me in a leadership capacity with SCLC. Why? First, I'm a woman. Also, I'm *not* a minister. And second . . . I knew that my penchant for speaking honestly . . . would not be well tolerated. The combination of the basic attitude of women in *their leadership setup* is—*that of taking orders, not providing leadership*—and the ego problems involved in having to feel that there is someone who . . . had more information about a lot of things than they possessed at that time. . . . This would never have lent itself to my being a leader in the movement there. (Quoted in Giddings 1984, 312, emphasis mine)

Septima Clark's experience did not differ much from Baker's. She would recall how her work in the SCLC was constantly challenged by churchmen:

The thing that I think stands out a whole lot was the fact that women could never be accorded their rightful place even in the Southern Christian Leadership Conference. I can't never forget Reverend Abernathy saying, "Why is Mrs. Clark on the executive board?" And Dr. King saying, "Why she designed a whole program." "Well I just can't see why you got to have her on the board!" They just didn't feel as if a woman, you know, had any sense. (Quoted in McFadden 1990, 93)

Josephine Carson, who collected the experiences of southern black women during the civil rights movement, recorded one woman's description of her experience in a South Carolina church: "Here the church is all a man's domain and the women really don't have much to say. They do a lot of work, they cook for the picnics and socials, and they raise the most money and they kind of keep the church going, but when you get to policy, the men have it all tied up. They don't want a woman in any kind of power"[4]

Because of their difficulties in becoming ministers in mainstream black denominations, many black women interested in preaching have started their own congregations, often in Pentecostal, Holiness, or Spiritualist churches that operate from storefronts in urban communities. Yet when these independent congregations are organized into formal religious associations, men tend to dominate the leadership positions. In his study of Spiritualist churches, Hans A. Baer finds that "[w]hile the black Spiritualist movement never fostered an updated version of the cult of true womanhood," it nonetheless "developed a contradictory pattern of both challenging patterns of male dominance and reinforcing them." This contradiction is reflected in the Spiritualist church associations. "As the Spiritual movement underwent a process of institutionalization," Baer reports, "women came to play a less significant role in many of its larger associations, despite the fact that they played a highly instrumental role in the establishment of the earliest Spiritual churches in cities such as Chicago, New Orleans, and Nashville" (1993, 79). As churches become institutionalized, they may pick up the gender bias of mainstream society, regardless of the more egalitarian gender practices of local congregations.[5]

Whether black women learn civic or organizing skills through independent churches that are relatively free of gender bias or through alternative spheres within more mainstream churches, those skills still enhance their participation in secular politics. Yet the enhancement may come in a form that encourages the maintenance of a separate women's political sphere. Throughout the twentieth century, black women have developed separate political spheres of their own through organizations like the National Association of Colored Women and the National League of Negro Women or created auxiliary organizations to political organizations and movements dominated by male leaders.

Women auxiliaries existed in Marcus Garvey's black nationalist movement, in A. Phillip Randolph's Brotherhood of Sleeping Car Porters (Chateauvert 1998), and as fundraising committees in local Urban League and NAACP chapters. Even the SCLC, despite Ella Baker and Septima Clark's criticism of its exclusion of women from leadership, still maintains a separate sphere of women's work through its auxiliary, SCLC Women.

ATTITUDES TOWARD WOMEN'S CLERICAL AND POLITICAL LEADERSHIP

How might the development of gendered norms and practices in Afro-Christianity influence attitudes toward black women's religious and political leadership? Support for women's clerical leadership shows its widest gap not between men and women, as we might expect, but between the male-dominated clergy and church members. In figure 9.1, support for women clerics among both ministers and the laity is presented for three denominations—COGIC, Baptist, and Methodist. The data for the clergy came from Lincoln and Mamiya's survey of black ministers (conducted between 1978 and 1983), which asked black ministers whether or not they approved (or strongly approved) or disapproved (or strongly disapproved) of women as pastors. The data for lay support came from the 1993 National Black Politics Study, which asked respondents: "Black churches or places of worship should allow more women to become members of the clergy—do you strongly agree, somewhat agree, somewhat disagree, or strongly disagree?" Estimates for both ministers and laity in figure 9.1 reflect positive responses (either strongly agree and somewhat agree or approve and strongly approve) in support of women being clerics.

Although the differences in dates and wording make it hard to compare these two surveys, the ministerial and lay support nevertheless seem rather large. While only half (52 percent) the black ministers surveyed thought that women should be "pastors," a huge majority of black church members (78 percent) supported women in the ministry. The Methodist ministers and laity seem to have parallel views, but whereas an overwhelming majority of lay Baptists (77 percent), Methodists (89 percent), and members of the COGIC (84 percent) favor women clerics, only about a third of Baptist ministers (29 percent) and a quarter of COGIC ministers support the idea.

The Baptist church and the COGIC have, far more than the Methodist, an alternative religious sphere for women. They also have ministers who are the least supportive of women clergy. The COGIC not only explicitly forbids women to be ordained ministers, but its denominational rules also explicitly exclude women from key decision-making positions in the denomination, including the position of church elder (Lincoln and Mamiya 1990, 287–288). The various Baptist de-

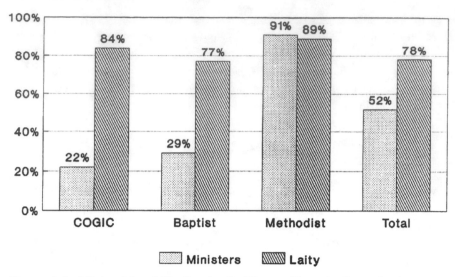

FIGURE 9.1. *Ministerial and Lay Support for Women Clergy, by Denomination. Source: Lincoln and Mamiya (1990) and the 1993 National Black Politics Study.*

nominations have no official rules that prevent women from becoming clergy, but "the general climate has not been supportive of women preaching and pastoring churches" (287).

In contrast to the Baptist and COGIC ministers, ministers from Methodist denominations (i.e., AME church, AME Zion, the CME church, and the United Methodist church) give nearly unanimous approval of women ministers. The solid support for women clerics in Methodism comes from its organizational structure and history of being relatively inclusive of women. The AME Zion church ordained women to preach in the late nineteenth century, at the same time that the Baptist and COGIC were creating separate spheres of women's work. And although the AME church and the CME church did not ordain women to preach until 1948 and 1954, respectively, women in those denominations had been pushing for inclusion in the church's leadership structure since the late nineteenth century. The denomination's response to demands for women's inclusion was to institute a separate—and not-so-equal—leadership role for women through the stewardess board. Unlike the stewards' board, however, membership in the stewardess board was not a step toward ordination until restrictions were dropped after World War II (Lincoln and Mamiya 1990, 285).

In contrast to the Baptist polity, where each local congregation determines its own policies and where ministers are accountable only to their members and not to a denominational authority, the episcopal polity of the Methodist churches promotes practices and norms throughout its member congregations. The uniform rules of Methodism and Methodism's relatively longer tradition of including

Table 9.1 Black Support for Women Clergy by Gender

I am going to read some questions and please tell me if you strongly agree, somewhat agree, somewhat disagree: Black churches or places of worship should allow more women to become members of the clergy.	Women	Men	Total
Strongly agree	41%	53%	45%
Somewhat agree	34%	30%	33%
Somewhat disagree	12%	6%	10%
Strongly disagree	12%	11%	11%
Total number of cases	735	405	1140

Source: 1993 National Black Politics Study.
Total sample = 1,206

women in the ministry undoubtably account for the nearly unanimous support for women clergy among both clergy and laity.

A look at gender differences among church members reveals another paradox: lay women are less likely to support women clergy than lay men. Table 9.1 shows that although slightly more than half of the male respondents (53 percent) to the National Black Politics Study "strongly agreed" that women should be allowed to be ministers, only 41 percent of women thought so, a difference of twelve percentage points. And while 17 percent of men either "disagreed" or "strongly disagreed" with the idea of women clerics, nearly a quarter of black women (24 percent) disagreed with the idea.[6] Women, who are the most committed and active in churches, are the least supportive of women clergy. Of black women who report attending church weekly, 73 percent support the idea of women clergy, compared to 80 percent of the black women who are less active in their churches—that is, attend church several times a month or less. This softer support for women clergy among women might be attributed to their socialization in an institution that has traditionally been led by men. Dolores Carpenter explains black women's opposition to women ministers as follows:

The image of God as Father exercises a very strong association in some women's minds with the images of their fathers. This image is readily transferred to the male minister. Additionally, and regrettably, most black women, observing the relative powerlessness of black women of our world, where men are treated with far greater respect, transfer this consciousness into the exalted image of the male preacher. This exalted image restores their confidence in black men in general, and, in turn, fills a great need for hopefulness in the face of societal and media emasculation of the black male. Given the inordinate focus upon black men who are unemployed, physically abusive, incarcerated, drug dealers, drug addicts, or gay, there is a need to identity strong male figures who speak with authority, wield power, and display moderate affluence. (1990–1991, 20–21)

Although black women are in general more likely than white women to support feminist principles, black women's support for feminist principles softens among black women who are the most active in their churches.

This group not only is less likely to favor women clergy, it is also less likely to favor black women's political leadership. Asked to choose which statement is most true, whether "Black women should share equally in the political leadership of the black community" or "Black women should not undermine black male leadership," 79 percent agreed that black women should share equally in political leadership. Exactly the same percentage of men give the same response. However, only 77 percent (N = 255) of black women attending church weekly support the idea of black men and women sharing political leadership, especially compared to 81 percent of women attending church once or twice a month (N = 164) and 90 percent of women attending only once or twice a year (N = 46).

A similar pattern emerges in asking the degree of attention that should be given black men's concerns. Asked whether the problems of black men "deserve special attention" or the problems of black men and women "deserve equal attention," the black women most active in church are more likely to agree that black males deserve special attention. Only 50 percent of black women who attend church weekly agree that the problems of black men and women deserve equal attention, compared to 63 percent of black women attending less than once a week.

The lower support that active church women give to the idea of gender equality is explained partly by differences in generations or active engagement in the church. If we look separately at women under and over age fifty, we find that the most active church women do not differ from the least active when questioned about black women's leadership. Of black women below fifty (N = 146) who attend church weekly, 81 percent are just as supportive of gender equality in political leadership as women below fifty who attend church less than once a week (N = 128). However, when estimating black women's views on whether the problems of black men deserve special attention, regular church attendance rather than generational differences is the factor that contributes most to black women's greater sympathy toward black men's problems.[7]

Bringing Men Back in: Masculinity and Patriarchy in Afro-Christianity

In a primer that encourages black men to "return" to black churches, community activist Jawanza Kunjufu lists twenty-one reasons why black men are not active in churches (1994). Although several of these explanations could be given by either men or women—for instance, the hypocrisy of ministers, the financial commitments that come with church membership, long church services, and formal dress codes—several other explanations had to do with masculinity. Comments from Kunjufu's focus group of unchurched black men reveal that many of them see Christianity as incompatible with "black manhood." Kunjufu reports that these men believe that the image of Christ is "wimpish" and encourages black men to "turn the other cheek" in response to racial injustice; that the traditions of "blond and blue-eyed" images of Christ reflect blacks' self-hatred and capitulation to white supremacy; that religious services are too emotionally driven because the churches are dominated by women, who "by nature" are emotional; and that, unlike the Nation of Islam, which among many unchurched men represents the essence of black manhood, black churches attract homosexuals.

These views on Christianity and masculinity are both a cause and a response to the respect that Louis Farrakhan and the Nation of Islam garner among black men. As the only religious organization in African-American society where men outnumber women, the Nation of Islam competes against black churches for the religious commitment of young black men. In response, rap artist Joseph "Run" Simmons of the rap group Run-DMC justifies his devotion to Christianity by countering the Eurocentric, "effeminate" images of Christ:

> [T]he picture of Jesus with the light blue eyes and blond hair and the 105 pounds is not the description given in the Bible. He had to carry that cross a long way to be some 105-pound skinny white man with blue eyes. Jesus was bad. He would walk in places where there was gambling in a temple and turn the tables over. The Bible talks about him having matted bronze-colored hair and bronze-colored skin, and he wasn't a punk. He was bad. (Linden 1993)

Contemporary gospel performer Kirk Franklin also reveals how young black males see Christianity as feminine space, and how he responded to participating in a church choir by asserting his manhood: "[W]hen I was growing up . . . the guys in the church were considered gay, sissies. So whatever it took for me to prove that I wasn't that, that's what I did. From trying to sleep around, drink, go to clubs, smoke. Man, when I was in high school, I was called gay so much that I used to wake up in the morning crying and begging my mother not to send me to school" (Light 1997).

Perhaps because of this widespread fear of the feminization associated with Christianity, churches that are the most successful at wooing black men tend to be the most patriarchal in their outlook. In his analysis of why black men are returning to church, Tucker Carlson cites "orthodox readings of the Bible" and the rejection of "modern forces" that allow black men to "reclaim their place in the home" (1992, 13). Writing three years before the Million Man March, which called black men to "reclaim their communities," Carlson argued that "the more feminized churches become, the less men want to join them." He argued that instead of joining churches that are dominated by women, black men "will opt instead to join other organizations where women are institutionally excluded from positions of leadership" (14).[8] Carlson saw fundamentalist churches drawing black men to church when they "teach that men are ordained by God to be the leaders of their families" and that "God governs the family directly through the husband, who in turn has the final word in decisions regarding his wife and children" (16).

These views on women's roles do not differ much from those of the Promise Keepers, an all-male movement of mostly white religious conservatives. Nor do they differ from those of nationalist leaders of the all-black Million Man March. Ben Chavis, one of the march organizers, who had been ousted from the presidency of the NAACP on charges of sexual harassment, seeks to reinforce the hegemonic ideology of patriarchy even as he opposes racial and economic injustice. A Christian who later converted to the Nation of Islam and who believes (like Supreme Court justice Clarence Thomas) that charges of sexual harassment have been used as a "weapon" against black men, Chavis thinks that it is "retardant to the African-American struggle for freedom . . . when sisters and brothers battle each other. . . . *Our problem is not gender.* . . . Our problem is racism. . . . Our problem is economic exploitation" (Powell 1994; my emphasis).

Louis Farrakhan, leader of the Nation of Islam and the Million Man March, asserts men's authority over women in his political discourse. Like many black ministers, he also believes in an alternative sphere of women's work. Writing *two years* before the Million Man March, Farrakhan gave a racialized and religious explanation to justify black men's "rule" over black women:

> Now, the qualities of a female that God gives her, sometimes in much more abundance than the male, because of her duty to nurture life, the female is much more tolerant, patient, forbearing, loving, long-suffering. All of these are feminine qualities. The male side are the attributes that deal with the power side, you know. Not that women don't have power, but the male should have more in order to rule. And since God made the man to rule and gave him power and dominion in order that he might exercise rule . . . when you take power and dominion away from the man, that is castrating the man.[9]

He then explained how women's resistance to male domination undermines men's masculinity and how white men have undermined black men's rule over black women:

> "By challenging his ability to rule, you are automatically casting him in a subordinate, dependent role such as the nature of the female. Ya'll alright?

What the white man wanted to do to us as black men is deprive us of the two things they don't want us to have: power and dominion. Why? Because if they're in power you can't have power. If they are the rule, they don't want you to rule. So the white man makes sure you never come into too much power to exercise any rule because this is the white man's world and the white man's house and everybody black in it must serve him. Well then if he castrates you how do you look in the eyes of your female? Just look at it, brothers.

THE PARTICIPATORY PARADOXES OF PATRIARCHAL STRUCTURES

Notwithstanding the gendered practices of local churches and denominational bodies and the masculinist perspectives on black men's lack of involvement in churches, black women politically benefit from their intensive participation in church activities. Through their church work, black women probably gain more civic and organizing skills than black men, white women and white men. Figure 9.2 shows the distribution of weekly church attendance by race and gender for five time periods, spanning the early 1970s to the early 1990s.

About a third of both black and white women report attending religious services at least once a week. This pattern in women's church attendance has been consistent for all four time periods. In contrast, black men's and white men's regular church attendance has hovered around 20 percent, although white men have a slight edge over black men. These patterns in men's regular church attendance challenge assumptions about the "recent" exodus of black men from churches. Black men's regular attendance at church services has remained much the same since the early 1970s. Moreover, their level of participation does not differ greatly from that of white men, having dropped by only 2 percent in three decades.

The gap in church attendance between black women and men may have political consequences. Although statistical models from survey data show no significant difference in black men and women's reported voter participation, government statistics on voter turnout show a small advantage to women. In almost every age category used by the Census Bureau to estimate voter turnout, black women report higher levels of turnout than black men. During the 1992 fall election, the gap between black women's voter turnout (56 percent) and black men's (51 percent) was five percentage points, while the gap between white men and women was two percentage points. Black women's relatively higher voter turnout defies conventional understandings of who votes. Since black women's average income and education levels are less than those of white women and black men, we would expect their voter activity to reflect their relatively low socioeconomic status.

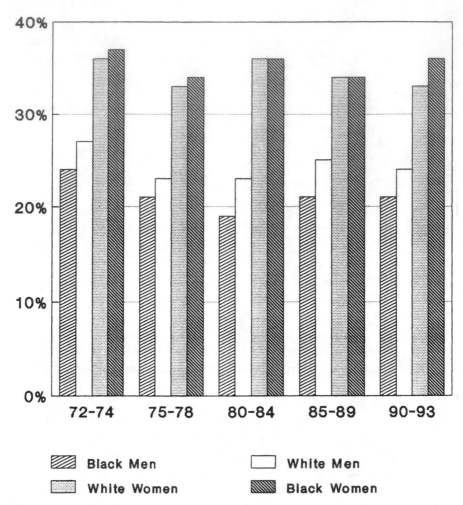

FIGURE 9.2. *Church Attendance by Race and Gender, 1970s–1990s. Source: General Social Survey, 1972–1983.*

Regular church attendance increases individuals' political participation in two ways. First, as I have argued throughout, church attendance encourages voter participation by fostering a sense of civic duty. Second, regular church attendance exposes churchgoers to political information, which in turn increases the likelihood that they will vote, campaign for candidates, and participate in community politics. Black churchgoers receive more information about politics than white churchgoers, giving black congregants who regularly attend church greater opportunities to be mobilized at their church than whites who do so.

Black women's regular church attendance may provide at least one explanation. Jesse Jackson's 1984 presidential election campaign, which relied on church networks to mobilize black voters, is instructive. In that election, black women's voter turnout rate was substantially higher than black men's, especially in the age groups in which black women substantially outnumber black men in church attendance. For instance, in the 18–20 age category, the male-female difference in reported voter turnout was eleven percentage points; in the 21–24 age group, gap was six points. For the 25–34 and 35–44 age groups the gap hovered around ten percentage points, but it narrowed considerably in the age groups where black men's church attendance is highest. For the 55–64 and 65–74 age groups, the gap in black men and women's voter turnout was less than two percentage points.[10]

Black women gain not only from their church attendance but also from their extensive participation in church work. Not only is black women's regular attendance in church services likely to boost their voting, so is their participation in church activities. As we have seen, participation in church organizations has a greater effect on fostering voter participation among blacks than whites. Figure 9.3 shows the degree of participation in church-affiliated groups by race and gender from the 1970s and the 1990s. Black women are more engaged in church work than white women, black men, or white men. During the 1970s, about 55 percent of all black women were members of church groups; by the early 1990s their rate of participation had declined to 45 percent, a drop of ten percentage points. White women's involvement in church work has remained relatively stable, hovering around 40 percent, but is still noticeably lower than black women's.

Although black men attend church less than white men, they are more involved in church-affiliated groups than white men. Their greater involvement here is probably explained by the attraction of the patriarchal power they can exercise in these groups. Even so, however, their participation may have eroded slightly since the 1970s. Their participation in church-affiliated groups fell from 43 percent in the mid-1970s to 37 percent in the early 1990s. Yet black women's participation in church life has declined still further, from 55 percent in the mid-1970s to 44 percent in 1990–1993. The different levels of black women's and men's participation in church life may partially account for the fact that black women are more engaged in politics than one would expect from their income and education.

The greater participation in church life by black women shows the unintended, positive benefits of the gendered norms and practices of churches. But those norms and practices come with a price. While the male-dominated clergy are "community leaders" and their mostly female members are "footsoldiers" for mobilization, the types of issues that ministers mobilize around can privilege men's concerns over women's. Elsa Barkley Brown calls this privilege in African-American politics and society the "masculinization of race progress" (1994, 145). When boxer Mike Tyson was tried for raping a Miss Black America beauty contest contestant, black ministers rallied to his support. A petition drive was circulated

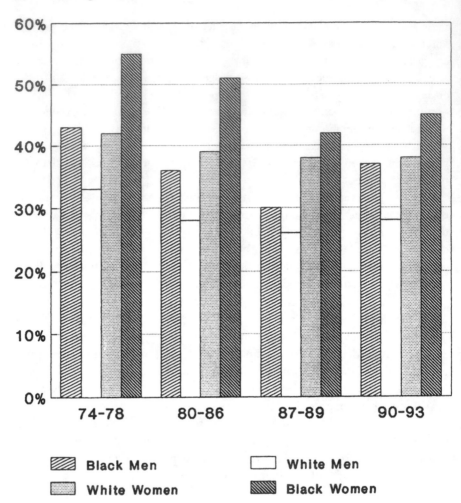

FIGURE 9.3. *Participation in Church-Affiliated Groups by Race and Gender, 1970s–1990s. Source: General Social Survey, 1974–1993.*

in black churches in Indianapolis, where Tyson's trial was held, asking the judge presiding over the trial to "consider that Mr. Tyson is one of a very few modern-day heroes. . . . It is very difficult, no matter what the reason, to see a fallen hero and not be affected."[11] The petition drive was headed by Reverend T. J. Jemison, who was then president of the National Baptist Convention and who had been active in the civil rights struggles of the 1950s and 1960s. The FBI later investigated Jemison for supposedly offering the plaintiff one million dollars to drop her case against Tyson. Ministerial groups also mobilized in behalf of fallen "male heroes" such as Clarence Thomas, O. J. Simpson, and Marion Barry, all of whom were publicly accused of exploiting women.

Finally, the gendered dynamics of churches also have consequences for black women's religious and political leadership. Although there has been much progress over the past two decades in the number of women clerics, the idea of an alternative sphere of women's work can have the negative effect of legitimizing male leadership in both the religious and political spheres. Rather than promoting the idea of shared leadership between black men and black women, the belief in an alternative sphere of women's work undervalues church women's contributions to black political activism. The words of Reverend Addie Wyatt are instructive here. Recounting women's participation in Harold Washington's 1983 Chicago mayoral campaign, she implicitly revealed part of the gender inequality inherent in the idea of an alternative sphere of women's work and provides hope for the day when church women's political activism will be adequately acknowledged:

> [W]omen are the majority in our churches. But those are the same women [who raised money for Harold Washington's campaign]. That's why I say that we gave more than one hundred thousand dollars because we helped to raise monies in our churches. . . . Wherever people were, we worked. We took credit for what we did as a women's organization or Women for Washington, but that wasn't all that women did. And you see in the church, we have always been included but not recognized to the extent that we should be. We built our churches; we make them and we really never ask for our share of recognition. And then we never challenge our male clergy. Because some of us feel that way. We never challenge ourselves to the word of God which calls us to be one.[12]

Epilogue

It Remains to Be Seen: Stability and Change in Religion and African-American Politics

Marion S. Barry! Forgiven by God! Marion S. Barry! Raised by God to be the mayor of our nation's capital!

> Voice from a campaign sound truck,
> Washington, D.C., 1994

We don't have a ministry of condemnation. We have a ministry of reconciliation. White people don't understand that in their institutions, so they pull down their [Jim] Bakkers and [Jimmy] Swaggarts.

> Reverend E. V. Hill, chairman of the Ethics
> Committee, National Baptist Convention, 1997

To equate forgiveness with absolution from personal responsibility is to cheapen biblical forgiveness and to deny biblical justice.

> Message from an Internet bulletin board
> on the Reverend Henry Lyons, 1998

And all the people answered together and said, "All that the Lord has spoken we will do." And Moses reported the words of the people to the Lord.

> Exodus 19:8

THIS STUDY OF RELIGION'S IMPACT on African-American political life provides an alternative perspective to the way scholars have traditionally thought about religion and black political activism. It shows that, far from subverting black political activism, Afro-Christianity stimulates black political activism. Over time religion's effects on black activism have depended on the political and social conditions facing black communities. Indeed, religiously based resources for black political activism have been deeply affected by the material and physical sanctions against political activity that were imposed before the civil rights movement. Critics of Afro-Christianity may have erroneously attributed the lack of black mobilization in the South during the Jim Crow era to the otherworldly tenets of Afro-Christianity. As I have argued throughout this analysis, when opportunities for participation emerged and sanctions against participation eased, religiously based resources were forged for black activism. These sources of action had their effects even when clerical leadership discouraged political mobilization.

My main concern in this book has been to show how religiously based resources affect black political participation rather than to assess the political behavior of black ministers and churches. While theological perspectives, congregation size, denominational affiliations, and the social class characteristics of ministers and congregations may well influence a church's or minister's political involvement, I have instead emphasized the ways in which individuals themselves become politically stimulated by their religion. Rather than viewing them as distinct, independent actors, I locate the clergy and church in an array of organizational resources that are embedded in religious institutions.

Taking a multidimensional and non-elite-oriented approach to the study of religion and black political activism demonstrates how religion can mobilize religious blacks both through church networks and independently of church networks. Skills developed in the course of church work, for instance, can be mobilized behind church-sanctioned support for political candidates or can be employed for political activities that require skills such as public speaking, planning meetings, or raising money. Religiously inspired feelings of political empowerment can be reinforced by a minister's sermon, but they can also be personally activated when activists themselves become unsure or fearful about their participation.

This study also shows the importance of religious rituals and symbols in black political activism. Using indigenous material from their belief in Christianity, African Americans have developed a rich oppositional culture that assists with mobilizing their resistance against racial domination. Though various biblical icons and scriptures have conveyed meaning to black political activism, the biblical story of the Exodus—which chronicles the Israelites' revolt against a repressive society—has been a continuous theme in African-American political culture.

The symbol of the Exodus story for black political activism conveys what I have described throughout as a civic culture of opposition. In his book on African-American political culture, political scientist Charles P. Henry notes that the Exodus story has been understood by African Americans as a struggle for inclusion, affirming their participation "in the larger society rather than their separateness" from it (1990, 61). As I discuss hereafter, a civic culture of opposition in African-American politics and society has had both positive and negative consequences. While providing the tools for actively resisting racial oppression in the United States, the religious basis of the civic culture of opposition has, on the other hand, undermined democratic processes in African-American politics and society. But before I discuss this point, I will first briefly address the implications this work has for the study of religion, American politics, and African-American politics.

IMPLICATIONS FOR THE STUDY OF RELIGION
AND AMERICAN POLITICS

Thinking of religion as a political resource allows us to reconsider the ways political scientists have generally thought about religion and politics in the United States. Most scholarship in the field takes an interest group or voting behavior approach, comparing the political attitudes and voting behavior of various religious groups and leaders. Indeed, the most important works in the field have examined the strategies of religious lobbies, the religious perspectives of presidential candidates, the impact of religion on opinion formation, the political behavior of religious elites, the emergence of the religious right, and the legal tensions in the separation of church and state.

Few studies, however, have investigated the effects of religious beliefs and practices on individual and collective forms of political action. We know little, for instance, of how privatized religious beliefs influence feelings of political empowerment throughout American political life. Nor do we know much about how religious rituals and symbols are constructed for political action. From the standpoint of collective action behavior, we have little knowledge of the links between religion, rationality, and collective action. Examining such links would raise important questions. It might be that religious beliefs, for instance, may reduce the material costs associated with an individual's decision to act cooperatively when that action is perceived in sacred terms. The belief in a protective sacred force may give assurance to political actors just as the assurance of cooperation with human actors encourages an individual to act cooperatively.

This study also raises questions about the meaning of civil religion and civic culture in American political life. We need to rethink our views on civic culture and civil religion by considering—more systematically than I have done in this study—how both the civic and the oppositional aspects of religion are linked to the quasi-religious dimensions of civic loyalty. Closer examination of the civic dimensions of those who revolt against the state, particularly those who are marginalized in American life, should produce a more complex and accurate picture of the way civil religion and civic culture function in liberal democratic societies.

The work of Sidney Verba, Kay Lehman Scholzman, and Henry Brady (1995), on the other hand, has expanded our understanding of the relationship between religion and political participation in the United States. It shows how the institutional design of religious institutions affects whether congregants will practice politically relevant political skills in their churches. Catholic churches, which are hierarchically structured, provide relatively fewer opportunities for congregants to develop politically relevant skills, while Protestant churches, which are likely to be run and managed by congregants themselves, give congregants the opportunity to learn and practice organizing skills.

However, like most scholars of religion and American politics, Verba, Scholzman, and Brady do not consider religion's influence on nurturing feelings of political efficacy, which, in turn, may stimulate political participation. Nor do they consider the ways in which religious rituals and symbols influence political participation. Sorting out the effects of religiously inspired feelings of political efficacy and religion's symbolic and ritualistic power in political activism would further our understanding of political participation in the United States.

THE IMPACT OF POLITICAL AND RELIGIOUS CHANGE

Transformations in African-American politics and Afro-Christianity since the civil rights movement may have cross-cutting effects on religion's capacity to furnish future resources for black political activism. The decline of party organizations and their diminished capability to mobilize voters and the rise in personality-centered politics opens black churches to political entrepreneurs seeking black support for their goals. Although black churches today are criticized for not being as politically active as they were during the civil rights movement (a charge that exaggerates the actual involvement of churches during the movement), the decline of party organizations and the increasing number of blacks seeking public office has probably stimulated more church-based political activism in black communities since the civil rights movement than took place during it. Black elected officials, who numbered less than fifteen hundred in the early 1970s and grew to more than seven thousand in the early 1990s, rely on the indigenous resources of churches to mobilize support behind their candidacies. As we have seen, black churchgoers are more likely than white churchgoers to hear political speeches and to be encouraged to register and vote at their place of worship.

In addition to being wooed by black and white political candidates, conservative religious organizations are beginning to mobilize black ministers and churches. The Christian Coalition, for instance, is forming alliances with black ministers over support for organized prayer in public schools, the use of public funds to subsidize private education, and opposition to municipal laws that protect the civil rights of gays and lesbians.[1] In just one example, Citizens Opposing Special Treatment, a political organization opposed to civil rights for gays and lesbians, collaborated in 1998 with an all-black ministerial organization in Ypsilanti, Michigan, to overturn an ordinance protecting the civil rights of gays and lesbians in that city. Four African-American celebrities who disapprove of homosexuality on religious grounds were recruited to mobilize support against the ordinance.[2]

Emerging trends in African-American religious life, on the other hand, may undercut political opportunities for greater church involvement. The rise of megachurches may undermine the one consistent political resource that blacks gain from their church participation—the practice of politically relevant skills. Megachurches, large Protestant congregations with more than two thousand members, are organizationally structured like corporations. Some of them are housed in edifices that resemble theaters and sports arenas. Many use corporate management principles and marketing strategies to manage church affairs and entice members.[3] In black communities across the country, megachurches are attracting the black middle class, who are lured by their "professional-quality gospel singers, well-educated pastors, and the multitude of services provided by [a] large paid staff."[4]

In contrast to congregationally organized churches, where lay members manage church affairs, megachurches hire their own finance directors, office managers, data processors, media personnel, executive assistants, administrative secretaries, and other full-time personnel to manage church affairs. Moreover, the management practices of megachurches not only provide fewer opportunities for lay members to practice civic skills, they also undermine the tradition of service that is a core belief in Afro-Christianity. Instead of fostering a spirit of service to others, many megachurches view their members as "consumers" who are in need of both secular and religious services.[5] Membership in megachurches, then, lowers the cost in time that congregants devote to church activities since it leaves church work to professionals. As religion scholar Wardell Payne explains, black "megachurches give you a smorgasbord. You can feel good about yourself, reduce the guilt, and not have an ongoing commitment to the traditional church."[6] Although the effects of megachurches on lay participation have implication for both black and white churchgoers, it is more consequential for blacks since they are more likely to be politically activated by their church work than whites.

The ideology behind the beliefs of some megachurches may have consequences for black political activism as well. Megachurches such as Atlanta's World Changers Ministries, Chicago's Christ Universal Temple, and Los Angeles' Crenshaw Christian Center preach a theology of material prosperity and positive thinking. The World Changers Ministries, for instance, urges its fifteen-thousand-plus members to pursue material wealth, claiming that they "can be rich, healthy and trouble free. . . . Jesus was rich and God wants you to be rich."[7] Religion scholars argue that theologies that encourage the pursuit of material prosperity may undermine collective action efforts to challenge racial inequality; "instead of pointing out how social and economic forces may be at the root of many of their followers' and clients' problems," these theologies "hold the individual solely responsible for his or her failures" (Baer and Singer 1992, 210).

Research by Mark Chaves and Lynn M. Higgins (1992) suggests that the growth in Pentecostal churches may also undermine the civic activities of black church-goers. In a national survey of the civic activities of churches, the authors found that although predominately black churches are more engaged in civic activities than predominately white churches, black churches founded during or after the civil rights movement were *less active* in civic activities than black churches with a longer history. Their findings are surprising, since we would expect churches founded during and after the 1960s to be, in theory, socialized by the civil rights and black power movements and thus more engaged in civic activities. However, the fastest-growing churches in Afro-Christianity today are Pentecostal churches, while the Baptists and Methodists have lost membership over the years. It may be that the changing of the guard in black Protestantism will also undercut the tradition of civic activism in black churches.

Aside from changes in black Protestantism, the growth in the number of black Catholics and the rise in the number of black Muslims may also have implications for the capacity of religion to mobilize religious African Americans in the future. There are an estimated 2.5 million black Catholics in the United States, up considerably since the 1960s. Catholics represent about 10 percent of all religious blacks, nearly outpacing members of the all-black Methodist denominations (Kosmin and Lachman 1993). As we have seen, Catholics are considerably less likely than Protestants to receive political stimuli from their churches. Moreover, like megachurches, the hierarchial organizational structure of the Catholic church provides relatively fewer opportunities for lay members to learn civic skills.

The increase in black Muslims may also have implications for black political activism. Although black Muslims represent less than 1 percent of all blacks who claim a religion, their numbers are rapidly increasing. This growth, however, is taking place in mainstream Islam rather than in the Nation of Islam, the black nationalist sect that was founded in the 1930s by Elijah Muhammad.[18] Since mainstream Islam has not been directly involved in either community-based activism or electoral mobilization in the United States, it is unlikely that it will generate the types of organizational resources that black Protestants receive from their church involvement.

The increasing popularity of the Nation of Islam, on the other hand, has provided the ideological and institutional resources for mobilizing black nationalist sentiments in black communities throughout urban America. The Nation of Islam's entrance into electoral politics began with Louis Farrakhan's support for Harold Washington's 1983 mayoral election in Chicago and his support a year later of Jesse Jackson's 1984 presidential campaign. The Nation of Islam's involvement in electoral politics is a departure from the group under the leadership of Elijah Muhammad, who believed that blacks should physically separate from American society and should therefore withdraw from the politics of a "corrupt" nation. Since the early 1980s, members of the Nation have run for public office, and units of the group's security forces have received government contracts to patrol public housing projects. The group's capacity to mobilize African Americans is evidenced by its success at drawing hundreds of thousands of black men to the nation's capital for the Million Man March in 1995.

Membership declines in mainstream black churches and membership increases in megachurches, Pentecostal churches, Catholic churches, and mainstream Islam may countervail the political inducements that black churches receive to directly engage in political activism. It remains to be seen, then, if religion will maintain its strong influence on black political activism in years to come.

THEOCRATIC NORMS IN PARTICIPATORY STRUCTURES

The belief in Afro-Christianity that clerical leadership communicates God's political will to believers undermines democratic processes in African-American politics. Religious traditions that legitimize clerical leadership's political authority are called theocracies. Theocratic practices (which are characteristic of most charismatic religious traditions) are believed to be extensive in politically active black churches and are related to what many have described as the autocratic leadership styles of black ministers. A generation ago, sociologist E. Franklin Frazier observed that "the pattern of control and organization of the Negro church has been authoritarian, with a strong man in a dominant position. . . . The petty tyrants in Negro churches have their counterparts in practically all other Negro organizations. . . . As a consequence Negroes have had little education in democratic processes" ([1963] 1974, 90). While the autocratic leadership styles that Frazier observed in the 1950s may have diminished since then, my observation of black churches for this study revealed many instances when politically active ministers were both theocratic and autocratic in their approach to politics.

The practice of theocratic and autocratic norms in Afro-Christianity presents a paradox. On the one hand, the participatory structures of many black churches give blacks the organizing skills to become politically active in the secular sphere. On the other hand, obedience to theocratic beliefs and autocratic leadership styles stymies collective decision making and leadership accountability—practices that are required of citizens in a democratic polity.

In his analysis of the 1984 Jesse Jackson campaign, Adolph Reed, Jr., argues that clerical authority is incompatible with democratic processes in African-American politics. "[B]ecause of the assumption of privileged clerical access to divine purposes mysterious to others," clerical authority "exonerates clerical leadership from susceptibility to secular criticism" (1986b, 56). Not only can the belief in clerical authority isolate clerical leadership from secular criticism, it may also short-circuit criticism that church members themselves have of religious leadership. For example, a church trustee affiliated with the COGIC reveals in a letter to his denomination's bishop how clerical authority can be used to undermine

democratic processes in church governance. Criticizing the minister for misman-
aging church funds, the trustee complains that his pastor has made "ongoing
prophesies of death" since his arrival as pastor in which the "prophesies seemed
always to coincide when questions are asked regarding church finances." [9]

Even when rules of accountability are incorporated in the formal structures
of congregations and denominational bodies, acquiescence to clerical authority
may supersede democratic practices. When Reverend Henry Lyons, president of
the National Baptist Convention, was found by a newspaper to have misappro-
priated funds intended for the denomination, church leaders rushed to his de-
fense. Drawing on the biblical themes of redemption and the oppositional aspect
of black civil society, Reverend Lyons's defenders attempted to deflect criticism
from him by blaming the "white press" for his problems. Lyons, who had run
his 1994 campaign for the presidency of the Convention on a pledge of financial
accountability, did not receive any sanctions by his local congregation or by
denominational leaders.

Asked if forthcoming indictments would move Lyons's congregants to ask for
his resignation, a church deacon reasoned that since his pastor had apologized
to the public and to his church there was no reason for him to give up the pulpit.
"We follow what the Bible says. . . . We have to forgive. . . . Everybody makes
mistakes."[10] After Lyons faced the Convention's ethics committee at the Convention's 1997 annual meeting to answer to multiple charges of marital infidelity and
financial mismanagement, all charges were dropped by the committee. Reverend
E. V. Hill, chairman of the committee and ally of conservative political activist
Reverend Jerry Falwell, excused Lyons on the grounds that black leaders such as
Martin Luther King and Adam Clayton Powell were wrongly investigated in the
past. "The fact that we may face an investigation is nothing new. Afro-American
people have been investigated ever since we hit this shore," said Hill, adding that
"as long as there is a white press, Negroes will be indicted and accused."[11]

Reverend Roscoe Cooper, the Convention's general secretary, echoed Hill's
support by complaining that people who "screw up" in American society are
given "no possibility of Redemption." [12] After having initiated the investigation
on Lyons after she set fire to a condo owned by him and another woman, Lyons's
wife, Deborah Lyons, asked the convention delegates to forgive her husband and
blamed *her* problem with alcoholism for *his* troubles.[13] Despite the vocal opposition of a small group of ministers who urged him to step down, Lyons received
a standing vote of confidence from a majority of convention delegates. Months
later Lyons was arrested and indicted for racketeering and grand theft.[14] Even
after indictments, many delegates to the following 1998 convention felt that they
had no right to punish Lyons. As one delegate said: "I'm not condemning him,
and I'm not praising him. That's for God to decide. God has the power to knock
him down. I don't." Another offered this explanation: "I don't know if he took
any money. I don't know if money is missing. If he used money inappropriately,

then he is going to have hell to pay. But not by us. Leave it to (God)."[15] Lyons was later convicted on state charges and pleaded guilty to federal charges.

The biblical theme of redemption can also assist with shielding political leaders from accountability. Marion Barry, who while mayor of Washington, D.C., was convicted on drug charges, was re-elected as mayor on the theme of Christian forgiveness. Immediately after his release from prison, Barry was greeted by a caravan of supporters led by the Reverend Willie Wilson, a popular minister of a Baptist church in one of Washington's poorest communities, who held many political rallies on Barry's behalf. In her analysis of Barry's political comeback, Jonetta Rose Barras observed how Barry used religion to win over black voters: "Barry, honing his redemption theme each day, frequently referred to God as if he were his personal friend, and to his own political resurrection as if he had been nailed to the cross and personally deserved the same adulation as Jesus Christ" (1998, 55).

DRAWING LESSONS FROM MOUNT SINAI

As I have already mentioned, the theocratic norms and autocratic leadership styles in Afro-Christianity present a problem for the practice of democratic processes in African-American politics and society. Michael Walzer, in his book *Exodus and Revolution*, points out that the biblical story of the Exodus has served as a paradigm for social change across time and in a variety of contexts. Walzer explains that the Israelites' revolt against a repressive society is not the only lesson that movements for social change can learn from the Exodus story. Treating the story as a problem of self-determination in which organized resistance is but the first step of a larger process of transformation leading to self-government, Walzer argues that the covenant at Sinai required God's people to make their own decisions. As they enter the land of milk and honey, Moses is no longer their leader, for "at Sinai . . . the entire people committed itself, not through representatives or proxies but each individual in his own voice" (1985, 79).

For African Americans, who throughout their history of political resistance in the United States have regarded themselves as Israelites revolting against a repressive society, the covenant at Sinai is instructive. The theocratic mindset of politically involved ministers must be challenged by church members. Institutional processes for holding clerical leadership accountable for their misdeeds as church leaders and for the political positions they take that are contradictory to the collective will of their congregants must be created or strengthened. Such practices would not only democratize local congregations and denominational bodies but would in turn strengthen democratic practices throughout African-American politics and society.

Proposals to fund government social services through inner-city churches should raise concerns. Only churches with a strong record of financial management should be funded, for even ministers with the best intentions may spend government funds intended for social services on church needs or appropriate them for their own personal use.[16] While the use of government monies to fund social services through churches raises constitutional questions about the separation of church and state, such funding may also encourage political corruption. As in the past, politicians may use church-based funding to build political alliances with black ministers. In Chicago, for instance, Mayor Richard J. Daley used funding provided by President Johnson's War on Poverty to gain the political loyalty of black ministers in Chicago. As a way to build support for his political machine, Daley dispensed poverty funds to black churches to keep them "pro-administration, or at least to keep them from becoming forums for [his] opponents"[17] Furthermore, even where government funding allocated to a local congregation may be successful and corruption-free, the demands of service provision may have the unintended effect of replacing church volunteers with social service professionals, undermining the very spirit of voluntarism that churches are celebrated for nurturing.

This study, like several recent analyses of social movements, locates the resources on which individuals can draw not only in the material world around them but also in their cognitive and cultural frameworks. To produce social change, groups and individuals need preexisting networks, meeting places, and leadership. They also need places to learn critical organizational skills. They need to draw on existing ideals, symbols, and rituals that give meaning to their lives and that can be adopted to the needs of the movement for change. For African Americans today, black churches fill many of these needs. They provide material resources, they provide training grounds, they provide psychological inspiration, and they provide the language of resistance. Although an individual's calculus of cost and benefit will usually produce the conclusion that political inaction is the most rational course, black churches direct blacks to act. In doing so, they draw on and regenerate their commitment to "something within."

Appendix A: The 1966 Harris-Newsweek Race Relations Survey Questions and Variables

The survey was obtained from the Louis Harris Data Center at the Institute for Research in Social Science at the University of North Carolina, Chapel Hill.

Dependent Variables

Voter Participation (Cronbach's alpha = .81)
  Are you a registered voter? (1 = Registered, 0 = Not registered)
  Did you vote in the election for president in 1964 when Johnson and Goldwater ran? (1 = voted in 1964, 0 = did not vote in 1964)
  Did you vote in the election for President in 1960 when Nixon and Kennedy ran? (1 = voted in 1960, 0 = did not vote in 1960)
Campaign Activism (Cronbach's alpha = .86)
  Have you ever:
    Worked for a political candidate? (1 = done, 0 = not done)
    Asked people to register to vote? (1 = done, 0 = not done)
    Asked people to vote for one candidate over another? (1 = done, 0 = not done)
    Gone to a political meeting? (1 = done, 0 = not done)
    Written or spoken to your congressman? (1 = done, 0 = not done)
    Given money to a political candidate? (1 = done, 0 = not done)
Protest Activism (Cronbach's alpha = 0.76)
  In the cause of Negro rights, have you personally or has any member of your family:
  Taken part in a sit-in ? (1 = done, 0 = not done)
  Marched in a demonstration (1 = done, 0 = not done)
  Picketed a store (1 = done, 0 = not done)
  Stopped buying at a store (1 = done, 0 = not done)
  Gone to jail (1 = done, 0 = not done)
Willingness to Protest (Cronbach's alpha = 0.90)
  If you were asked would you:
    Take part in a sit-in? (3 = would, 2 = not sure, 1 = would not)
    march in a demonstration? (3 = would, 2 = not sure, 1 = would not)
    Picket a store? (3 = would, 2 = not sure, 1 = would not)
    Stop buying at a store? (3 = would, 2 = not sure, 1 = would not)
    Go to Jail? (3 = would, 2 = not sure, 1 = would not)

Separatist Black Nationalism (Cronbach's alpha = 0.62)
>   Some people are saying that Negroes have tried to work out their problems with white
>   people and there's been a lot of talk but not much action. Now, they say, Negroes
>   should give up working together with whites and just depend on their own people.
>   Do you tend to agree or disagree with people who say this?
>   (3 = agree, 2 = not sure, 1 = disagree)
>   On the whole, do you approve or disapprove of the Black nationalists?
>   (3 = approve, 2 = not sure, 1 = disapprove)
>   On the whole, do you approve or disapprove of the Black Muslim movement?
>   (3 = approve, 2 = not sure, 1 = disapprove)
> Some Negro leaders have proposed that whites and Negroes won't live well together so
> the only solution is to set up a separate Negro state or states in this country or in Africa.
> Do you favor or oppose this idea? (3 = approve, 2 = not sure, 1 = disapprove)

Political Violence (Cronbach's alpha = 0.44)
>   Some Negro leaders have said that Negroes can only succeed in winning rights if they
>   use non-violent means to demonstrate. Others disagree.
>   Do you personally feel Negroes today can win their rights without resorting to vio-
>   lence or do you think it will have to be an eye for an eye a tooth for a tooth?
>   (3 = will have to use violence; 2 = not sure; 1 = can win without violence)
>   Do you think the riots that have taken place in Los Angeles and other cities have
>   helped or hurt the cause of Negro rights or don't you think it makes a difference?
>   (3 = helped; not much difference = 2; not sure = 2; hurt = 1)
>   Would you join something like that (a riot)?
>   (3 = would join; 2 = not sure; 1 = would not join)

Independent Variables

Religious Dimensions
>   Deeply Religious
>   Do you feel deeply about religion, or isn't it that important to you?
>   (dichotomous: 1 = important, 0 = not important)
>   Church Attendance
>   How often do you go to church? (5 = more than once a week, 4 = once a week,
>   3 = two or three times a month, 2 = once a month, 1 = less often)
>   Denominations
>   What is your religion? What church do you attend? (dichotomous: 1 = Baptist,
>   0 = not Baptist 1 = Methodist, 0 = not Methodist; 1 = Catholic, 0 = not Catholic,
>   1 = other religion, 0 = not other religion, 1 = no religion, 0 = religion)

Organizational Resources:
>   What organizations are you a member of or active in?
>   Religious/quasi-religious:
>   Church Group, (1 = church group member, 0 = not member)
>   Masonic (1 = member of Masons or Eastern Stars, 0 = not member)
>   Political
>   Civil rights, 1 = member of NAACP, CORE, or Urban League, 0 = not member
>   of civil rights group)
>   Partisan/citizen, (1 = member of Democratic Club, Republican Club, civic league,
>   or voters league, 0 = not member of partisan/civic group)

Table A.1 Correlation Matrix Based on the 1966 Harris-Newsweek Survey

	Campaign activism	Protest activism	Separatist nationalism	Political violence
Voter participation	.38	.20	−.17	−.07
	p = .000	p = .000	p = .000	p = .027
Campaign activism		.55	−.05	−.01
		p = .000	p = .116	p = .590
Protest activism			−.01	.03
			p = .846	p = .280
Separatist nationalism				.24
				p = .000

Nonpolitical secular groups (1 = college fraternity, YMCA, Negro improvement organizations, PTA, NEA, professional organization, senior citizens club, American Legion, or Boys Club, 0 = Not a member of nonpolitical secular groups)

Control Variables

Region (1 = South, 0 = non-South)
Gender (1 = Male, 0 = female)
Education (1 = did not attend school, 2 = 1st-2nd grade, 3 = 3rd-4th grade, 4 = 5th-8th grade, 5 = some high school, 6 = completed high school, 7 = some college, 8 = college graduate)
Age (1 = 18–20, 2 = 21–34, 3 = 35–49, 4 = 50–64, 5 = 65 and over)
Urban (1 = central city and suburb, 0 = rural and town)

THE 1966 HARRIS-NEWSWEEK RACE RELATIONS SURVEY: CORRELATIONS BETWEEN VARIABLES MEASURING BLACK PARTICIPATION AND THOUGHT

Table A.1 presents the intercorrelations among the indexes. The two conventional modes of political activism, represented by voter participation and campaign activism, are moderately correlated with one another (r = 0.38, < 0.001), but the unconventional mode of protest-demand activism is also moderately correlated with both of these conventional modes. Indeed, the two most closely related modes of political activism (r = 0.55, < 0.001) are campaign activism and protest-demand activism. As Sidney Verba and Norman Nie explained (in examining a similar relationship between campaign activism and communal-cooperative activities), these modes of activism "require initiative and are the major ways by which citizens attempt to influence political outcomes of broad scope" (1972, 75).

While all forms of conventional and protest-demand activism are significantly correlated with one another, support for political violence is uncorrelated or negatively correlated with all of them, except for support for black autonomy. Support for black autonomy is significantly and positively related to support for political violence and is negatively related to voter participation, reflecting the antithetical relationship between civic-oriented activism and the withdrawal politics of black separatist ideology.

Appendix B: The National Survey of Black Americans, 1979

ESTIMATING CAUSAL LINKAGES BETWEEN RELIGIOSITY,
PERSONAL EFFICACY, AND PARTICIPATION

Figures B.1 and B.2 represent the empirical data that derives from part of the model in figure 5.1 (in chapter 5), which illustrates the theorized links between internal religiosity, a sense of personal self-esteem, a sense of personal efficacy, a sense of political efficacy, and political activism. Only a part of the theoretical model can be empirically tested since measures of political efficacy are not included in the National Survey of Black Americans. Figure B.1 shows among African Americans the statistically significant causal linkages between internal religiosity, a sense of personal efficacy, and neighborhood activism. As predicted, internalized religious activities—independent of SES and demographic factors—are positively linked to self-esteem and feelings of personal efficacy among African Americans, although the magnitude of the coefficients is modest. These findings on religiosity and personal self-esteem and sense of efficacy are consistent with Hughes and Demo's analysis (1989) of the self-perceptions of African Americans.

Internal religiosity has an independent direct effect on neighborhood activism, but this relationship may be partially attributed to the spurious effect of the organizational components of religion that are also positively linked to participation (Peterson 1992). Similarly, as figure B.2 indicates, internalized religious activities have some causal linkages to communal political activism. Nonpolitical psychological resources can promote other kinds of political involvement, also through feelings of personal self-worth and efficacy. The link between a sense of personal efficacy and communal political activism is small. As is the case with neighborhood activism, internalized religiosity is directly linked with broader political activism, but again this relationship may be partially explained by the institutional aspects of religion.

THE QUESTIONS AND VARIABLES

Dependent Variables

Political Activism (Cronbach's alpha = 0.61)
    Did you vote in the last presidential election? (1 = voted, 0 = did not vote)
    Did you vote in any state or local election last year? (1 = voted, 0 = did not vote)

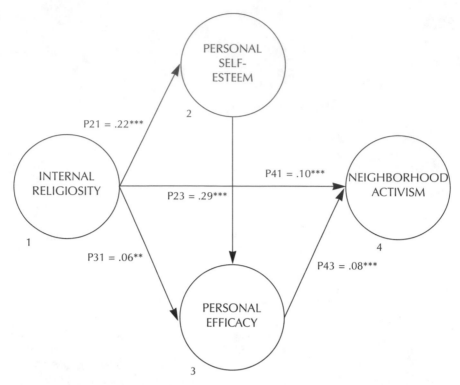

FIGURE B.1. *Causal Model of Religiosity, Personal Efficacy, and Neighborhood Activism among Blacks.* ***$p < .001$; **$p < .01$; *$p < .10$; adjusted $R^2 = .05$. Paths from exogenous variable are controlled for education, income, gender, age, region, and urban location. *Source:* 1979 National Survey of Black Americans.

Have you ever worked for a political party or campaigned for a political candidate? (1 = yes, 0 = no)

Have you ever called or written a public official about a concern or problem? (1 = yes, 0 = no)

Neighborhood Activism (Cronbach's alpha = .79)

How many (neighborhood groups) are you involved in? (7 = seven or more, 6 = six, 5 = five, 4 = four, 3 = three, 2 = two, 1 = one, 0 = zero)

Do you hold an office or post in this group/any of these groups? (1 = yes, 0 = no)

Independent Variables

Personal Self-Esteem (Cronbach's alpha = 0.66)

I am a useful person to have around. Would you say this is almost always true, often true, not often true, or never true for you? (4 = almost always true, 3 = often true, 2 = not often true, 1 = never true)

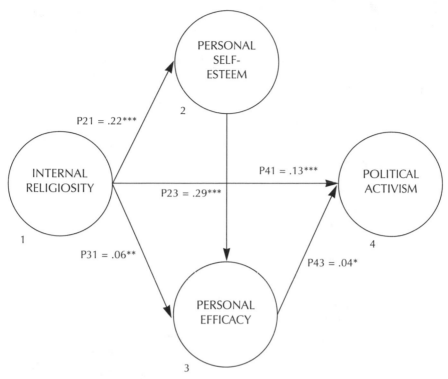

FIGURE B.2. *Causal Model of Religiosity, Personal Efficacy, and Political Activism among Blacks.* ***p < .001; **p < .01; *p < .10; adjusted R² = .20. Paths from exogenous variable are controlled by for education, income, gender, age, region, and urban location. *Source:* 1979 National Survey of Black Americans.

I feel that I am a person of worth. Would you say this is almost always true, often true, not often true, or never true for you? (4 = almost always true, 3 = often true, 2 = not often true, 1 = never true)

I feel I can't do anything right. Would you say this is almost always true, often true, not often true, or never true for you? (4 = never true, 3 = not often true, 2 = often true, 1 = almost always true)

I feel that my life is not very useful. Would you say this is almost always true, often true, not often true, or never true for you? (4 = never true, 3 = not often true, 2 = often true, 1 = almost always true)

I feel I do not have much to be proud of. Would you say this is almost always true, often true, not often true, or never true for you? (4 = never true, 3 = not often true, 2 = often true, 1 = almost always true)

As a person I do a good job these days. Would you say this is almost always true, often true, not often true, or never true for you? (4 = almost always true, 3 = often true, 2 = not often true, 1 = never true)

Personal Efficacy (Cronbach's alpha = 0.57)

Do you think it is better to plan your life a good ways ahead, or would you say that life is too much a matter of luck to plan ahead very far? (3 = plan ahead, 2 = both, 1 = too much luck to plan)

When you do make plans ahead, do you usually get to carry out things the way you expected, or do things usually come up to make you change your plans? (3 = carry out way expected, 2 = both, 1 = have to change plans)

Have you usually felt pretty sure your life would work out the way you want it to, or have there been times you haven't been sure about it? (3 = pretty sure, 2 = both, 3 = haven't been sure)

Some people feel they can run their lives pretty much the way they want to, others feel the problems in life are sometimes too big for them. Which one are you most like? (3 = can run own life, 2 = both, 1 = problems of life too big)

Internal Religiosity (Cronbach's alpha = 0.73)

How often do you pray? (5 = nearly every day, 4 = a few times a week, 3 = a few times a month, 2 = a few times a year, 1 = never)

How often do you ask someone to pray for you? (5 = nearly every day, 4 = a few times a week, 3 = a few times a month, 2 = a few times a year, 1 = never)

How often do you read religious books or other religious materials? Would you say nearly every day, at least once a week, a few times a month, a few times a year, or never? (5 = nearly every day, 4 = at least once a week, 3 = a few times a month, 2 = a few times a year, 1 = never)

How often do you watch or listen to religious programs on TV or radio? Would you say nearly every day, at least once a week, a few times a month, a few times a year, or never? (5 = nearly every day, 4 = at least once a week, 3 = a few times a month, 2 = a few times a year, 1 = never)

How often do you usually attend religious services? Would you say a few times a week, at least once a week, a few times a month, a few times a year, or never? (5 = a few times a week, 4 = at least once a week, 3 = a few times a month, 2 = a few times a year, 1 = never)

Control Variables

Education (coded 0–17 for years of school completed; 17 represents education beyond four years of college)

Urban-city (1 = urban resident, 0 = non–urban resident

Gender (1 = male, 0 = female)

Region (1 = South, 0 = non-South

Age (reported in years)

Notes

1. Introduction

Parts of this introduction are taken from my article "Something Within: Religion as a Mobilizer of African-American Political Activism" (1994a).

1. These accounts are from my own observations as a participant at the ministerial breakfast for Carol Moseley Braun; the breakfast took place on August 1, 1992. I would like to thank Father Martini Shaw for inviting me to the event.

2. Brazier 1969. For records on Bishop Brazier's campaign contributions, see Richard Daley's campaign finance disclosure records for 1991 (Illinois State Board of Elections). For further reading on Bishop Brazier's political activities during the sixties, see Lehmann 1991 and Ralph 1993.

3. Reverend Charles Adams, "Burden of Black Religion," Hartford Memorial Baptist Church, Detroit, Michigan, Sunday, April 12, 1992, cassette tape.

4. I was directed to this body of literature through Hans Baer's excellent and exhaustive bibliographic work on the social scientific scholarship on African-American religion. The works listed include community studies with extensive discussions of black religion, studies of black churches in specific cities and towns, research on the pattern and trends of black religious behavior over time, as well as scholarship on black clergy and the effects of religion on black activism. See Baer 1988. Few scholars provided an alternative view of African-American religion during this period (see Mays and Nicholson ([1933] 1969), Thurman (1981).

5. See, for example, Madron, Nelsen, and Yokley (1974), Hunt and Hunt (1977), Reed (1986), Lincoln and Mamiya (1990), and Ellison (1991).

6. See Cone (1969), Cone ([1970] 1986), Cone (1972), Harding (1983), Paris (1985), West (1982), and West (1988).

7. See Tate (1993, table 4.5).

8. See Lenski (1961), Yinger (1970), Glock and Hammonds (1973), Wilcox (1986), and Jelen (1989).

9. For a review of black protest before the emergence of the modern civil rights movement, see Meier and Rudwick (1989).

10. I explore this concept in more detail in Harris (1997).

2. *When a Little Becomes Much*

1. See Merrill Goozner, "Mississippi Strike Takes on Civil Rights Character," *Chicago Tribune*, October 1, 1990.

2. See Wyatt, "The Role of Women in the Harold Washington Story," 95–103.

3. See Lynn Sweet and Mark Brown, "Black Clerics Back Hofeld; Steinem Stumps for Braun," *Chicago Sun-Times*, March 11, 1992. Reverend White had also favored a white candidate over popular black candidate Harold Washington during the 1983 Chicago mayoral election. When asked why he preferred Richard Daley over Washington at an endorsement session for Daley attended by over 150 black ministers, Reverend White responded that the election of black mayors in other cities had caused economic devastation to those cities, maintaining that "[w]e know what happened in Cleveland, Gary, and Detroit. When Mayor Richard Hatcher was elected, the white officials took all the money to Merrillville, Indiana. Gary is now a ghost town." He insisted that Daley would "pull together businesses to generate jobs."

One of Reverend White's colleagues at the ministerial endorsement session for Richard Daley, Reverend E. J. Jones, echoed these sentiments, saying that the election of a black mayor in Chicago would be futile. Speaking on behalf of the group, Reverend Jones claimed: "It is our spiritual insight and my better judgement—and I am not an Uncle Tom, but I believe the homework should be done [on Washington's potential election as mayor]. I guess we got too excited with the extra few thousand voter registration." See Mitchell Locin and Jane Fritsch, "Black Clergy for Washington Hit Pro-Daley Colleagues,"*Chicago Tribune*, January 13, 1983.

A paid political advertisement in the *Chicago Sun-Times* made public the political divisions among black clerics over whether to endorse Richard Daley, Harold Washington, or incumbent Jane Byrne. Referring to other politically active ministers as the "splinter group which backs the 'Daley regime' who opposed Dr. [Martin Luther] King" and the "other splinter group which rolls over and plays dead in the face of insult after insult to the Black community from the 'Byrne regime,' " Harold Washington's clerical supporters proclaimed that—unlike the other two groups of ministers—they were "not looking for 'political favors' or plums from the patronage orchard." See "The Black Church Supports Harold Washington for Mayor !!!" *Chicago Sun-Times*, February 12, 1983.

For insights into the political behavior of black ministers in the post-Washington era of Chicago politics, see Dinges (1989); Ray Hanania, "Twelve Ministers to Boycott King Affair," *Chicago Sun-Times*, January 10, 1990; Chinta Strausberg, "Ministers Split on Mayoral Support," *Chicago Defender*, January 30, 1991.

4. See McClory (1989).

5. Reverend Jordan stated that his role in the campaign was merely that of facilitator, insisting that black ministers of the United Methodist Church in Chicago "were sensing the need for my support," noting that "my pastors were on the front line. They were the ones that were knocking on the doors and doing the precinct work, going to the meetings and so forth," acknowledging that his role was "not that of a campaign worker." See Charles Wesley Jordan, "The Role of the District Superintendent in the Harold Washington Story," in Young (1988, 30–34).

6. Sunday morning service, Vernon Park Church of God, Chicago, Illinois, November 1, 1992; cassette tape.

7. Thomas Hardy and Steven Johnson, "Senate Foes Don't Let up on Attacks," *Chicago Tribune*, November 2, 1992. Michael Briggs and Ray Long, "Senate Rivals Work Strongholds," *Chicago Sun-Times*, November 2, 1992.

3. Prophetic Fragments

1. For a fuller discussion of the role of religion in the southern labor movement, see Billings (1990). For religion's role in the formation of social movements in Latin America see Levine (1992).

2. Omega Baptist Church, Sunday, February 24, 1991.

3. In addition, religious institutions may also directly facilitate civic activism by disseminating political information to congregants through church networks, thus acting as a direct stimulant to individual and collective forms of political action (Verba, Schlozman, and Brady 1995).

4. In her discussion of why African Americans believe in the American dream, Hochschild (1996, 168) implicitly acknowledges the duality of Afro-Christianity as both an agent of integration in American society and as a source of opposition to class and racial domination. She notes that the "conservative interpretations of the Bible emphasize personal virtue, hard work and humility," factors that support the prevailing ideology of the social order. On the other hand, the "radical interpretations of the Bible emphasize the fundamental equality of all God's children, the joyous strength associated with righteous rebellion, and the virtue of pursuing collective well-being." These religious forces nurture oppositional dispositions that challenge the dominant society's attitudes toward subordinates.

4. Religion Reconsidered

1. In direct response to Hare's criticism, Reverend Charles H. King, Jr., a Baptist minister from Indiana, countered that the black church had played a crucial role in mobilizing direct action campaigns in the South. King argued that "the backbone of the entire Negro Revolt was the Negro church and its minister." He claimed further: "If the jails could speak they would tell the story of their inhabitants. They would declare that their cells contained in virtually every southern state the sons, the daughters of the church, and the black prophets who led them there" (1963, 15).

2. Marx combined two samples for his analysis. One group of respondents was taken from a random metropolitan sample of 492 respondents, while a supplementary sample was developed from representative surveys in Chicago, New York, Atlanta, and Birmingham. According to Marx, these cities were "among the most important urban centers of the Negro population." The combined surveys netted 1,119 respondents for Marx's analysis (1967a, xxiii–xxvii).

3. One of the most important findings of the Harris-Newsweek survey emerges simply from the intercorrelations of the dependent variables. Although most research on political participation distinguishes sharply between conventional and unconventional behavior, this study reveals instead that, at least among African Americans in the mid-sixties, the primary cleavage was between *inclusive* conventional and unconventional behaviors or attitudes on the one hand and *exclusive* attitudes on the other. This survey was particularly fortunate in asking, during this crucial period, sufficient numbers of questions on each of

these dimensions to let us analyze their internal relations. See appendix B for further discussion of the inclusive and exclusive measures of black political thought and action.

4. See Wald, Owen, and Hill (1988), Wald, Owen, and Hill (1990), Jelen (1989), Jelen (1991), Wald, Kellstedt, and Leege (1993), and Gilbert (1993).

5. See McAdam (1982), Morris (1984), Morris, Hatchett, and Brown (1989), Allen, Dawson, and Brown (1989), Tate (1993), Brown and Wolford (1994), and Calhoun-Brown (1996).

6. For an analysis of the structure of post–civil rights black activism see Smith (1981). Smith argues that after the civil rights and black power movements, black protest organizations transformed themselves into mainstream interest groups.

5. Blessed Assurance

1. George James, "Police Honor a Preacher for Fight against Crime." *New York Times*, September 27, 1991, A14.

2. Lincoln and Mamiya's research on African-American religion hints at the role of religion as a nurturer of political efficacy (1990, 232–233). Noting that "[d]iscussions about the black church and politics often miss the role of a believer's individual faith in nurturing and sustaining political activity over time," the authors speculate that there is a positive relationship between private faith and political action.

3. For an extended discussion of the counter-hegemonic modes of resistance to white domination by southern African Americans during the Jim Crow period, see Robin D. G. Kelley 1993.

4. Jay MacLeod notes that the mobilization of resistance in Holmes County, Mississippi, during the initial stages of the movement developed without the organizational resources of local black churches. MacLeod describes local black churches as "belated, reluctant convert(s) to the Movement" because of the economic dependency of part-time ministers on the white elite, which allows churches to function merely as a "field of white domination" (1991, 15). Septima Clark, who organized citizenship schools throughout the south during the movement, also noted that some religious leadership undermined organizing efforts (1986, 69). However, as MacLeod notes and as participants in the movement reveal, other components of religion did help the movement. Both cultural and psychological aspects of religion were employed as resources during the process of mobilization (MacLeod 1991, 15).

6. Rock in a Weary Land

I would like to thank the late Colin Murry, then a curator at the Harold Washington Library in Chicago, for making available the Harold Washington Papers cited in this chapter and for encouragement in the six days I spent plowing through them.

1. Bunche's book ([1940] 1973) is indispensable for its insight into black political mobilization in both the North and South. See especially chapter 14, "Negro Voting in Selected Southern Cities"; chapter 17, "Southern Negroes and the Rewards of Politics"; and chapter 18, "Negro Political Activity in the North."

2. See Morris (1984) for further discussion (30–35). In South Carolina, it was illegal for school teachers to be members of the NAACP immediately after the *Brown* decision. See Septima Clark (1986, 35–40) for a personal account on South Carolina.

3. However, as Kilson points out, Chicago was an exception to this exclusionary pattern. Here blacks were incorporated into the party organization structure and black party leaders wielded considerable patronage. But this incorporation into machine politics came at a cost for blacks, because white machine leaders and their black subordinates avoided civil rights issues, especially open housing. This legacy undermined the success of Martin Luther King's movement against segregated and slum housing in Chicago a generation later and facilitated a black electoral insurgency against the Democratic establishment that culminated with Harold Washington's mayoral victory in the early 1980s (Pinderhughes 1987; Kleppner 1985; Ralph 1993).

4. Pamphlet, Fannie Lou Hamer Papers, 1917–1977, Amistad Research Center, Tulane University, roll 4. Microfilm copy at Northwestern University Library.

5. For further details on the organizational structure of black Protestant denominations and how they influenced protest activism, see Payne (1995).

6. Bulletin, Second Baptist Church, Evanston, Illinois, February 25, 1990. I would like to thank Miasha Goss for assistance in compiling church bulletins for this research during 1990 and 1991.

7. Reverend Dr. Charles G. Adams, "What Do These Stones Mean?" Hartford Memorial Baptist Church, Detroit, Michigan, November 1, 1992, cassette tape. I would like to thank Don R. Weston for providing me with this tape.

8. For further details and examples of religious institutions disseminating political information see Harris (1994b).

9. The *Herald*, Progressive Community Center, Chicago, Illinois, October 7, 1990.

10. Morning worship service, Mt. Vernon Baptist Church, Chicago, Illinois, March 13, 1994, participant observation.

11. For an itemized list of church and clerical contributions to Harold Washington's 1983 mayoral campaign, see Harris (1994b).

12. For details, see Harris (1994b).

13. Letter dated May 11, 1992, in my possession.

14. Letter dated July 16, 1992, in my possession.

15. Bulletin, Abyssinian Baptist Church, New York, New York, March 28, 1993.

16. See Vernon Jarrett, " 'Hired' Preachers Don't Always Win Votes," *Chicago Sun-Times*, December 20, 1988.

17. For details on itemized contributions to churches from the Richard M. Daley campaign committee see Harris (1994b).

18. Jerry Gray, "Rollins Gives Sworn Denial on Vote Ploy," *New York Times*, November 21, 1993. See also Jerry Gray, "Rollins Says He Fabricated Payoff Tale to Irk Foes," *New York Times*, November 20, 1993.

19. Bishop David L. Ellis, Greater Grace Broadcasts, Detroit, Michigan, November 1, 1992, 12:00 P.M. service, cassette tape.

20. Pastor Anderson Culbreath, "Fear And How to Deal with It," Tryed Stone Missionary Baptist Church, Cincinnati, Ohio, November 1, 1992, 10:00 A.M. service, cassette tape.

21. See Young (1988) for Reverend Hilliard's comments about Harold Washington's meeting with the black clerical group during the 1983 mayoral campaign (140–143).

22. NBC News/Associated Press national poll, taken October 8–10, 1980.

23. The questions for the five indicators of campaign participation had response categories of "yes" and "no." The index has a numeric range of zero to five and was com-

muted by the positive responses of each question on campaign activity. The index has a population mean of 0.77. The questions asked: "So far this year, have you, yourself, done any of the following things in any one of the political campaigns or primaries, either national or local:

> Distributed literature for a candidate?
>
> Gone to a political meeting or rally?
>
> Given money to a candidate?
>
> Called on the telephone on behalf of a candidate?
>
> Helped to register voters?"

24. See chapter 4 for a discussion of how church attendance functions as a civic-oriented resource for voter participation.

25. For further readings on religion and black electoral mobilization in the post–civil rights era, see Dawson, Brown, and Allen (1990).

26. These survey results are from the 1991 Chicago Area Survey conducted by the Northwestern University Survey Laboratory from April 28 to June 6, 1991. For further details concerning the survey, see Harris (1994b). Results on Latinos may be biased by their small representation in the survey (N = 42) and by the surveying of only English-speaking respondents. Questions 2, 3, and 4 were partially replicated from the 1984 National Black Election Study at the University of Michigan. Exact questions from the survey are as follows:

1. How often does your (minister) (priest) (rabbi) discuss political issues as part of the service? Does this happen nearly all the time, frequently, sometimes, rarely, or never?
2. How often do political candidates visit your place of worship during election time? Would you say frequently, only sometimes, or basically never?
3. Has your place of worship ever encouraged members to vote in any election?
4. Has your place of worship ever taken up a collection for any political candidates during any election?

27. The reported frequencies for Latinos should be read with caution given the small number of Latinos in the population sample (N = 42) and the even smaller number who reported being members of a church (N = 22). Again, interviewers surveyed only English-speaking respondents.

28. To access the educational variations for racial/ethnic religious groups, an institutionally based activism index was constructed from the standardized z-scores that were composed from the four modes of church-based activism. The activism index has a Cronbach's alpha reliability coefficient of 0.50.

29. See Putnam (1993) for further discussion.

7. Ties That Bind

1. This chapter was taken from my previously published article (1994).

2. I chose to use the GSS because, with a 1987 oversample of 353 black respondents, in addition to the regular cross-section, it yields a total of 544 blacks, more than most national surveys.

3. In a factor analysis, these indicators clustered around two broadly defined constructs. The first was church activism—intensive and extensive organizational involvement in church life. The second was internal religiosity—private, internalized religious behavior. A third factor, church attendance, reflected both public and private commitment to religion, affirming the distinctiveness of church attendance as a factor separate from either strictly organizational or psychological religious behavior. A principal component analysis using a varimax orthogonal (uncorrelated) rotation was employed to sort out the relationship of each of these indicators to one another. All items in the analysis were standardized before factoring, and the missing cases were substituted with the mean of that variable, giving each missing value a score of zero. The factor scores for church activism and internal religiosity are reported respectively: being a member of in a church organization (0.90, 0.25); being a member of a church group that solves problems (0.90, 0.19); being active in church organizations (0.89, 0.20); being, of all organizational affiliations, most active in a church group (0.71, 0.12) praying frequently; (0.14, 0.81); having feelings of closeness to God (0.01, 0.80); having feelings of commitment to a particular religion (0.27, 0.62); and attending church (0.44, 0.65). The internal religiosity scale has a standardized Cronbach's alpha of 0.68, while the Cronbach's alpha for the church activism scale is 0.89. Although the religious constructs are closely related to one another, their association does not create problems of multicollinearity. Correlations between the religion measures are 0.53 for church activism and internal religiosity, 0.38 for internal religiosity and church attendance, and 0.48 for church attendance and church activism.

The multidimensional aspects of religion are not limited to church organizational involvement, internalized religious behavior, and church attendance. Other dimensions of religion, like denominational orientations and affiliations (Brady1989), theological teachings, and religions other than Christianity, also belong to the varied universe of religious behavior and beliefs that might influence political action. Future work in the realm of race, religion, and political action should tease out the denominational dimensions of political action, allowing an analysis of sects, like Pentecostals and Jehovah's Witnesses, that have explicitly otherworldly orientations. For African Americans, who are overwhelmingly Christian and Protestant, other religious orientations, like the Nation of Islam and the Black Hebrews, should also promote resources for political action. Given that these particular religious sects are racially nationalistic, they should serve, in theory, as psychological resources for participation by promoting and shaping the racial identity and consciousness of its members. However, these sects have traditionally advocated withdrawal from participation in mainstream and protest politics (Lincoln 1961; Essien-Udon 1962; Baer and Singer1992).

4. The exact wording of questions and their frequency distributions appear in the 1987 General Social Survey codebook. Indicators of the operational definitions of voting, communal-cooperative activities, psychological involvement, political knowledge, and the sense of political efficacy may be found in appendixes C and D of Verba and Nie 1972. In my analysis, the modes of political participation and cognitive resources for participation are constructed as follows: voting: VOTE80 + VOTE84 + LOCVOTE; Communal-cooperative activities: LOCGRP + LOCPROB; psychological involvement: INTPOL + TALKPOL1; political knowledge: GOVERNOR + USREP + SCHLHEAD; internal political efficacy: LOCINFLU. The variable LOCVOTE measures the frequency of voting in local elections through a four-category response asking whether respondents never, rarely, mostly, or always vote in local elections.

5. Causal inferences regarding this analysis are taken from nonexperimental data and assume that the underlying causal associations between religious factors, intermediary resources for participation, and modes of political participation are recursive and independently related.

6. Regression on the religious measures shows that the race of the respondent (black = 1, white = 0), independent of SES, age, and gender, has a positive and significant effect on church activism and internal religiosity. These findings show that blacks are clearly more strongly involved with religious beliefs and practices than whites.

7. I have used OLS regression estimates.

8. Interviews conducted at the Apostolic Faith Church, Chicago, Illinois, April 21, 1991.

9. Although church activism is posited as being causally linked to secular participation, the causal relationship between the two constructs in the model might actually be reciprocal rather than one-sided. Notwithstanding the causal ambiguity, the association between secular and religious organizational life provides evidence that supports the theory that intensive involvement in church organizational life, at least among African Americans, is not antithetical to participation in the secular world. In fact, the model demonstrates that church organizational participation has a greater effect on frequency of voting among blacks than does participation in secular organizations does.

10. Although my causal model of religion and political action posits a reciprocal relationship between organizational and cognitive resources, the empirical representation from the 1987 GSS does not allow for a more extensive investigation of the model. For this analysis, the empirical representation of the model assumes that church organizational activism promotes knowledge of public affairs ($P73 = 0.08$), representing a one-dimensional relationship between psychological and organizational resources. The causal linkages between church activism and psychological involvement in politics ($P53$), as well as political efficacy ($P63$), were not significantly related, suggesting that church activism does not promote these psychological resources for political action. However, other cognitive resources for participation, like group consciousness and identity, would theoretically have a reciprocal relationship to church organizational activism. Allen, Dawson, and Brown, in their study of racial belief systems (1989), discovered a strong linkage between religiosity and racial identity and consciousness, reinforcing the view of the African-American church as an authentic "race institution" (Woodson [1921] 1945; Mays and Nicholson [1933] 1969; Drake and Cayton [1945] 1970; Frazier [1957] 1967). Unfortunately, the 1987 GSS did not include measures of racial consciousness and identity.

11. Since the inclusion of interactive terms with their component parts in the same regression equation may create problems of multicollinearity, tolerance scores are reported alongside each regression coefficient, indicating the degree of intercorrelation within the regression model. The model representing the interaction effects is expressed as follows:

Political Activism = a + B1(INTERNAL RELIGIOSITY) + B2(CHURCH ATTENDANCE) + B3(CHURCH ACTIVISM) + B4(SECULAR PARTICIPATION) + B5(EFFICACY) + B6(INTEREST) + B7(KNOWLEDGE) + B8(EDUC) + B9(INCOME) + B10(AGE) + B11(SOUTH) + B12(GENDER) + B13(RACE) + B14(INTERNAL RELIGIOSITY × BLACK) + B15(CHURCH ATTENDANCE × BLACK) + B16(CHURCH ACTIVISM × BLACK)

12. If trust in government, a promoter of civic attitudes, is strongly related to regular church attendance, regular church attenders might be discouraged from participating in

community-based action that is geared toward solving community problems. In theory, citizens who are more trusting of government are probably more likely to leave problem-solving to government officials, than to community efforts. If so, church attendance would function as a religious factor that supports the civic order rather than as a catalyst that fosters participation that opposes or challenges government officials and institutions. As previous research has detailed, feelings of distrust toward government, a political orientation that has been viewed as a suppressor of conventional political activity, can serve as a facilitator of political participation. Shingles (1981) demonstrates how feelings of distrust of government among blacks, in combination with feelings of internal political efficacy, contributes to racial consciousness, thus promoting more demanding modes of political action beyond voting. The thesis that church attendance promotes government trust is speculative. Further research investigating the interactions of race, government, trust, and church attendance on communal collective action would shed light on the impact of church attendance on civic culture.

8. The Last Shall Be First

1. Interfaith Religious Commemoration of Dr. Martin Luther King, hosted by the Chicago NAACP and First Church of Deliverance-Spiritual, Chicago, Illinois, January 20, 1992, participant observation.

2. Second Baptist Church, Evanston, Illinois, February 25, 1990, cassette tape.

3. Thomas Hardy, "Race for Mayor Ends on Heated Note," *Chicago Tribune*, April 2, 1991.

4. Omega Missionary Baptist Church, Chicago, Illinois, February 24, 1991, participant observation.

5. Secular forms of culture are also employed for political mobilization. For instance, political actors use the folk art of storytelling to construct strategies for political action and to articulate opposition to systems of domination. In a church-sponsored rally for mayoral candidate Danny Davis at the Stone Temple Baptist Church in Chicago on January 20, 1991, remarks by a local minister demonstrated how to assemble a narrative in an oppositional frame of reference for political action. Telling the congregation that "the Lord can work miracles . . . and I believe the Lord can put Danny in office," Reverend Charles Murry told the audience:

> I remember when I was on program with Mayor Harold Washington when he was running [for mayor] . . . and I told a story about [my friends] in Arkansas. This same boy I was talking about named Snoop—it was three of us sitting on the creek, and Honey was darker than Danny, he was black and he had red eyes. We were sitting there on the creek fishing for crawfish. . . . We didn't have [fishing] hooks, we had nails. We were too poor to buy hooks. We put the nail on the string. . . . So we were sitting there fishing for crawfish. So one of the boys said, "You know, if I was white, I could fly that plane" that was flying over. Honey wouldn't say a word. Snoop said, "If I was white, I would want to be a policeman." I said that "if I was white, I [would] want to be an engineer on a train." About that time all three of us had spoken. Honey looked around at us— and he was dangerous [looking], even white and black [people] were afraid of him. He looked at us with those red eyes. He said, "You know one thing? I could do all three of them y'all talking about black as I am if I only had a

chance" [laughter and applause]. I believe Danny can run it as black as he is, and he sure is black. God bless you. (Participant observation)

For further perspectives on the use of narrative as a form of political resistance, see Couto (1993). For recent research on skin color and social and economic stratification among African Americans, see the informative article by Herring and Keith (1991).

6. Rally for Danny K. Davis, Bethel African Methodist Episcopal Church, Chicago, Illinois, November 24, 1990, participant observation.

7. Bishop Paul S. Morton, Sr., "Take Heed," Greater St. Stephen Ministries, New Orleans, Louisiana, November 3, 1991, cassette tape no. 253.

8. The metaphor of the promised land has deep roots in American political culture. Like Bishop Morton's discussion of African-American destiny in the "last days," Revolutionary War sermons used the Exodus metaphor to describe American destiny. See Cherry (1971).

9. In My Father's House

1. See "Souvenir Journal for the 109th Annual Session of the National Baptist Convention, U.S.A., Inc.," New Orleans, Louisiana, September 4–10, 1989.

2. See Mansbridge and Tate (1992).

3. These verses were taken from Carpenter (1990–1991).

4. Quoted in Carpenter (1990–1991, 20), quoting in Josephine Carson, *Silent Voices: The Southern Negro Women Today* (New York: Delacorte Press, 1969), 108.

5. This pattern in gender leadership is fairly typical in white churches as well as in grassroots politics. For a religious perspective, see Lehman (1985) and Falk and Childs (1985).

6. Of male respondents (N = 122), 30 percent "somewhat agreed," 6 percent (N = 23) "somewhat disagreed," and 11 percent (N = 46) "strongly disagreed." Of female respondents (N = 252), 30 percent "somewhat agreed," 12 percent (N = 89) "somewhat disagreed," and 12 percent "strongly disagreed." The total number of respondents for this question was 405 men and 735 women.

7. In a logistic regression model estimating black women's support for gender equality, age positively predicted support for the idea that black women's leadership undermined black men's leadership. Education is negatively related, while region (the South) and church attendance have no effect. On the question of special versus equal attention, church attendance positively predicted support for special attention of black men's problems. Age and region have no effect; however, education positively predicts the idea among black women that black men's problems deserve special attention, suggesting that middle-class black women are more sympathetic to the plight of black men than poor and working-class women.

8. For an example of how patriarchal structures in churches are used as an incentive to recruit black men into churches, see Freedman (1987).

9. Louis Farrakhan, "The Problem of Suicide and the Causes of Homosexuality," Muhammad University of Islam, Wednesday, April 7, 1993, cassette tape.

10. See Cavanagh (1985, Table 7, 24). Black men's reported church attendance by age mirrors their reported voter participation rates. In the 1993–1994 National Black Politics Study, 41 percent of black men in the 18–20 (N= 17) and 21–24 (N = 17) age groups reported attending church weekly, while 51 percent of black men in the 55–64 cohort (N

= 37) and 60 percent of the black men in the 65–74 cohort (N = 27) reported attending weekly church services.

11. See "Indy Clergy Seek Mercy for Tyson," *Chicago Defender*, February 19, 1992.

12. "The Role of Women in the Harold Washington Story," in Young (1988).

Epilogue. It Remains to Be Seen

1. Katharine Q. Seelye, "Conservative Religious Group Reaches out to Black Leaders, *New York Times*, May 11, 1997. See also "Mississippi Fights Ban on School Prayer," *New York Times*, December 7, 1993.

2. Those celebrities were professional football player Reggie White, Martin Luther King, Jr.'s, niece Alveda King, and gospel singers Angie and Debbie Winans. Rhonda Smith, "Ypsilanti Voters Defeat Measure," *Washington Blade*, May 15, 1998.

3. Gustav Niebuhr, "The Minister as Marketer: Learning from Business,"*New York Times*, April 18, 1995.

4. Deborah Kovach Caldwell, "Megachurches: The Fastest-Growing Congregations Drawing Middle-Class Blacks," *Dallas Morning News*, June 8, 1997.

5. Gustav Niebuhr, "The Minister as Marketer: Learning from Business,"*New York Times*, April 18, 1995.

6. Deborah Kovach Caldwell, "Megachurches: The Fastest-Growing Congregations Drawing Middle-Class Blacks," *Dallas Morning News*, June 8, 1997.

7. Rick Sherrell, "Cult or Christianity?" *Creative Loafing*, December 6, 1997.

8. Don Terry, "Black Muslims Enter Islamic Mainstream," *New York Times*, May 3, 1993.

9. Letter in my possession.

10. Mike Wilson, Craig Pittman, and David Barstow, "I Have Sinned," *St. Petersburg Times*, December 4, 1997.

11. Waveney Ann Moore, David Barstow, Mike Wilson, and Monica Davey, "Ouster Attempt Fails; Lyons Wins," *St. Petersburg Times*, September 4, 1997.

12. Mike Wilson, David Barstow, and Waveney Ann Moore, "Lyons' Backers Successfully Use Race as a Political Strategy," *St. Petersburg Times*, September 4, 1997.

13. Waveney Ann Moore, David Barstow, Mike Wilson, and Monica Davey, "Ouster attempt fails; Lyons Wins," *St. Petersburg Times*, September 4, 1997. See also Dyson (1998).

14. Monica Davey, Craig Pittman, Mike Wilson, and David Barstow, "Lyons Arrested," *St. Petersburg Times*, February 26, 1998. For a brief discussion of financial corruption in the history of the National Baptist Convention, see Burkett (1994).

15. Monica Davey and David Barstow, "Why His Church Still Backs Rev. Lyons," *St. Petersburg Times*, September 9, 1998.

16. Josh Barbanel, "Rep. Flake's Indictment: Good Works or Greed," *New York Times*, August 8, 1990.

17. Melvin Holli quoted in Dinges(1989).

References

Aberbach, Joel D., and Jack L. Walker. 1970. "A Comparison of White and Black Interpretations of a Political Slogan." *American Political Science Review* 64 (June): 367–388.

Abramson, Paul R. 1977. *The Political Socialization of Black Americans: A Critical Evaluation
of Research on Efficacy and Trust.* New York: Free Press.

Allen, Richard L., Michael C. Dawson, and Ronald E. Brown. 1989. "A Schema-Based
Approach to Modeling an African-American Racial Belief System." *American Political
Science Review* 83:421–441.

Almond, Gabriel A., and Sidney Verba. 1963. *The Civic Culture.* Boston: Little Brown.

Appiah, Kwame Anthony. 1992. *In My Father's House: Africa in the Philosophy of Culture.*
New York: Oxford University Press.

Babchuk, Nicholas, and Ralph V. Thompson. 1962. "Voluntary Associations of Negroes."
American Sociological Review 27:647–655.

Baer, Hans A. 1988. "Bibliography of Social Science Literature on Afro-American Religion
in the United States." *Review of Religious Research* 29 (June):413–430.

———. 1993. "The Limited Empowerment of Women in Black Spiritual Churches: An
Alternative Vehicle to Religious Leadership." *Sociology of Religion* 54:1 65–82.

Baer, Hans A., and Merrill Singer. 1992. *African-American Religion in the Twentieth Century.*
Knoxville: University of Tennessee Press.

Barker, Lucius J. 1988. *Our Time Has Come: A Delegate's Diary of Jesse Jackson's 1984
Presidential Campaign.* Urbana: University of Illinois Press.

Barnes, Samuel H., and Max Kaase. 1979. *Political Action: Mass Participation in Western
Democracies.* Beverly Hills: Sage.

Barras, Jonetta Rose. 1998. *The Last of the Black Emperors: The Hollow Comeback of Marion
Barry in the Age of New Black Leaders.* Baltimore: Bancroft Press.

Bellah, Robert N. 1967. "Civil Religion, in America." *Daedalus* 96 (Winter):1–21.

———. 1980. "Religion and the Legitimation of the American Public." In *Varieties of Civil
Religion*, edited by Robert N. Bellah and Phillip Hammond. San Francisco: Harper and
Row.

Berelson, Bernard R., Paul F. Lazerfeld, and William N. McPhee. 1954. *Voting.* Chicago:
University of Chicago Press.

Berenson, William W., Kirk W. Elifson, and Tandy Tollerson III. 1976. "Preachers in

Politics: A Study of Political Activism among the Black Ministry." *Journal of Black Studies* 6 (June):373–392.

Bergman, Peter M. 1969. *The Chronological History of the Negro in America.* New York: Harper and Row.

Billings, Dwight B. 1990. "Religion as Opposition: A Gramscian Analysis." *American Journal of Sociology* 96:1–31.

Billings, R. A. 1934. "The Negro and His Church: A Psychogenetic Study." *Psychoanalytic Review* 21:425–441.

Bobo, Lawrence, and Frank Gilliam. 1990. "Race, Sociopolitical Participation, and Black Empowerment." *American Political Science Review* 84:377–393.

Brady, Henry E. 1989. "Religious Fundamentalism and Political Participation." Paper presented at the Annual Midwest Political Science Association Meeting, Chicago, Illinois, April 13–15.

Branch, Taylor. 1988. *Parting the Waters: America in the King Years, 1954–1963.* New York: Simon and Schuster.

Brazier, Arthur M. 1969. *Black Self-Determination: The Story of The Woodlawn Organization.* Grand Rapids: Eerdmans.

Briggs, Michael, and Ray Long. 1992. "Senate Rivals Work Strongholds." *Chicago Sun-Times*, November 2.

Brink, William, and Louis Harris. 1964. *The Negro Revolution in America.* New York: Simon and Schuster.

———. 1967. *Black and White.* New York: Simon and Schuster.

Brown, Elsa Barkley. 1994. "Negotiating and Transforming the Public Sphere: African-American Political Life in the Transition from Slavery to Freedom." *Public Culture* 7: 107–146.

Browning, Rufus P., Dale Rogers Marshall, and David Tabb. 1984. *Protest Is Not Enough.* Chicago: University of Chicago Press.

Bryant, Christopher G. A. 1995. "Civic Nations, Civil Society, and Civil Religion." In *Civil Society: Theory, History, and Comparison*, edited by John Hall. Cambridge: Polity Press.

Bunche, Ralph J. [1940] 1973. *The Political Status of the Negro in the Age of FDR.* Edited by Dewey W. Grantham. Reprint, Chicago: University of Chicago Press.

Burkett, Randall. 1978. *Garveyism as a Religious Movement.* Metuchen, N.J.: Scarecrow Press.

———. "The Baptist Church in the Years of Crisis: J. C. Austin and the Pilgrim Baptist Church, 1926–1950." In *African-American Christianity: Essays in History*, edited by Paul E. Johnson. Berkeley, Calif.: University of California Press.

Calhoun-Brown, Allison. 1996. "African American Churches and Political Mobilization: The Psychological Impact of Organizational Resources." *Journal of Politics* 58:4, 935–53.

———. 1998. "The Politics of Black Evangelicals: What Hinders Diversity in the Christian Right." *American Politics Quarterly* 26:31–109.

Campbell, Angus, Philip Converse, Warren Miller, and Donald Stokes. 1960. *The American Voter.* New York: Wiley.

Carlson, Tucker. 1992. "That Old-Time Religion: Why Black Men Are Returning to Church." *Policy Review* 67:13–17.

Carpenter, Dolores C. 1990–1991. "Black Women in Religious Institutions: A Historical Summary from Slavery to the 1960s." *Journal of Religious Thought* Winter-Spring, 47: 2, 7–27.

Carter, Stephen L. 1993. *The Culture of Disbelief: How American Law and Politics Trivialize Religious Devotion.* New York: Basic Books.

Cavanagh, Thomas E. 1985. *Inside Black America: The Message of the Black Vote in the 1984 Elections.* Washington, D.C.: Joint Center for Political and Economic Studies.

Cavanagh, Thomas E., and Lorn S. Foster. 1984. *Jesse Jackson's Campaign: Primaries and Caucuses.* Washington, D.C.: Joint Center for Political Studies.

Cavanagh, Thomas E., ed. 1987. *Strategies for Mobilizing Black Voters: Four Case Studies.* Washington, D.C.: Joint Center for Political Studies.

Chateauvert, Melinda. 1998. *Marching Together: Women of the Brotherhood of Sleeping Car Porters.* Urbana: University of Illinois Press.

Chaves, Mark, and Lynn Higgins. 1992. "Comparing the Community Involvement of Black and White Congregations." *Journal for the Scientific Study of Religion* 31:4, 425–440.

Cherry, Conrad, ed. 1971. *God's New Israel: Religious Interpretations of American Destiny.* Englewood Cliffs, N.J.: Prentice-Hall.

Childs, John Brown. 1980. *The Political Black Minister: A Study in Afro-American Politics and Religion.* Boston: G. K. Hall.

Chong, Dennis. 1991. *Collective Action and the Civil Rights Movement.* Chicago: University of Chicago Press.

Clark, Septima. 1986. *Ready from Within: Septima Clark and the Civil Rights Movement.* Edited by Cynthia Stokes Brown. Navarro, Calif.: Wild Trees Press.

Cleage, Albert B., Jr. 1972. *Black Christian Nationalism.* New York: Morrow.

Cohen, Jean, and Andrew Arato. 1995. *Civil Society and Political Theory.* Cambridge: Massachusetts Institute of Technology Press.

Collins, Patricia Hill. 1991. *Black Feminist Thought.* New York: Routledge.

Cone, James H. 1969. *Black Theology and Black Power.* New York: Seabury Press.

———. 1972. *The Spiritual and the Blues.* New York: Seabury Press, 1972.

———. [1970] 1986. *A Black Theology of Liberation.* Reprint, Maryknoll, N.Y.: Orbis.

Conway, M. Margaret. 1985. *Political Participation in the United States.* Washington, D.C.: CQ Press.

Corbin, David Alan. 1981. *Life, Work, and Rebellion in the Coal Fields: The Southern West Virginia Miners, 1880–1922.* Urbana: University of Illinois Press.

Couto, Richard. 1993. "Narrative, Free Space, and Political Leadership in Social Movements." *Journal of Politics* 55:57–79.

Cross, William E., Jr. 1991. *Shades of Black: Diversity in African-American Identity.* Philadelphia: Temple University Press.

Crotty, William J. 1978. *Decision for the Democrats: Reforming the Party Structure.* Baltimore: Johns Hopkins University Press.

Dawson, Michael C. 1994a. *Behind the Mule: Race and Class in African-American Politics.* Princeton: Princeton University Press.

————. 1994b. "A Black Counterpublic? Economic Earthquakes, Racial Agenda(s), and Black Politics." *Public Culture* 7:195–223.

Dawson, Michael C., Ronald E. Brown, and Richard Allen. 1990. "Racial Belief Systems, Religious Guidance, and African-American Political Participation." *National Political Science Review* 2:22–44.

Dawson, Michael C., and Ernest J. Wilson III. 1991. "Paradigms and Paradoxes: Political Science and African-American Politics." In *The Theory and Practice of Political Science, Political Science: Looking to the Future*, edited by William Crotty, vol. 1. Evanston, Ill.: Northwestern University Press.

Dent, Gina, 1992. *Black Popular Culture*. Seattle: Bay Press.

Dinges, Barnaby. 1989. "Mayor Daley Courting Black Ministers." *Chicago Reporter*, December 18.

Dollard, John. [1937] 1949. *Caste and Class in a Southern Town*. Reprint, New York: Doubleday.

Drake, St. Clair. 1940. *Churches and Voluntary Associations in the Chicago Negro Community*. Chicago: Work Projects Administration.

————. 1970. *The Redemption of Africa and Black Religion*. Chicago: Third World.

Drake, St. Clair, and Horace R. Cayton. [1945] 1970. *Black Metropolis*. Vol. 2. Reprint, New York: Harcourt, Brace.

Draper, Theodore. 1970. *The Rediscovery of Black Nationalism*. New York: Viking Press.

DuBois, W. E. B. 1903. *The Negro Church*. Atlanta: Atlanta University Press.

————. 1970. *The Gift of Black Folk*. New York: Washington Square Press.

Durkheim, Emile. [1915] 1946. *The Elementary Forms of Religious Life*. Reprint, Glencoe, Ill.: Free Press.

Dunson, John. 1985. *Freedom in the Air: Movement Songs of the Sixties*. New York: International Press.

Dyson, Marcia L. 1998. "When Preachers Prey." *Essence*, May.

Edelman, Murray. 1985. *The Symbolic Uses of Politics*. Urbana: University of Illinois Press.

Ellison, Christopher. 1991. "Identification and Separatism: Religious Involvement and Racial Orientations among Black Americans." *Sociological Quarterly* 32:477–494.

Essien-Udon, E. U. 1962. *Black Nationalism: A Search for an Identity in America*. Chicago: University of Chicago Press.

Evans, Sara M., and Harry C. Boyte. 1986. *Free Spaces: The Sources of Democratic Change in America*. New York: Harper and Row.

Falk, Nancy, and Rita Child. 1985. *Unspoken Words: Women's Religious Lives*. Belmont, Calif.: Wadsworth.

Fauset, A. H. 1944. *Black Gods of the Metropolis: Negro Religious Cults of the Urban North*. Philadelphia: University of Pennsylvania Press.

Foner, Eric. 1988. *Reconstruction: America's Unfinished Revolution, 1863–1877*. New York: Harper and Row.

Franklin, John Hope. 1980. *From Slavery to Freedom: The History of Negro Americans*. 5th ed. New York: Knopf.

Frazier, E. Franklin. [1957] 1967. *Black Bourgeoisie*. Reprint, New York: Collier Books.

————. [1963] 1974. *The Negro Church in America*. Reprint, New York: Knopf.

Freedman, Samuel. 1987. *Upon This Rock: The Miracles of a Black Church*. New York: HarperCollins.

Gallup, George, Jr., and Jim Castelli. 1989. *The People's Religion: American Faith in the Nineties*. New York: Macmillan.

Garrow, David. 1986. *Bearing the Cross: Martin Luther King, Jr. and the Southern Christian Leadership Conference*. New York: Morrow.

———, ed. 1989. *Chicago 1966: Open Housing Marches, Summit Negotiations, and Operation Breadbasket*. Brooklyn: Carlson Publications.

Gehrid, Gail. 1979. *American Civil Religion: An Assessment*. Society for the Scientific Study of Religion, Monograph Series, number 3.

Genovese, Eugene D. 1974. *Roll, Jordan, Roll*. New York: Vintage Books.

Geertz, Clifford. 1973a. "Religion as a Cultural System." In *The Interpretation of Cultures*. New York: Basic Books.

———. 1973b. "Ethos, World View, and the Analysis of Sacred Symbols." In *The Interpretation of Cultures*. New York: Basic Books.

George, Luvenia A. 1992. "Lucie E. Campbell: Her Nurturing and Expansion of Gospel Music in the National Baptist Convention, U.S.A., Inc." In *We'll Understand It Better By and By: Pioneering African American Gospel Composers*, edited by Bernice Johnson Reagon. Washington, D.C.: Smithsonian Institution Press.

Giddens, Anthony, ed. 1972. *Emile Durkheim: Selected Writings*. Cambridge: Cambridge University Press.

Giddings, Paula. 1984. *When and Where I Enter: The Impact of Black Women on Race and Sex in America*. New York: Bantam.

———. 1988. *In Search of Sisterhood: Delta Sigma Theta and the Challenge of the Black Sorority Movement*. New York: Morrow.

Gilbert, Christopher P. 1993. *The Impact of Churches on Political Behavior: An Empirical Study*. Westport, Conn.: Greenwood Press.

Gilkes, Cheryl Townsend. 1980. "The Black Church as a Therapeutic Community: Suggested Areas for Research into the Black Religious Experience." *Journal of the Interdenominational Theological Center* 8:29–44.

———. 1994. "The Politics of 'Silence': Dual-Sex Political Systems and Women's Traditions in African-American Religion." In *African-American Christianity: Essays in History*, edited by Paul E. Johnson. Berkeley: University of California Press.

———. 1997. "The Roles of Church and Community Mothers: Ambivalent American Sexism or Fragmented African Familyhood?" In *African-American Religion: Interpretive Essays in History and Culture*, edited by Timothy E. Fulop and Albert Raboteau. New York: Routledge.

Glenn, Noval D. 1964. "Negro Religion and Negro Status in the United States." In *Religion, Culture, and Society*, edited by L. Schneider. New York: Wiley.

Glenn, Noval D., and Erin Gotard. 1977. "The Religion of Blacks in the United States: Some Recent Trends and Current Characteristics," *American Journal of Sociology* 83: 443–451.

Glock, C. Y., and P. E. Hammonds, eds. 1973. *Beyond the Classics: Essays in the Scientific Study of Religion*. New York: Harper and Row.

Goodwyn, Lawrence. 1978. *The Populist Movement: A Short History of the Agrarian Revolt in America*. Oxford: Oxford University Press.

Gordon, Ethel M. 1976. *Unfinished Business: Bits of History That Go Back as Far as the Past Seventy-five Years of the Women's Convention Auxiliary to the National Baptist Convention, U.S.A., Inc., with Special Emphasis on the Past Five Years*. Detroit: Harlo Press.

Gordon, Eugene. [1927] 1972. "A New Religion for the Negro." In *A Documentary History of the Negro People in the United States*, edited by Herbert Aptheker, vol. 3. New York: Citadel Press.

Gosnell, Harold F. [1935] 1967. *Negro Politicians: The Rise of Negro Politics in Chicago*. Reprint, Chicago: University of Chicago Press.

Gosnell, Harold F., and Robert E. Martin. 1963. "The Negro as Voter and Officeholder." *Journal of Negro Education* 32:415–425.

Green, Charles, and Basil Wilson. 1989. *The Struggle for Black Empowerment in New York City: Beyond the Politics of Pigmentation*. New York: Praeger.

Grier, W. H., and P. M. Cobbs. 1971. *The Jesus Bag*. New York: McGraw-Hill.

Griffith, Ezra E. H., Thelouizs English, and Violet Mayfield. 1980. "Possession, Prayer, and Testimony: Therapeutic Aspects of the Wednesday Night Meeting in a Black Church." *Psychiatry* 43 (May):120–128.

Gurin, Patricia, Shirley J. Hatchett, and James S. Jackson. 1989. *Hope and Independence: Blacks' Response to Electoral and Party Politics*. New York: Russell Sage Foundation.

Hamilton, Charles V. 1972. *The Black Preacher In America*. New York: Morrow

Hanania, Ray. 1990. "Twelve Ministers To Boycott King Affair," *Chicago Sun-Times*, January, 10.

Harding, Vincent. 1983. *There Is a River: The Black Struggle for Freedom in America*. New York: Vintage Books.

Hardy, Thomas, and Steven Johnson. 1992. "Senate Foes Don't Let Up on Attacks," *Chicago Tribune*, November 2.

Hare, Nathan. 1963. "Have Negro Ministers Failed Their Roles?" *Negro Digest* (July):11–19.

Harris, Fredrick C. 1994a. "Something Within: Religion as a Mobilizer of African-American Political Activism." *Journal of Politics* 56: 42–68.

———. 1994b. "Something Within: Religion in African American Political Activism." Ph.D dissertation, Northwestern University.

———. 1997. "Will the Circle Be Unbroken? The Erosion and Transformation of African-American Civic Life." College Park. Working Paper no. 9, National Commission on Civic Renewal, Institute for Philosophy and Public Policy, University of Maryland.

Henry, Charles P. 1990. *Culture and African American Politics*. Bloomington: Indiana: University Press.

Herring, Cedric, and Vera M. Keith. 1991. "Skin Tone and Stratification in the Black Community." *American Journal of Sociology* 97:760–778.

Higginbotham, Evelyn Brooks. 1993. *Righteous Discontent: The Women's Movement in the Black Baptist Church, 1880–1920*. Cambridge: Harvard University Press.

Hill, Kenneth. 1989. "The Political Behavior of African Methodist Episcopal Church Members: Detroit." Paper presented at the Midwest Political Science Association Annual Meeting, Chicago, Illinois, April 13–15.

Hochschild, Jennifer. 1996. *Facing Up to the American Dream: Race, Class and the Soul of the Nation.* Princeton: Princeton University Press.

Holden, Matthew, Jr. 1973. *The Politics of the Black "Nation."* New York: Chandler.

Houghland, J. G., and J. A. Christenson. 1983. "Religion and Politics: The Relationship of Religious Participation to Political Efficacy and Involvement." *Sociology and Social Research* 67: 405–420.

Hughes, Michael, and David H. Demo. 1989. "Self Perceptions of Black Americans: Self-Esteem and Personal Efficacy." *American Journal of Sociology* 95: 132–159.

Hunt, L. L., and J. G. Hunt. 1977. "Black Religion as Both Opiate and Inspiration of Civil Rights Militance: Putting Marx's Data to Test." *Social Forces* 86: 1–14.

Hunter, Tera. 1997. *To 'Joy My Freedom: Southern Black Women's Lives and Labors after the Civil War.* Cambridge: Harvard University Press.

Hurston, Zora Neal. 1983. *The Sanctified Church.* Berkeley: Turtle Island.

Jelen, Ted G. 1991. *The Political Mobilization of Religious Beliefs.* New York: Praeger.

———. ed. 1989. *Religion and Political Behavior in the United States.* New York: Praeger.

Johnson, Charles S. [1934] 1966. *Shadow of the Plantation.* Reprint, Chicago: University of Chicago Press.

———. [1941] 1967. *Growing Up in the Black Belt.* Reprint, New York: Schocken Books.

Johnson, Ruby Funchess. 1956. *The Religion of Negro Protestants: Changing Religious Attitudes and Practices.* New York: Philosophical Library.

Johnston, Ronald. 1971. "Negro Preachers Take Sides." In *The Black Church in America,* edited by Hart M. Nelson and Raytha L. Yokley. New York: Basic Books.

Joint Center for Political Studies. 1988. *Blacks and the 1988 Democratic National Convention.* Washington, D.C.: Joint Center for Political Studies.

Kelley, Robin D. G. 1990. *Hammer and Hoe: Alabama Communists during the Great Depression.* Chapel Hill: University of North Carolina Press.

———. 1993. " 'We Are Not What We Seem': Rethinking Black Working-Class Opposition in the Jim Crow South." *Journal of American History* 80:75–112.

Kerner Commission. 1968. *Report of the National Advisory Commission on Civil Disorders.* Washington, D.C.: U.S. Government Printing Office.

Kertzer, I. David. 1980. *Comrades and Christians: Religion and Political Struggle in Communionist Italy.* New York: Cambridge University Press.

———. 1988. *Ritual, Politics, and Power.* New Haven: Yale University Press.

Key, V. O., Jr. 1949. *Southern Politics.* New York: Vintage Books.

Kilson, Martin. 1971. "Political Change in the Negro Ghetto, 1900–1940s." In *Key Issues in the Afro-American Experience,* edited by Nathan I. Huggins, Martin Kilson, and Daniel M. Fox. New York: Harcourt Brace Jovanovich.

King, Charles H. 1963. "Negro Ministers Have Not Failed—Have Sociologists?" *Negro Digest* (November): 12–16.

King, Martin Luther, Jr. 1958. *Stride toward Freedom: The Montgomery Story.* New York: Ballantine Books.

Kleppner, Paul. 1985. *Chicago Divided: The Making of a Black Mayor.* DeKalb: Northern Illinois University.

Kosmin, Barry A., and Seymour P. Lachman. 1993. *One Nation under God: Religion in Contemporary American Society.* New York: Crown.

Kubik, Jan. 1994. *The Power of Symbols against the Symbols of Power: The Rise of Solidarity and the Fall of State Socialism in Poland*. University Park: Penn State University.

Kunjufu, Jawanza. 1994. *Where Are You Adam! Why Black Men Don't Go to Church*. Chicago: African American Images.

Laitin, David D. 1988. "Political Culture and Political Preferences." *American Political Science Review* 82: 589–1593.

Lane, Robert E. 1959. *Political Life: Why People Get Involved in Politics*. Glencoe Ill.: Free Press.

Leege, David C., Joel A. Lieske, and Kenneth D. Wald. 1990. "Toward Cultural Theories of American Political Behavior: Religion, Ethnicity and Race, and Class Outlook." In *Political Behavior, Political Science: Looking to the Future*, edited by William Crotty, vol. 3. Evanston, Ill: Northwestern University Press.

Lehman, Edward C., Jr. 1985. *Women Clergy: Breaking through Gender Barriers*. New Brunswick, N.J.: Transaction Books.

Lehmann, Nicholas. 1991. *The Promised Land: The Great Black Migration and How It Changed America*. New York: Vintage Books.

Lenski, Gerhard. 1961. *The Religious Factor*. Garden City, N.Y.: Doubleday.

Levine, Daniel. 1992. *Popular Voices in Latin American Catholicism*. Princeton: Princeton University Press.

Levine, Lawrence W. 1977. *Black Culture and Black Consciousness: Afro-American Folk Thought from Slavery to Freedom*. New York: Oxford University Press.

Light, Alan. 1997. "Say Amen, Somebody!" *Vibe*, October.

Lincoln, C. Eric. 1961. *The Black Muslims In America*. Boston: Beacon Press.

———. 1974. *The Black Church Since Frazier*. New York: Schocken.

Lincoln, C. Eric, and Lawrence H. Mamiya. 1990. *The Black Church in the African-American Experience*. Durham, N.C.: Duke University Press.

Linden, Amy. 1993. "Niggas with Beatitude." *Transition* 62: 176–187.

Locin, Mitchell, and Jane Fritsch. 1983. "Black Clergy for Washington Hit Pro-Daley Colleagues." *Chicago Tribune*, January 13.

Logan, Rayford W. 1968. *The Betrayal of the Negro: From Rutherford B. Hayes to Woodrow Wilson*. New York: Collier Books.

Macaluso, Theodore F., and John Wanat. 1979. "Voting Turnout and Religiosity." *Polity* 12: 158–169.

MacLeod, Jay, ed. 1991. *Minds Stayed on Freedom: The Civil Rights Struggle in the Rural South, an Oral History*. Youth of the Rural Organizing and Cultural Center. Boulder: Westview Press.

Madron, Thomas W., Hart M. Nelsen, and Raytha L. Yokley. 1974. "Religion as a Determinant of Militancy and Political Participation among Black Americans." *American Behavioralist Scientist* 17: 783–796.

Malcolm X. 1965. "Message to the Grassroots." In *Malcolm X Speaks*. New York: Grove Press.

Mansbridge, Jane J. 1991. "On the Relation of Altruism and Self-Interest." In *Beyond Self Interest*, edited by Jane J. Mansbridge. Chicago: University of Chicago Press.

Mansbridge, Jane, and Katherine Tate. 1992. "Race Trumps Gender: The Thomas Nomination in the Black Community." *PS* 15:488–493.

Marable, Manning. 1983. *How Capitalism Underdeveloped Black America*. Boston: South End Press.

———. 1989. "Religion and Black Protest Thought in African American History." In *African American Religious Studies*, edited by Gayraud S. Wilmore. Durham, N.C.: Duke University Press.

Martinson, Oscar B., and E. A. Wilkening. 1987. "Religious Participation and Involvement in Local Politics throughout the Life Cycle." *Sociological Focus* 20: 309–318.

Marx, Gary T. 1967a. *Protest and Prejudice*. New York: Harper and Row.

———. 1967b. "Religion: Opiate or Inspiration of Civil Rights Militancy among Negroes." *American Journal of Sociology* 81:139–46.

Marx, Karl. 1963. "Contribution to the Critique of Hegel's Philosophy of Right." [1884] In *Karl Marx: Early Writings*, edited and translated by T. B. Bottomore. New York: McGraw-Hill.

Matthews, Donald R., and James W. Prothro. 1966. *Negroes and the New Southern Politics*. New York: Harcourt, Brace, and World.

Mays, Benjamin E. [1938] 1968. *The Negro's God as Reflected in His Literature*. New York: Atheneum.

Mays, Benjamin E., and Joseph N. Nicholson. [1933] 1969. *The Negroes' Church*. New York: Russell and Russell.

McAdam, Doug. 1982. *Political Process and the Development of Black Insurgency: 1930–1970*. Chicago: University of Chicago Press.

McCartney, John T. 1992. *Black Power Ideologies: An Essay in African-American Political Thought*. Philadelphia: Temple University Press.

McClory, Robert. 1989. "The Holy Terror of Saint Sabina's: What's a White Boy Like Mick Pfleger Doing in a Parish Like This?" *Chicago Reader* 19 (November 17).

McConahay, J. B. 1970. "Attitudes of Negroes toward the Church following the Los Angeles Riot." *Sociological Analysis* 31:12–22.

McFadden, Grace Jordan. 1990. "Septima P. Clark and the Struggle for Human Rights." In *Women in the Civil Rights Movement: Trailblazers and Torchbearers, 1941–1965*, edited by Vicki L. Crawford, Jacqueline Anne Rouse, and Barbara Woods. Brooklyn: Carlson.

McGuire, Meredith. 1983. "Discovering Religious Power." *Sociological Analysis* 44:1–9.

Meier, August. 1963. "Negro Protest Movements and Organizations." *Journal of Negro Education* 32:437–450.

———. 1970. Editor's introduction to *The Transformation of Activism*. Chicago: Aldine.

Meier, August, and Elliott Rudwick. 1969. "The Boycott Movement against Jim Crow Street Cars in the South, 1900–1906." *Journal of American History* 55:756–775.

———. 1979. *Black Detroit and the Rise of the UAW*. Oxford: Oxford University Press.

———. 1985. "The Origins of Nonviolent Direct Action in Afro-American Protest." In *We Shall Overcome: The Civil Rights Movement in the United States in the 1950s and the 1960s*, edited by David Garrow. Brooklyn: Carlson.

Milbrath, Lester W., and M. L. Goel. 1977. *Political Participation*. Chicago: Rand McNally.

Miller, Arthur H., Patricia Gurin, Gerald Gurin, and Okasana Malanchuk. 1981. "Group Consciousness and Political Participation." *American Journal of Political Science* 25:494–511.

Morris, Aldon D. 1984. *The Origins of the Civil Rights Movement: Black Communities Organizing for Change*. New York: Free Press.

————. 1992. "Political Consciousness and Collective Action." In *Frontiers in Social Movement Theory*, edited by Aldon D. Morris and Carol McClurg Mueller. New Haven: Yale University Press.

Morris, Aldon D., Shirley J. Hatchett, and Ronald E. Brown. 1989. "The Civil Rights Movement and Black Political Socialization." In *Political Learning in Adulthood*, edited by Roberta S. Sigel. Chicago: University of Chicago Press.

Mueller, Carol McClurg. 1992. "Building Social Movement Theory." In *Frontiers in Social Movement Theory*, edited by Aldon D. Morris and Carol McClurg Mueller. New Haven: Yale University Press.

Mukenge, Ida Rousseau. 1983. *The Black Church in Urban America: A Case Study in Political Economy*. Lanham, Md.: University Press of America.

Muraskin, William Alan. 1975. *Middle-Class Blacks in a White Society: Prince Hall Freemasonry in America*. Berkeley: University of California Press.

Myrdal, Gunnar. 1944. *An American Dilemma*. New York: Harper.

Nelsen, Hart M. 1988. "Unchurched Black Americans: Patterns of Religiosity and Affiliation." *Review of Religious Research* 29:398–412.

Nelsen, Hart M., and Anne K. Nelsen. 1975. *The Black Church in the Sixties*. Lexington: University of Kentucky Press.

Nelsen, Hart M., Thomas W. Waldron, and Raytha L. Yokley. 1975. "Black Religion's Promethean Motif: Orthodoxy and Militancy." *American Journal of Sociology* 81:139–146.

Olsen, Marvin E. 1970. "Social and Political Participation of Blacks." *American Sociological Review* 35:682–697.

Olson, Mancur. 1971. *The Logic of Collective Action: Public Goods and the Theory of Groups*. Cambridge: Harvard University Press.

Orum, Anthony M. 1966. "A Reappraisal of the Social and Political Participation of Negroes." *American Journal of Sociology* 72:32–47.

Paris, Peter J. 1985. *The Social Teachings of the Black Churches*. Philadelphia: Fortress Press.

Payne, Charles. 1990. "Men Led, but Women Organized: Movement Participation of Women in the Mississippi Delta." In *Women in the Civil Rights Movement: Trailblazers and Torchbearers, 1941–1965*. Brooklyn: Carlson.

Payne, Charles M. 1995. *I've Got the Light of Freedom: The Organizing Tradition and the Mississippi Freedom Struggle*. Berkeley: University of California Press.

Payne, Wardell J., ed. 1991. *Directory of African American Religious Bodies*. Washington, D.C.: Howard University Press.

Peck, Gary R. 1982. "Black Radical Consciousness and the Black Christian Experience: Toward a Critical Sociology of Afro-American Religion." *Sociological Analysis* 43:155–167

Peterson, Steven A. 1992. "Church Participation and Political Participation." *American Politics Quarterly* 20:123–139.

Pinderhughes, Dianne M. 1987. *Race and Ethnicity in Chicago Politics: A Reexamination of Pluralist Theory*. Urbana: University of Illinois Press.

Poinsett, Alex. 1962. *Common Folk in an Uncommon Cause: Liberty Baptist Church*. Chicago: Lakeside Press.

Pollock, Philip H., III. 1982. "Organizations as Agents of Mobilization: How Does Group

Activity Affect Political Participation?" *American Journal of Political Science* 26: 483–503.

Powdermaker, Hortense. [1939] 1968. *After Freedom: A Cultural History of the Deep South.* Reprint, New York: Viking Press.

Powell, Kelvin. 1994. "Soul on Ice." *Vibe*, November.

Putnam, Robert D. 1993. *Making Democracy Work: Civic Traditions in Modern Italy.* Princeton: Princeton University Press.

———. 1995. "Bowling Alone: America's Declining Social Capital." *Journal of Democracy* 6: 1 65–78.

Raboteau, Albert. 1978. *Slave Religion: The "Invisible Institution" in the Antebellum South.* New York: Oxford University Press.

Raines, Howell. 1977. *My Soul Is Rested.* New York: Putnam.

Ralph, James. 1993. *Northern Protest: Martin Luther King, Jr., Chicago, and the Civil Rights Movement.* Cambridge: Harvard University Press.

Randolph, A. Phillip. 1990. "Negro Labor and the Church." [1929] In *A Documentary History of the Negro People in the United States*, edited by Herbert Aptheker, volume 3. New York: First Carol.

Reagon, Bernice Johnson. 1990. "Women as Culture Carriers in the Civil Rights Movement: Fannie Lou Hamer." In *Women in the Civil Rights Movement: Trailblazers and Torchbearers, 1941–1965*, edited by Vicki L. Crawford, Jacqueline Anne Rouse, and Barbara Woods. Brooklyn: Carlson.

Reed, Adolph, Jr. 1986a. Editor's Introduction to *Race, Politics and Culture: Critical Essays on the Radicalism of the 1960s*. New York: Greenwood Press.

———. 1986b. *The Jesse Jackson Phenomenon: The Crisis of Purpose in Afro-American Politics.* New Haven: Yale University Press.

Richey, Russell E., and Donald G. Jones, eds. 1974. *American Civil Religion.* New York: Harper and Row.

Roof, Wade Clark. 1979. "Concepts and Indicators of Religious Commitment: A Critical Review." In *The Religious Dimension: New Directions in Quantitative Research*, edited by Robert Wuthnow. New York: Academic Press.

Rosenstone, Steven, and John Mark Hansen. 1993. *Mobilization, Participation, and Democracy in America.* New York: Macmillan.

Rustin, Bayard. 1971. "From Protest to Politics: The Future of the Civil Rights Movement." In *Down the Line: The Collected Writings of Bayard Rustin.* Chicago: Quadrangle Books.

Sata, L. S., D. A. Perry, and C. E. Cameron. 1970. "Store Front Churches in the Inner City." *Mental Hygiene* 54:256–260.

Scott, James. 1985. *Weapons of the Weak.* New Haven: Yale University Press.

———. 1990. *Domination and the Arts of Resistance.* New Haven: Yale University Press.

Shingles, Richard D. 1981. "Black Consciousness and Political Participation: The Missing Link." *American Political Science Review* 75:76–91.

Smith, Robert C. 1981. "Black Power and the Transformation from Protest to Politics." *Political Science Quarterly* 96:431–443.

Sniderman, Paul M. 1975. *Personality and Democratic Politics.* Berkeley: University of California Press.

Snow, David E., Burke Rochford, Jr., Steven K. Worden, and Robert Benford. 1986. "Frame

Realignment Processes, Micromobilization, and Movement Participation." *American Sociological Review* 51: 464–481.

Snow, David, and Robert D. Benford. 1992. "Master Frames and Cycles of Protest." In *Frontiers in Social Movement Theory*, edited by Aldon D. Morris and Carol McClurg Mueller. New Haven: Yale University Press.

Spilka, Bernard, Ralph W. Hood Jr., and Richard L. Gorsuch. 1985. *The Psychology of Religion: An Empirical Approach.* Englewood Cliffs, N.J.: Prentice, Hall.

St. George, Arthur, and Patrick H. McNamara. 1984. "Religion, Race, and Psychological Well-Being." *Journal for the Scientific Study of Religion* 23:351–363.

Strate, John M., Charles H. Parrish, Charles D. Elder, and Coit Ford III. 1989. "Life Span Civic Development and Voting Participation." *American Political Science Review* 83: 443–464.

Sweet, Lynn, and Mark Brown. 1992. "Black Clerics Back Hofeld; Steinem Stumps for Braun." *Chicago Sun-Times*, March 11.

Swidler, Ann. 1986. "Culture In Action: Symbols and Strategies." *American Sociological Review* 51:273–286.

Tarrow, Sidney. 1992. "Mentalities, Political Cultures, and Collective Action Frames." In *Frontiers in Social Movement Theory*, edited by Aldon D. Morris and Carol McClurg Mueller. New Haven: Yale University Press.

Tate, Katherine. 1991. "Black Political Participation in the 1984 and 1988 Presidential Elections." *American Political Science Review* 85: 1159–1176.

———. 1993. *From Protest to Politics: The New Black Voters in American Elections.* Cambridge: Harvard University Press.

Tate, Katherine, and Ronald Brown. 1991. "The Black Church and Political Participation." Paper presented at the Annual Midwest Political Science Association Meeting, Chicago, Illinois, April 13–151.

Tate, Katherine, Shirley J. Hatchett, and James S. Jackson. 1988. *The 1984 National Black Election Study Sourcebook.* Ann Arbor: Institute for Social Research, University of Michigan.

Taylor, Clarence. 1994. *The Black Churches of Brooklyn.* New York: Columbia University Press.

Thompson, Michael, Richard Ellis, and Aaron Wildavsky. 1990. *Cultural Theory.* Boulder: Westview Press.

Thurman, Howard. 1955. *Deep River: Reflections of the Religious Insight of Certain of the Negro Spirituals.* New York: Harper.

———. 1981. *Jesus and the Disinherited.* Richmond, Ind.: Friends United Press.

United States Commission on Civil Rights. 1968. *Political Participation.* Washington, D.C.: U.S. Government Printing Office.

Van Deburg, William L. 1992. *New Day in Babylon: The Black Power Movement and American Culture, 1965–1975.* Chicago: University of Chicago Press.

Verba, Sidney, and Norman H. Nie. 1972. *Participation In America.* New York: Harper and Row.

Verba, Sidney, Kay L. Schlozman, Henry Brady and Norman Nie. 1993. "Race, Ethnicity and Political Resources: Participation in the United States." *British Journal of Political Science* 23: 453–497.

Verba, Sidney, Kay Lehman Schlozman, and Henry Brady. 1995. *Voice and Equality: Civic Voluntarism in American Politics.* Cambridge: Harvard University Press.

Wald, Kenneth D. 1987. *Religion and Politics in the United States.* New York: St. Martin's Press.

———. 1990. "Political Cohesion in Churches." *Journal of Politics* 52: 197–215.

Wald, Kenneth D., Lyman A. Kellstedt, and David C. Leege. 1993. "Church Involvement and Political Behavior." In *Rediscovering the Religious Factor in American Politics*, edited by David C. Leege and Lyman A. Kellstedt. Armonk, N.Y.: M. E. Sharpe.

Wald, Kenneth D., Dennis E. Owen, and Samuel S. Hill, Jr. 1988. "Churches as Political Communities." *American Political Science Review* 28: 531–547.

Walker, Clarence E. 1982. *A Rock in a Weary Land: The African Methodist Episcopal Church During the Civil War and Reconstruction.* Baton Rouge: Louisiana State University Press.

Walker, Wyatt Tee. 1979. *Somebody's Calling My Name.* Valley Forge: Judson Press.

Walton, Hanes, Jr. 1972. *Black Political Parties: An Historical and Political Analysis.* New York: Free Press.

———. 1975. *Black Republicans: The Politics of the Black and Tans.* Metuchen: Scarecrow Press.

Walzer, Michael. 1985. *Exodus and Revolution.* New York: Basic Books.

Washington, Harold M. Papers. Harold Washington Library, Chicago.

Washington, James M. 1985. *Frustrated Fellowship: The Black Baptist Quest for Social Power.* Macon: Mercer University Press.

———. 1986. "Jesse Jackson and the Symbolic Politics of Black Christendom." *Annals of American Academy of Political and Social Science* 480: 89–105.

West, Cornel. 1982. *Prophesy Deliverance! An Afro-American Revolutionary Christianity.* Philadelphia: Westminster Press.

———. 1988. *Prophetic Fragments.* Trenton, N.J.: Africa World Press.

Wesley, Charles H. 1953. *The History of Alpha Phi Alpha: A Development in College Life.* Washington, D.C.: Foundation.

———. 1961. *The History of the Prince Hall Grand Lodge of Free and Accepted Masons of the State of Ohio 1849–1960.* Wilberforce, Ohio: Thomkins.

Wilcox, Clyde. 1986. "Fundamentalist and Politics: An Analysis of the Effects of Differing Operational Definitions." *Journal of Politics* 48: 1041–1051.

———. 1990. "Religious Sources of Politicization among Blacks in Washington, D.C." *Journal for the Scientific Study of Religion* 29: 387–394.

Wilcox, Clyde, and Leopoldo Gomez. 1990. "Religion, Group Identification, and Politics among American Blacks." *Sociological Analysis* 51:271–285.

Williams, Dolores S. 1993. *Sisters in the Wilderness: The Challenge of Womanist God-Talk.* Mayknoll, New York: Orbis Books.

Wills, Gary. 1990. *Under God: Religion and American Politics.* New York: Simon and Schuster.

Wilmore, Gayraud S. 1983. *Black Religion and Black Radicalism.* 2nd ed. Maryknoll, N.Y.: Orbis Books.

Wolfinger, Raymond, and Steven Rosenstone. 1980. *Who Votes?* New Haven: Yale University Press.

Woodard, Michael D. 1987. "Voluntary Association Membership among Black Americans: The Post–Civil Rights Era," *Sociological Quarterly* 28:285–301.

Woodson, Carter G. [1921] 1945. *The History of the Negro Church*. Reprint, Washington, D.C.: Associated Publishers.

Woodson, Carter G. 1985. "Things of the Spirit." [1930] In *Afro-American Religious History: A Documentary Witness*, edited by Milton C. Sernett. Durham: Duke University Press.

Yinger, J. Milton. 1970. *The Scientific Study of Religion*. New York: Macmillian.

Young, Henry J., ed. 1988. *The Black Church and the Harold Washington Story*. Bristol, Ind.: Wyndham Hall Press.

Index